IMUS

Also by Kathleen Tracy

Ellen: The Real Story of Ellen DeGeneres

*Elvis: Top Secret: The Untold Story of Elvis Presley's
FBI Files* (with Earl Greenwood)

*The Boy Who Would Be King: An Intimate Portrait of
Elvis Presley by His Cousin* (with Earl Greenwood)

*The Girl's Got Real Bite: Unofficial Guide to
Buffy's World*

Home Brewed: The Drew Carey Story

Jerry Seinfeld: The Entire Domain

Matt Damon

Antonio Banderas

IMUS

AMERICA'S COWBOY

Kathleen Tracy

CARROLL & GRAF PUBLISHERS, INC.
NEW YORK

First Carroll & Graf edition 1999

Carroll & Graf Publishers, Inc.
19 West 21st Street
New York, NY 10010-6805

Library of Congress Cataloging-in-Publication Data is available.
ISBN: 0-7867-0608-2

Manufactured in the United States of America

Acknowledgments

The author would like to acknowledge Valerie Milano for her assistance in researching this book. And a special thanks to Troy Augusto for his tireless assistance.

Introduction

THE COWBOY AS MYTHIC FIGURE OF THE OLD WEST IS AS MUCH A PART of the American psyche as the symbolism of mom, baseball, and apple pie, embodying traits that from a romantic distance are distinct and unambiguous, even poetic. Lured to the West by the wide open spaces, where individuality ruled supreme, the cowboy was also seen as a rugged outdoorsman who appreciated and respected the land he was trying to tame. He was also a larger-than-life figure, able to hold his whiskey, shoot the wings off a fly, and leave a trail of brokenhearted ladies in his wake. Most important, though, while the cowboy could be both outlaw and hero, he was ultimately defined by a personal code of honor, willing to live with the consequences of his life choices without complaint. He was, in short, his own man.

Ironically, the romantic view of the John Wayne-esque Marlboro Man loses some of its sheen upon closer scrutiny. In reality, cowboys were the largely uneducated hired hands of cattle ranchers, who worked grueling hours for very little pay. And although cowboys and the West have been forever intertwined, the reign of the cowboy was less than a generation, with the majority of cowboys disappearing after the nineteenth-century cattle barons gave way to smaller landowners. However, the image of the cowboy way of life endured and became romanticized and rose-tinted, a hard way of life forever woven into the fabric of American culture and identity. Nowhere is the cowboy myth more embraced than in the Southwest, where cattle still roam and where many like to say young children are taught to ride before they can walk.

John Donald Imus, Jr., grew up in such a place, surrounded by modern-day cowboys who tended to the cattle on the Imus family ranch. Naturally rebellious, he identified with the image of the lone figure forging his own path and found an identity in ranch life that would remain with him even when he left to pursue his ambitions in the world of big cities and cramped concrete spaces. Two parts originator, one part agitator, Imus has always done things his way, both to his detriment and his unbridled success. He grew up an angry young man who learned early on to use words as his weapon of choice and humor to win favor from his friends, and even his enemies. Rather than be tamed by the corporate world of radio, Imus continued to be the rugged individualist living by his own code, and, many times over, wound up suffering the consequences of his actions. Addictions to both alcohol and cocaine in the midst of his meteoric rise in radio came shockingly close to ending this truly original success story.

Although Imus hasn't necessarily gotten mellow with age, he has gotten wiser, finally realizing that self-destruction isn't honorable by anybody's code. The most heroic individual is the one who can confront his demons and face them head-on. While his cowboy mentality may have alienated him from many over the course of his life, it is also what ultimately makes him a remarkable survivor.

Not only has Imus turned his personal life around, he has also reinvented himself professionally. Unlike the cowboy heroes of his childhood past, Don Imus simply refuses to drift away. More popular than ever, he boasts some fifteen million followers strong, and with his undiluted opinions and shoot-from-the-hip style, there is little indifference to Imus; you either love him or don't get him. Like his personality, Imus's humor is always witty but often prickly, tinged with a cutting meanness that comes from his refusal to temper his views in order to spare anybody's feelings, regardless of their gender, religious views, or ethnicity.

As a result, to some Don Imus is a misogynist and a racist, to others he's a keen humorist and social commentator. Jeff Greenfield offers a different view. "He's the court jester. The court jester to the powerful. The job of the court jester was to prick the pretentions and the pomposity of the royal court, and [he] could say things nobody else could. And that's what Imus does."

In the early days of his career, Imus was a deejay who gained popularity by doing outrageous on-air stunts and pushing the envelope of good taste. But over the years he has transformed himself from being an in-your-face shock jock to his current status as an acutely intelligent political observer, riding high in the saddle as the media's most feared curmudgeon and perhaps America's last true cowboy.

Chapter One

IN MANY WAYS, SOUTHERN CALIFORNIA HAS BECOME A SELF-PERPETU-ated fiction. Invoke the name and it congers *Baywatch*-esque images of swaying palm trees, sandy beaches, the Pacific Coast Highway, Hollywood, and Beverly Hills. But travel east and in less than an hour a very different and typically unseen Southern California emerges, one with scrub-brush landscapes, mobile home parks, and hardscrabble towns with glamour-challenged names like Calimesa, Belmont, and Hemet. Even today these small communities lie in relatively remote rural areas and, except for those looking to buy gas or get a snack at a 7 Eleven, are barely noticed by passing drivers on nearby Interstate 10.

But fifty years ago Los Angeles was actually the anomaly when viewed in the context of the entire southern region of the state. California was, and for that matter still is, primarily an agricultural state. Farms and ranches dotted the landscape, and the nose-to-the-grindstone lifestyle was as far removed from that of movie stars as it was from English tea and finger sandwiches. For the most part, the areas east of the coastal cities were isolated and rustic. The few residents who inhabited the sparsely settled land identified not with the developing fantasy that was known as Hollywood but with the legacy of the Old West, where men were the masters of their destiny and where hard work would be rewarded.

At the same time, however, there was also a subtle but definite unforgiving nature to both the land and the residents. Human failings weren't likely to be excused because of a difficult childhood, and an affliction such as alcoholism was seen not as a disease needing treatment but as a weakness of moral character. And once a family was marked with a particular reputation, it stuck to them like branding on the backside of a steer.

Perris, California, is such a community; it is also Don Imus's hometown. John Donald Imus, Jr., was born on July 23, 1940, in the small enclave located not far from the Riverside County seat. His parents, John, Sr., and local beauty Frances Elizabeth, had been married a year earlier, in 1939. Family friend Michael Lynn remembers Frances as "one of the terrific, outspoken women who had also a very quick and incisive wit."

"We had a funny family. Mother and Dad were both funny," says Don's brother, Fred, who is younger by just eighteen months. "In fact, the ones that weren't funny were crazy."

"I don't know," counters Don. "I mean, we had great parents."

At the time, Frances no doubt thought she had made a good catch in John, who was a third-generation cattle rancher and who came from hardy family stock. The Imuses' presence in California can be traced back to 1850, and the story of the family's trek west shows the mettle of the people who were compelled to settle the untamed land west of the Rockies.

The move west was initiated in 1849 by Hiram Imus, Sr., and his son, Hiram, Jr., who had married a Quaker from Pennsylvania, Eliza, with whom he sired eleven children. At the time, both father and son were living in Illinois, but after hearing the glorious tales of the California gold rush, dreamed of taking a herd of cattle west, where they could set themselves up as ranchers. Plus, Hiram, Jr.'s, brother Charles and Hiram's son, also named Charles, had already moved to California. So on May 3, 1849, the younger Imus, together with his parents and another family, the Rices, left Galena, Illinois, with a wagon train consisting of cattle, horses, and mules packed high with provisions they believed were sufficient to last through their journey to California.

In the early stages of the trip, the travel was easy. There was plentiful grass for the cattle to graze on and the weather was temperate. Along the way the Imus party passed several other groups who were also California bound, as well as trains of Mormons heading for their promised land of Utah. But at the Platte River in Nebraska, the Imuses' luck began to take a turn.

They had made camp near the river and spent an uneventful night. But as they were cooking breakfast the following morning, the ground beneath them began to shake, as if an earthquake were trembling the land. Then suddenly a herd of buffalo came stampeding through their camp, charging through the cattle and pushing them not only upriver but across the river. The stampede lasted several hours, and when the last of the buffalo ran through, all their cattle were gone.

The horses that fled during the chaos were rounded up and the badly shaken party packed up and moved on, while a few of the men rode off to see if they could find any of the scattered cattle. Only a handful was ever retrieved.

In Utah the Imus party traveled to Salt Lake City, where they planned to rest and restock their provisions before undertaking what they knew would be the most difficult part of the journey, in part because of the weather and in part because of pockets of hostile Indians. Several wagon trains had been forced back to Salt Lake because of deadly encounters with the local Indian tribes. However, the city wasn't set up or equipped to handle a large influx of travelers, so the Imuses and other parties were strenuously urged to move on, and in December 1849 continued their way west. It has become part of Imus family lore that at some point on their journey the Imuses met up with the Donner party, but in fact the Donner disaster had occurred two years earlier, during the winter of 1846 to 1847.

But as it was, the Imus party themselves barely survived. As they plodded through the arid deserts of the West, skeletons of fallen horses and oxen—as well as crude graves—were vivid reminders of the peril they were in. For weeks they passed piles of furniture and other personal belongings that had been left behind by previous groups in order to lighten the burden of the failing pack animals who were slowly starving to death. As the Imus party animals lost strength, their train covered fewer and fewer miles in a day, prolonging an already endless trip and forcing them to stretch meager provisions even thinner. The first thing they ran out of was salt, then their food supply was so precious, it was actually kept under lock and key so people, now on strict rations, wouldn't be tempted to steal.

Finally, the decision was made to send three members on the three strongest horses ahead to Los Angeles, then a small outpost of a city, for provisions. There they were able to locate the Rollins ranch, where the three men were given food to take back to those who'd been left stranded. Once nourished, what remained of the Imus party made their way back to the Rollins ranch, where they stayed until both the people and animals had recuperated.

Rollins, who owned the ranch, was a friend of Hiram, Sr.'s, son, Captain Charles Imus, who had settled in Santa Cruz, California, after his military service. And it was to Santa Cruz that the Imuses headed when they left the Rollins ranch on May 3, 1850, exactly a year to the day they had left Illinois.

Charles Imus had originally come to California in the summer of 1831 with Henry Rice and his wife, settling on a claim at the mouth of the Wolf River, in Stockton County—an area that would play an important part in Don Imus's life over a century later. But in 1832 Imus and the Rices were forced to return to Illinois for the duration of the Black Hawk Wars. In 1845 Charles had returned to California with his nephew and settled permanently.

Once in Santa Cruz, the rest of the newly transplanted Imus

clan settled in and made the area its home. However, the adventuresome spirit that had prompted the family to come to California lived on in Hiram, Jr.'s, sons, Edwin, Charles, and William. In 1854 the three young brothers packed a few horses and left the family ranch, Quien Sabe, and set off south along the ruggedly beautiful but often inhospitable northern California coast. They first spent time at the Gould ranch, then moved on to Rancho del Chorro, where William lived for many years with his wife, Sarah.

In the early summer of 1875 Charles and Edwin were once again on the move, this time with a cattleman named Jake Harden. The three men intended to drive their cattle from California all the way to Arizona, a risky proposition at best, considering the lack of plentiful water. They spent the winter in Carson Valley, Nevada, then continued on their journey, which took them through Rock Springs, then Eldorado Canyon (located near the Grand Canyon), where they had to cross the Colorado River, two mountain ranges, and go through Union Pass, until they at last settled at Camp Willows, an abandoned soldiers' camp located near Kingman, Arizona.

"The original Willows was an army post, and it was connected to Fort Whipple out of Prescott," explains George Davis, whose grandmother was Edwin's daughter. "The cavalry was based there and then they abandoned it. That's when my great-grandfather came through and homesteaded the Willows, living in that old adobe shack that was the army post."

After purchasing Camp Willows and settling his stock in, Edwin returned to California and married Rose Hunt, then brought his bride back to Arizona, where they would make their home. With verve and determination Edwin worked to make his land a successful cattle ranch. Eventually the property became known as the Willows ranch, with Edwin's the first white family to lay claim to the area. "The Imuses have a lot of history in there," Davis notes. "Historically, May was the first white lady born in Mohave County. She later married my namesake, George Davis, who came out of Idaho and brought a herd of horses down into that Kingman area."

It's easy to see what attracted men like George Davis and Edwin Imus to settle in that part of Arizona. First, although it is part of the Mohave Desert, with summer temperatures hovering in the mid-nineties, the area's low humidity helps keep the heat surprisingly bearable. At the same time, because it's nestled in a valley, the winters are relatively cool, which means that the saguaro cactus that many people associate with the southwest desert does not thrive there.

And then there was the land itself. Not only was it vast enough to hold a man's dreams, but it was also just naturally awe-inspiring. At dusk, the nearby Hualapai Mountains take on a pinkish cast, while off to the west, the sun goes down in a blaze of brilliant reds, oranges, and pinks reflecting off the brown and beige landscape to create a spectacular palette of color. It's hard not to feel both humbled and inspired by the sheer beauty of it all.

Although they were bound by both the land and by blood, the Imus and the Davis sides of the family slowly drifted apart, and by the time George was born in 1939, the estrangement was complete. He notes that even today he doesn't "know any of the Imuses. They still have an Imus family reunion, but I just never had the opportunity to know that side of the family."

The Imus clan felt that they had found their home and looked forward to laying down permanent roots, and by 1885 William Imus had joined his brother Edwin at Willows. Five years earlier, brother Charles had died en route to California at Eldorado Canyon. William, who had been his brother's business partner, disposed of Charles's property in California, then came to Arizona and took over his holdings there. Cattle ranching, though, is a difficult and uncertain business, fraught with risk. Nor is it as lucrative as one might think. While thirty-five thousand acres sounds like a vast expanse of land to most people, by ranching standards it's not. And the value of any land is not merely its overall size but how many acres are actually suitable for grazing and how many are unusable scrub. For all its splendor, Willows ranch, which would have been an operation with three to four hundred mother cows, would have been hard pressed to comfortably support more than one family.

"As far as I know," laughs George Davis, "there wasn't too many wealthy Imuses."

The reality was, neither Edwin nor his brothers nor their progeny ever became rich men cattle ranching, but they were comfortable enough; their land allowed them to be self-sufficient and provide for their large families, and most important, they were their own bosses.

Over the years the ranch passed between various family members, but with each succeeding generation the fate of the Willows seemed more and more precarious. Eventually the family fortunes would take a devastating turn with the generation that included Don's father, John Imus. As John grew older, it became obvious to everyone around him that what his friends and family discreetly referred to as a drinking problem was far more serious than that. John was a full-blown alcoholic, as much an addict as a heroin junkie and just as in need of help. But the days of understanding the true nature of the affliction and how to treat it were still decades away. So, the Imuses did what most other families of the time did: ignore the truth and pretend it wasn't affecting their lives.

One of the properties John had inherited was the family home in Perris, California. And like Imuses before him, he would regularly take his sons to the Willows during summers, where they would enjoy the fruits of their ancestors' labors. As youngsters, Don, Jr., and Freddie were still blissfully unaware of their family's skeletons or the uncertainty that the Willows ranch was facing. All they knew was that the ranch, fifty miles from the nearest town, was their personal playground, a real-life theme park, where boys really did grow up to be cowboys. Even in its early years, though, the ranch was primarily a summer residence, where family members would come for the season, then retreat to other residences during the colder, winter months.

"I love horses and cattle and I remember that as being great fun, growing up on a cattle ranch," Don would say years later. "That's all I remember about it. But it was great because we grew up about half the time on a cattle ranch."

Although they would later develop a symbiotic closeness more associated with twins than mere siblings, as young children Don would lord his age and size over Freddie by regularly beating up on him—until baby brother fought back one day.

"I broke his foot with a shoe," laughs Fred. "It's been a pretty good relationship ever since."

It needed to be. For one thing, because of their relative isolation on the ranch, they had no children to play with, which prompts Fred to note: "I guess that's why we get along so well."

"Even when we weren't out on the ranch we spent a lot of time together," Don adds. "And we're still very close."

With few other friends for the boys and no television to act as entertainment, Don's parents, who were both college educated, made sure Don and Fred had plenty of books to read. So as a young boy Don was exposed to a wide variety of literature, including Hemingway's *For Whom the Bell Tolls, The Story of Civilization* by Will and Ariel Durant, and the works of Aldous Huxley, F. Scott Fitzgerald, and Herman Wouk. Once Don was into a book, it was hard for him to put it down until he finished it.

His love of books may have also been a form of escapism, because his family life was often unsettled. One curious incident that other family members recall was the two-year absence of the boy's mother. "My grandmother May helped watch Don and Fred during that time," says George Davis. "What happened was, Frances went to Europe for a couple of years and left the boys and John behind."

As they grew older and their family would slowly start to deteriorate further, the boys would often have only each other to turn to for comfort and support, forging a bond that no person or circumstance would ever be able to break.

According to relatives, Don, Sr., tried to follow in the family business with a spread of his own in Perris. But he simply didn't have the necessary passion for ranching the way his grandfather and father had had. As the years unfolded, whatever promise Frances once thought Don held was broken by his drinking and his inability to turn much of a profit, until their life had more in common with *Of Mice and Men* than it did *Dallas*. The hopes they once had for the future were now just bitter pipe dreams.

Money was a particular sore spot. There was just never enough of it, a situation Frances was not accustomed to, because she had come from a wealthy family. Ironically Don's efforts to maintain his wife's standard of living may in fact have helped hasten their financial downfall.

"You could tell she came from wealth," says a relative. "Just the way she carried herself and the air about her. I'm just speculating, but I think that was a lot of the problem; Don tried to keep her in the manner to which she was accustomed."

Between his drinking and her desire for a standard of living that was beyond their means, money became increasingly tighter and the relationship between Frances and her husband grew increasingly strained. The family fallout had a pronounced effect on Don, who began acting out in school, exhibiting an aggressive, sharp-witted—and sharp-tongued—nature.

"I was a horrible adolescent," Don admits easily. "I was always the rotten kid who made fun of the fat kid in school. I was an obnoxious little bastard."

Powerless to stop his family's downward spiral, he did his best to be the master of his environment everywhere else. He would dress and talk the way he wanted and, whenever possible, try to be the one in charge, leading the way.

However, not everyone always appreciated the experience. In the eighth grade Don enjoyed his first taste of popularity when he was elected class president. But just a short time later he was impeached and removed from office for being too dictatorial.

"He had a definite attitude and a point of view of what he thought, and he didn't mind saying it," Fred acknowledges.

But Don was more than just opinionated. He was angry and confrontational, and looking back he admits he "was a problem child. I was bounced from one hideous private school to another." Sometimes he would leave because of family circumstance; sometimes he would be asked to go. Don's attitude toward authority figures was such that he recalls his wealthy grandmother once "predicted I would end up in prison."

At that point Frances was more worried about her children ending up in the poorhouse than in the big house. Although there are conflicting stories as to exactly how it happened, eventually John Imus lost everything. There was no longer a personal family home in Perris and no Imus family Willows ranch.

Some say John lost most of his money to tax troubles. Others say it was mostly a self-inflicted financial wound.

"The story was that Don's father just kept borrowing against his so-called legacy," says Phil Oelze, a friend from high school. He recalls Don and Fred revealing that their father's brother had been keeping the family afloat "all those years John had a drinking problem and ultimately he spent his legacy."

George Davis has a similar recollection. "John and his brother didn't get along, but I had the impression he was supporting his brother." Davis says that it was after they lost the ranch that "they started milling around a little bit."

As an adult George would have the chance to visit the ranch he'd heard so much about growing up. "The original site isn't there, but the Willows ranch is still there," he says, then adds with a sigh, "In fact, they're subdividing it now and I hate to see that."

Freddie was able to graduate from grammar school in Perris, but with no land to call their own, Frances and Don were forced into an itinerant lifestyle, moving from place to place, town to town. Since California had little left to offer the family other than unhappy memories, Don decided to return to his native state, spending some time in Scottsdale, Arizona, before moving on to Prescott, where he had some relatives who might help the family adjust.

While in Scottsdale, Don attended Scottsdale High and was befriended by a fellow student, Freddie Parker, who is now deceased. "Freddie had what we call command presence," says a college buddy of Parker's. "He was a good athlete and an interesting fellow. Don idolized Freddie, and Freddie used to laugh a lot about Don. They had a lot of fun together."

Which made it all that much more difficult for Don to be uprooted once again, especially to a town 110 miles from Scottsdale that any teenager would consider to be in the middle of nowhere. When the Imuses arrived in Prescott during the summer of 1956, it was a small community of less than twenty thousand people. Named after noted historian William Hickling Prescott, the town had played an important part of the area's history, a story well known by locals, who were proud of their heritage. After the discovery of gold led to Arizona becoming a United States territory, the provisional seat of the territorial government was established at Fort Whipple in Chino Valley on January 22, 1864. Nine months later it was moved twenty miles away to a little mining community named Prescott. The capital moved to Tucson in 1867 for ten years, then shifted back to Prescott, until it moved permanently to Phoenix in 1889.

Located over a mile above sea level in the Bradshaw Mountains among the largest stand of ponderosa pines in the world, Prescott lies within central Arizona's Yavapai County, which was one of the original four created when Arizona was still only a territory. Once a massive 65,000 square miles, Yavapai County now covers "only" little more than 8,125—an area as large as New Jersey.

Early settlers were attracted to Prescott because of the ponderosa pines; the wide, open ranges needed for the ever-present cattle ranchers; and minerals such as copper. As miners and ranchers swelled the town's population, some enterprising businessmen established Whiskey Row, which featured numerous saloons and restaurants that stayed open twenty-four hours a day, giving Prescott a true Dodge City feel. The current residents of the area are proud of their town's rich history and have taken pains to preserve their links to the past, which is why many areas, such as Whiskey Row, remain standing today as they did a century ago.

A community such as Prescott clings tenaciously to its past and doesn't readily welcome change of any kind, a painful lesson Don would soon experience first-hand. Like the cowboys and miners who first settled the area, the longtime residents believed there was a proper way of acting and behaving and anyone not abiding by the local standards was viewed with skepticism and wariness.

It's seldom easy being the new kid in town even for those who naturally fit in. For someone like Don, who seemed to go out of his way *not* to conform, it's nearly impossible. Although he would eventually establish close ties with a small group of guys, in many respects Don would remain an outsider throughout his time in Prescott, setting a pattern he would follow his entire life.

Chapter Two

————————— ▆▆▆▆▆ —————————

S INCE DON WASN'T PARTICULARLY OUTGOING AMONG STRANGERS, IT was left to George Davis to help his cousin try to settle in his new town, which the chamber-of-commerce types liked to call "Everyone's Hometown!" Although George and Don hadn't known each other while growing up and met for the first time in Prescott, they took an immediate liking to each other, which made the trauma of moving to yet another new place a little easier for Don. Like Fred, George was an easygoing youth with a gentle air about him, although he also had a bit of a hell-raiser in him, an appealing combination that made him popular among both his peers and adults.

George spent most of his time running around with a nearly inseparable handful of teenage boys who were similar in temperament and demeanor, and it was this group of young men who would become Don's closest Prescott friends. Which was somewhat surprising, considering that the group was somewhat taken aback by Don when George first introduced them.

"One day we were all going somewhere together," recalls Phil Oelze, "and George asked if would it be okay if his cousin Don Imus came along. And it's like, you know, who's Don Imus?"

Oelze says he and the others were taken aback a bit the first time they saw Don strut into view, because in the summer of 1956 he was going through what can be described only as his Elvis phase. "The sides of his hair were carefully slicked, with the front adorned by a big DA. His Levis were pressed down real low to where they're almost ready to fall down around your ankles, he had a shirt with the collar up and a little bit of a swagger to his manner and whatnot.

"When George revealed this was his cousin, everybody, I think, was a bit shocked, because George was like the rest of us, pretty clean-cut and interested in a good time. But we said sure, bring him along. We were pretty democratic. So he came along with Fred. Fred was always there. He never went *anywhere* without Fred."

Of the two, Fred had the easier time being accepted, in part because he looked like the other Prescott boys with short-cropped hair and a polite manner and because he had a very open, likable personality. Although he tended to hang back and let Don take the lead in social situations, acting almost as Don's straight man, Fred would step up to the fore whenever he sensed his brother was getting in over his head.

"Fred would always explain Don's eccentricities," says Phil. "If Don did or said something or behaved in a certain way, it seemed kind of Fred's job to explain it to everybody."

George Davis also remembers Fred being "a kick" and a calming influence on his brother. "Don was the big brother and Freddie knew his place there but Freddie had the common sense to keep things under control."

And in return Don kept an eye on Fred. "Don wouldn't let anything happen to Freddie, and still won't, from what I see. He was always a mother hen in that sense. He probably raised Freddie, truth be known. I still have a big place in my heart for them not because they were family but because they were darn good friends. The two of them together would just keep you rolling."

But of all the members of George's group, it was Phil who would become the closest to Don. "I enjoyed Don, I really did," Oelze says with obvious affection. What made the friendship surprising is that Phil was an insider, a respected student who would be voted Most Popular in his senior class.

Because of the way Don dressed and swaggered, Oelze says the boys quickly gave him a nickname. "Everybody started hazing Don, calling him Rat Pack. But he kind of took it in stride and gave it back a bit and kind of enjoyed that repartee. So the deal was done. He became a member of our crowd."

George Davis says of their crowd, "We had a good group of guys and had a lot of fun. I related to the *Happy Days* group, although we were probably a little worse than those guys."

As Don soon discovered, there wasn't a lot of organized activities in Prescott, so teenagers were left to entertain themselves, which on Friday and Saturday nights usually consisted of drinking beer and driving around.

"We used to drink quite a bit for kids in those days," Oelze laughs. "Of course, in our little community, you only needed a couple of beers to get you oiled. We could get the whole gang pretty well on its way on half a case of beer."

Once they were feeling buzzed, the boys would cram into a car and cruise the town from one end of town to the other, which took no more than ten or fifteen minutes. Cruising also allowed them to keep an eye out for any out-of-town intruders who dared come on their turf.

"We were rowdy. There used to be a lot of young kids who came up from Phoenix to Prescott on weekends, and one of the games we would play would be to chase these guys out of town," explains Phil.

Taking full advantage of Don's ability to piss people off, he would be the driver. While the other boys would scrunch down in the seats to hide, Don would pull aside the other car, roll down his window, and start talking until he goaded them into challenging him to a fight. But once both cars pulled over, Don's buddies would come spilling out of the car and chase the intruders away.

"It was mostly pushing and shoving and talk more than any-thing else, but we did get into a couple of whizzbangs," Phil says. "We bit off more than we could chew occasionally and got into some real mean fights, but we didn't do it all the time; we weren't sociopaths. Fighting was just a way you kind of proved your prowess." Although even then Imus seemed to prefer ver-bal jabs to physical sparring.

Even though they were always on the lookout to defend their home territory, most of the time they would just end up driving around talking, joking, and listening to the radio, which from the time they were young boys had also been one of Don's and Fred's favorite shared interests. On Saturday nights most of the boys were allowed to stay out past midnight, so once the local station would go off the air at eleven P.M., they scanned the dial for anything they could pick up in their remote area.

The strongest signals came from high-powered stations lo-cated along the Texas/Mexico border, such as the 250,000-watt XELO out of Del Rio, Texas. Although technically based in the United States, the transmitter was actually located in Juarez, Mexico, which made the broadcasts exempt from FCC regula-tions—a fact not lost on an up-and-coming deejay named Wolfman Jack.

In addition to the howlings of the Wolfman, the stations also offered a steady diet of programs featuring evangelists, reli-gious P. T. Barnums who in between preaching sold "every-thing from baby chickens to prayer clothes and authentic pic-tures of Jesus."

As they drove endlessly back and forth across town, the boys would spin stories and make social commentary. "Our task on a Saturday night in 1956 and '57 was to ferret out these things, the hypocrisy of certain things, and expose them as to how we really saw them. We all had a fairly sharp and critical view of what was going on in the world," says Phil, who remembers how they would also spend hours and hours making up their own parodies and takeoffs of the advertising evangelicals, creating new characters or combining real people with fictional characters, such as a "hellfire and damnation preacher who we would deride. That's what we did to entertain ourselves. There was nothing else going on. We had a lot of fun with it."

One of the objects of their wit was a man named Billy Sol Estes, who was involved in the notorious "salad oil scandal," in which Estes was accused of selling railroad cars that were supposed to be filled with salad oil but were found to be empty.

Years later Don would appropriate their late-night game and make it his professional signature. But back in Prescott it was simply a way to pass the time, a diversion that allowed Don to show off his wit and humor. But although Don had found a measure of acceptance with Phil, George, and the others in the group, his contact with other kids was somewhat limited because he had arrived during summer break. He had yet to face the special scrutiny that comes with being the new kid in school, an experience that would prove emotionally brutal. In the fall of 1956 Don enrolled at Prescott High School as a junior, a year behind George and the others, who were starting their senior year.

"He was an object of derision," admits Oelze. "When you're a teenager and don't look or act like anybody else, then obviously there's something wrong with you."

Kids would laugh at Don as he passed by, sarcastically taunt him, mimic his walk, and make fun of his doo-wop hair. Occasionally Don would talk back, and the jawing occasionally turned physical, with Don getting pushed and roughed up a bit in the halls. Although he was quick with a remark, Don was less prone to escalate a physical altercation.

"Don wasn't a vicious kid. He was no worse than any of the rest of them," explains Fred, who smilingly admits Don did get into scrapes. "Why? Oh, I suppose it was because of something he said."

It's telling, however, that although Imus found himself under almost constant scrutiny, part of him seemed to thrive on being controversial. Phil says his friend enjoyed the notoriety "because he gained a certain sense of celebrity from it.

"I look back over my life, and my friendships have been to some extent a collection of eccentric characters. And he certainly is one. He was definitely different. Even as part of our crowd he was still different."

And that difference was immediately noticed by the town's elders. Prescott was such a small, insular community in the mid-1950s that residents thought of Scottsdale, Arizona, as the "big city." And in the end, many in town would hold Don up as a living example of everything that was wrong with big-city life. Part of that perception would come from Don himself and his refusal to tone down, which resulted in Don's becoming a source of concern for many parents.

"He had a street kid's mouth and attitude, when our little darling innocents up here in the mountains didn't know about anything," remembers high school teacher Ethel Tyson. "They all kept him at arm's length, except for these six or seven boys.

"And a lot of parents, they didn't understand Don and they didn't want their children associating with him because of his streetwise attitude and his really vulgar language—scatological things that we hadn't heard before. It was shocking to our kids, who were really isolated on this mountain and pretty innocent in 1957. He was all the things that we didn't know anything about yet."

Not that the others in his group, or the other teenagers in town, were complete angels. Tyson admits that "almost all our boys drank beer, for sure. We had the darnedest time trying to keep that away from dances and picnics."

Even the parents of his friends had their reservations about Don, including Oelze's. "Don was terribly unpolished in a lot of ways. You went on your reputation in those days, and he was known as Rat Pack. But my parents were great people and they kind of let me have my head. I don't think the parents were aware of the beer consumption and whatnot. Or if they did, they didn't say anything."

Not only were parents keeping a wary eye on Don, his teachers at Prescott instinctively, and, as it turned out, justifiably singled him out as a potential troublemaker. Don admitted to George that he was kicked out of a school once when he was younger, although, "he never elaborated. He would just joke about it, but that's what he did with everything. That was Don's escape," Davis says, then adds, "He's not a whole lot different now than he was then; he has the same personality."

Ethel Tyson says it was obvious the boys found Don "very amusing, but I don't think the rest of the school thought he was very funny. Nor did the administration."

Even though Don managed to stay out of trouble, he still succeeded in rubbing many teachers and school administrators the wrong way. "He was one of those kids who always thought he knew more than the teachers did," Fred sighs.

It's somewhat surprising, then, that Don actually made an effort to get involved in some school activities. Encouraged by George, who was a member of the Thespians Club, Don got a part in the Christmas play, which was directed by Mrs. Tyson. Although she was aware of his reputation, Ethel says that Don always behaved appropriately in her presence.

"He didn't say obscenities in my classroom—I wouldn't have stood for that. Although I don't know what he did backstage when he wasn't onstage and I wasn't dealing with him. A lot goes on backstage while you're out front," she says with a wry laugh. "I had good stage managers, but they *were* kids."

The holiday play was titled *Why the Chimes Rang* and was based on a medieval pageant about a couple of very poor children. On their way to church on Christmas Eve, a little boy gives a traveler directions and is given a penny in return. The boy's brother suggests they go buy some candy, but the first boy thinks it should go to the Christ child because it was Christmas Eve. At the cathedral the wealthy people of the town have filled the church with jewels and money and flowers. But when the little boy puts his single penny on the plate, the chimes ring.

Don had a nonspeaking role as a soldier but enjoyed the experience so much that he appeared in two other plays that school year, and never once did Ethel have to reprimand him.

"He must have had an interest in theater and what it meant to face an audience because he was willing to be directed. He did his lines, came to rehearsals on time, and behaved himself, or I'd have booted him."

That taste of being onstage and the center of everyone's attention spurred Don to pursue his real passion—being a singer. He formed the Don Imus Combo and enlisted his buddies to back him up: Gene Neil on saxophone, Bob Baller on drums, Richard Franks on piano and cousin George Davis on bass.

"He wasn't a singer, but then, I wasn't a musician even though I played the bass in his combo," laughs Davis, who said he understood even then how badly Don needed attention and validation. "Don wanted, really wanted, the limelight. He wanted to be center stage. It was important to him."

Don would get his opportunity to stand in the spotlight at Prescott High's annual talent show, which was basically a performance free-for-all. Some participants would play a musical instrument, others would sing, and, of course, there was the inevitable baton twirler. Once again it was Ethel Tyson who ran the program. And when she saw who was in Don's combo, she admits it took her aback.

"It was amazing. Bob Baller was the boyfriend of a minister's daughter and Richard Frank's father was very well known in the community, so Richard was reared carefully. Gene was another one of my kids who did plays for me. So Don must have been musical enough that the kids put up with him as the leader of that band."

Whatever skepticism the student body had when Don and his band first got onstage was soon forgotten. Doing a set of Fats Domino songs, Don and his friends had the audience jumping and won the talent show hands down.

"He was a real ham up there and they loved him," remembers Phil, who enjoyed seeing so many surprised faces watching his friend's moment in the spotlight, none more shocked than the teachers and administrators.

"I don't suppose anybody knew Don had it in him," Ethel admits. "I think it was probably the best thing that happened to him all year, because he got accolades from the audience."

But to the guys who rode with Don every Saturday night, listening to the radio, it was no surprise. "No," said George, "because we had observed him doing those kinds of things lots of times."

What should have been Don's greatest moment, however, quickly became mired in controversy. Traditionally Prescott High and Flagstaff High would swap talent show winners, offering the acts a kind of mini victory tour. But school officials in Prescott initially balked at the idea of Don representing the school in any kind of official capacity.

"Yes, there was resistance from the administration," Ethel recalls, and says she immediately went to bat for Don because he had won the competition fairly and deserved the opportunity to perform in Flagstaff. "He got to go, but I had to sponsor the trip."

If Don was bothered by the official opposition to his going, he never let on to it. Instead, he just focused on winning over the Flagstaff student body.

"He got a big hoorah there," says George. "In fact, we stayed a little after the show and did an encore. This has always been his ambition, to be an entertainer."

The experience of performing in front of an audience was even greater the second time and convinced Don that his future would be found in performing. And it didn't matter whether anyone else believed he could do it or not.

"If you'd taken a vote in school, he'd probably have been voted the least likely to succeed in anything," comments Oelze, who says that back then nobody realized that "in this culture, you get paid for outrageous behavior. You get very well rewarded."

However, had they been told he would grow up to be the original shock jock, the most surprised might have been Don, who had set his sights on a singing career. It was a goal he wasn't shy talking about and would spend many nights visualizing himself center stage.

Apparently, though, the vision didn't include groupies. While it's true that the boys were almost inseparable, most of them still managed to carve out some time to spend with girls every now and then. "They'd be out at some campgrounds with a nice campfire and then off into the bushes with the girls. They were in the backseats of cars all the time, those kids, or out in the bushes," chuckles Mrs. Tyson.

Except Don. When he wasn't with the gang, he was with Fred. But according to both George and Phil, Imus never had anyone even close to resembling a girlfriend.

"Cute as he was—he had kind of a darling little face," Ethel says, then adds, "Mothers didn't like him much."

In retrospect, though, it might not have been Don individually who concerned the parents of Prescott as much as it was his family situation. In the Eisenhower years most Americans were still careful not to expose any family skeletons or, for that matter, even acknowledge they exist. Today there are twelve-step programs, counseling options, rehabs, and even medical options to help treat alcoholism. Moreover, there is also extensive assistance available to those other family members affected by their loved one's disease. But in 1956 and 1957, it was a taboo subject among proper people. So even though Don Imus, Sr., had a drinking problem, nobody ever talked about it openly. But everyone was aware of it.

"I think the objection parents had was based on that to some extent," agrees Phil. "It was a question of family values and moral commitment. I'm sure the parents were just concerned because you're kind of known by the company you keep. Don was acting out a bit and had that reputation and Fred was along for the ride. They didn't know that Don and Fred were really pretty good folks. I know Don is a fairly decent guy, and when you shake him right down to the elements, he's a good person."

As his alcoholism grew more debilitating, Mr. Imus would spend less and less time in Prescott. When he went on a lengthy binge, he would head for Los Angeles, disappearing for weeks and possibly months at a time. Then he would come back, and the family would have to adjust to his return. Occasionally he would take his sons with him to bars on Whiskey Row, where they would sit with their father as he drank.

"Except we weren't drunk like he was," Fred says, then jokes, "At least not yet."

Because he tended to leave town when bingeing, Mr. Imus was able to keep a lower profile. Says one resident: "Prescott has always had an assortment of characters anyway, but the father wasn't around Prescott enough to gain any particular notoriety as the town alcoholic or anything like that. He was a guy who'd come home to Prescott, spend a few weeks, then take off again."

Although they didn't talk much about their family, it was obvious, says Phil, that "it was a devastating problem and very difficult on Don and Fred. They did their best to cope with it, of course."

For the most part, coping meant both avoiding the issue themselves and making sure others didn't find out the full extent of the problem. Even George, who was related to them, says it was a subject they never talked about openly. "You know, I've probably learned more about Don over the years from reading, because it was stuff we just didn't talk about. Never. Like I say, they were kind of loners.

"Being a kid, you didn't look for those kinds of things. I can look back now and see how his family was and I don't want to be talkin' out of church but it was rough. I know it was rough. People might have been aware of it, but people didn't bring it up and talk about it. And like I say, as a kid it didn't matter. But there were undoubtedly a lot of problems there."

Even to the most casual observer it was obvious that the Imuses were struggling, particularly on a material level. "Although, there was always a bit of banter between Don and Fred about money in the family somewhere, these kids were so deprived, even by 1956 and '57 standards. They didn't have what the rest of us had—a family automobile, clean clothes for school, money in your pocket, and a stable family life."

Because there was so little money, they were also forced to live in a series of small rental homes, which Phil remembers as being nearly ramshackle.

"They lived in several different places in Prescott in the time we were palling around together. They didn't live among wreckage, but it certainly wasn't a middle-class existence. The furniture was old and dilapidated. They lived in such a disheveled manner that the boys wouldn't want to take us inside the house. It was only on one or two occasions that we ever did."

It was then that Phil and George first met the elusive Mrs. Imus, whom both remember as friendly. "She didn't really have any friends, but she was pretty articulate," adds Phil, "and when I first met her, I recall she was a rather slender lady, with a full head of hair and who had some very striking features. At one time she was a very handsome woman. Don looks more like his father."

Oelze also remembers meeting Mr. Imus on a couple of occasions. "He was never unfriendly, but he was not usually sober. Or he was sick. He was sick a lot. We were aware his family had problems."

Ironically, while the adults in town did little in the way of offering any help or support to either the family in general or the boys in particular, Don and Fred's gang of friends did look after them the best they could. On occasions some of the gang gave Don and Fred money so they'd have some cash in their pockets. Another time they were moved to go to even greater lengths.

"I remember the Thanksgiving of that particular year, Don and Fred wanted to do a Thanksgiving dinner so all the gang got together and took up a collection amongst our families and arranged to help them put together a Thanksgiving dinner," Oelze recalls. "I remember taking a large broiler over to Don's house. And I think there were other things given to the family, to the boys, to help them in this dinner.

"I think they were looking forward to their father being there, but I don't remember that he was. If they cooked anything, the boys were the ones who probably did it. I don't know that the mother was involved much."

Perhaps the bigger secret that Don and Fred shared wasn't about their father but concerned their beloved mother. During their time in Prescott, Frances stayed to herself, never making friends, nor, to anybody's recollection, did she work. Instead, she mostly stayed home. But those who did have some contact with her, such as the Davises, were aware that Frances, too, was no stranger to drinking. "They used to come to our house, not the father, though, and we'd visit with them occasionally before his dad died," George says. "And there again, his mother, and I loved her dearly, but she had a problem."

It wasn't until he was an adult that Phil Oelze became aware of any problem with Mrs. Imus. "Years later I picked up some comments from some of the older people in the community, when I was a young parent myself, where it was suggested she had a drinking problem too."

This goes a long way in explaining the extremely close bond that developed between Don and Fred and why Don was so protective of his baby brother. "Don wouldn't let anything happen to Freddie, and still won't, from what I see," George comments. "He was always a mother hen in that sense. He probably raised Freddie, truth be known."

It's more than a little ironic that even though John's alcohol consumption was the primary reason for her world's collapse, Mrs. Imus found her own solace in a bottle as well. But though both parents drank, it was the father who earned the animosity of the sons, because when drunk, Mr. Imus could become abusive. Or, as George Davis puts it: "Their dad was a little bit harsh with them, for lack of a nice word." Again, because of the times, talking about such things would have been unseemly. But because these issues weren't addressed, Mr. Imus's drinking and abuse were allowed to continue unabated.

Behind the closed doors of their run-down home, Don and Fred were isolated and alone, powerless to make their home life better and with no hope of outside help. All they could do was try to assist their mom the best they could and dream of a day when they would be able to make her life, and theirs, better.

Chapter Three

NOWHERE IS THE EXPRESSION "BOYS WILL BE BOYS" TAKEN SO TO heart than in small towns like Prescott. Although officially parents and law enforcement frowned on beer drinking, cruising, and the rough play teenage boys sometimes engaged in, for the most part it was more a mere wink and a nod. Such behavior was considered a rite of passage and a way for the young men in town to blow off a little steam.

Sometimes, however, an ill-advised display of chest-thumping bravado could escalate into punches thrown, resulting in little more than scraped knuckles, bloody noses, and bruised egos. One notable time Don and his friends found themselves in the middle of a potentially dangerous brawl. In the early spring of 1957, Don's regular gang along with another carload of boys drove up to Flagstaff, where many of their female classmates in the school band and chorus were attending a musical festival.

"We went up there to ride herd on the local ladies," Phil explains. "What happened was, we were up there and shouldn't have been."

When they arrived in Flagstaff, the group split up, with half the boys—those who fancied themselves ladies' men—heading off to a local dance. Don, Fred, Phil, George and the less socially inclined others decided to just hang out and wander about the town that had been the setting of Don's earlier talent show triumph. While their stroll through the streets of Flagstaff was uneventful, the rest of their group found themselves in the eye of a storm. On the other side of town, the Prescott boys at the dance were confronted by a group of locals who didn't take kindly to the intrusion—and who were no doubt eager to return the hospitality shown them on their unsolicited excursions to Prescott. A fight broke out that was quickly taken care of by the police, who merely told the boys to move on.

"In small towns in Arizona in those days, it was just something they knew boys were going to do," says Phil. "The police didn't consider it a criminal behavior. It was just young kids doing what young kids do. And boys will be boys, right?"

Reunited, Don and his friends loaded into their cars and drove around downtown, looking for a place to eat. At the restaurant they were once again confronted by a group of locals that by this time had swelled to almost fifty youths. George remembers looking around him and realizing how badly outnumbered they were, so he, Don, and Fred wisely tried to hang back, waiting for the first opportunity to get out of there. But before they could get to their cars, the fighting broke out.

"Things really got out of hand," recalls Oelze. "It may well have been that we started it. That was dumb. I remember yelling, trying to shove these Flagstaff guys away myself, trying to get all of our people into their cars and out of there.

"Gary Denny, another friend, who was a kind of notorious badass, was with our gang that evening and it's fortunate he was there, because he could really handle himself. He kind of held them at bay as I moved the truck full of guys out and back onto the highway and drove way down the road quite a ways before we pulled over and did an inventory."

What they saw wasn't good. "We just got the stuffing kicked out of us. It was tough stuff. A couple of our guys got hurt and one of us ended up in the hospital."

Most seriously hurt was a boy named George Keeley, who had several teeth knocked out and another young man, who almost lost the sight of one eye. On their way back to Prescott, they stopped at an emergency center to patch the more seriously wounded boys up, then took them back home, where Keeley would be hospitalized. No charges were ever filed.

In later years it became the conventional wisdom of the town that the Flagstaff brawl led to several of the boys, including Don, being told either to join the marines or face criminal prosecution. Oelze says this simply isn't the case.

"People might tie it to that, but I don't think there was ever any ultimatum given to anybody. In fact, I don't know what there would have been to handle other than charges against the fellows in Flagstaff. Our county attorney at the time was incensed that the Flagstaff guys would use such force. In his opinion, we probably shouldn't have been up there, but we had every right to be there, if you really wanted to press it."

Another persistent rumor was passed along by Ethel Tyson, who says she heard "those seven boys got very, very drunk and went down and signed up."

The actual chain of events is much less colorful. The fact was, in the mid-1950s there were no voluntary armed forces as there is today. All able-bodied young men were required to serve for two years of military service. It was merely a question of when they chose to go or waited to be drafted. In June 1957 everyone but Don and Fred, who were one and two years behind respectively, were graduating from Prescott High and were deciding when they should do their stint. Cousin George decided to enlist immediately after school was over.

"Another friend of ours, Bud Ernst, and I went into the service first," Davis recalls. "We went into the Marine Corps together five days after we got out of school. It was a while later that Don and Phil and everybody else decided to join too."

In the early days of that summer, it was assumed that Phil and another member of the group, Bert Schenberger, would delay their military hitch to attend college first, while Don would complete his senior year and graduate. But the thought of losing his only group of friends had to weigh heavily on Imus; they were all going off on one kind of adventure or another, either college or the marines, while he and Fred would be stuck, alone, in Prescott.

Plans began to change after George and Bud wrote their buddies back home, regaling them with tales of life in the military. The camaraderie, the training, the adventure of simply being away from home on their own for the first time, sounded exciting and exotic. And a lot more interesting than watching the wildlife in Prescott. As the long summer dragged by, the idea of being one of the few and the proud became a siren song to Don and his friends.

Oelze explains how it was they all decided to enlist together. "Bert and I had already enrolled in PLC program, which was the Marine Corps's leadership program at the University of Arizona, because that's where we were going to go to school.

"But as the summer wore on and we got a little bit crazier and a little bit more bored and in reading the letters from our pals who were already in, Bert and I decided we would go ahead and do our hitch earlier. The feeling was, we ought to do it sooner rather than later. At some point Don got involved in the conversation and then another friend, Stan Mason, got caught up in the whole thing and before you know it we were daring each other and off we went."

Because Don was only seventeen, he was required to get written parental permission, which his mother gave. His father didn't sign for Don because in March of that year, he and his mother had officially separated, with the elder Imus taking off once again for Los Angeles. If there was any downside for Don about leaving Prescott for the service, it was that he'd be leaving Fred behind. But they both understood somebody needed to look after Frances, so they agreed Fred would take care of their mom and finish school, which he eventually would, graduating in 1959. Although curiously his senior picture does not appear in that yearbook.

It's interesting to note that of all the boys in their group, Don was the least interested in actual academics, even though he was acknowledged as being just as intelligent as those who were eventually college-bound. Nor did it surprise anyone that Don would choose to forgo his senior year and the chance to graduate with his class.

"I just don't think school was important to Don," Phil says. "He never spent any time with the books, certainly. He wasn't a motivated student, wasn't interested, but he has a very quick mind. Like the rest of us, he was ready for an adventure."

There were few at Prescott High who mourned the loss of Don's presence. And the feeling was obviously mutual. Even after Imus had long since left the town and had become a celebrity, he would conjure no nostalgia for his time there. Although he would remain etched in the minds of many in Prescott, including Ethel Tyson.

"I must have associated with fifteen hundred or two thousand kids after him," she notes, "but one of the reasons I remember him, I think, is because when he first got to be famous, my kids came to me and said, 'Do you remember having Don Imus in class?' Evidently somebody called him on the phone and asked if he remembered being in Prescott and he was kind of slight about it. He wasn't gracious or warm about it. Maybe it wasn't a great year for him, I don't know."

The would-be marines lived out the waning days of their youth the way they always had—cruising the main drag, drinking beer, making fun of the late-night radio preachers, commenting on the world at large, and being a source of endless amusement for one another. Shortly before Don and the others were due to report for duty, the gang took a camping trip up to the White Mountains.

"In Arizona, as a youngster, you really led an outdoor existence. I had a pickup truck and our friend Bert had a pickup truck and we drove with four or five guys in each pickup for a long weekend," Phil recalls. "It was our last big outing before we went into the Marine Corps. It was the rainy season and we spent five days holed up in a tent as the rain came pouring down. But we still caught a few fish and I'm sure ruined a lot of good food."

They also spent a lot of time telling stories, recalling past exploits and just enjoying one another's company. Fred was particularly enjoyable that trip, and they thought of how much they would miss his humor and common sense. Although nobody mentioned it openly, they were all aware that this chapter of their lives was about to close.

In the third week of July 1957, Don, Phil, Bert, and Stan went to the marine recruiting depot and were officially enlisted in the Marine Corps. Because they joined at the same time, they were assigned to the same platoon, Marine Recruit Platoon 187, which meant they would sleep in the same barracks, eat in the same mess hall, and drill and train together. Like George and Bud, who were together in a different unit, they were stationed at Camp Pendleton, near San Diego.

Their first exercise in humility was the traditional initiation of having their heads shaved. Although his hair had always been a source of vanity, whether admitted or not, all Don could do was laugh when he saw how they looked. There was a comfort and security in numbers, and they gave one another moral support. If one guy could do something, they all believed they could do it. If one guy could scale a wall, then it couldn't be that hard. Don and the others first went through recruit training, better known as boot camp, then through the infantry training regiment, which is combat training.

Even early on, though, Don was at a disadvantage when compared to the other Prescott boys. A major part of combat training is handling guns, and Imus had far less experience than his friends, who had all grown up schooled as hunters. "You know, that was the macho thing to do," Oelze says wryly. So while the others were qualified as sharpshooters or expert riflemen, Don struggled. It was his first clue that perhaps military life wasn't going to be quite what he expected.

Even though Don had willingly enlisted and understood that the essence of military life demands conformity and an adherence to the rules, he was never able to completely subjugate himself to those requirements. Although he completed boot camp with no physical problems and had the aptitude to learn the various drills, the truth was he was having a difficult time adjusting to military life. And in typical Imus fashion, he hid his turmoil behind a curtain of biting humor so that the depth of his conflict was not immediately apparent, even to his closest friends.

"It was very difficult for Don to conform anyway, so, conforming in dress and manner was difficult for him," Phil comments. "In the hours away from the program, like at night, he was up to his antics. He would act out, mimicking the drill instructor. He was a comedian, a clown."

Even George was aware that his cousin was gaining a certain reputation. Again. "I know he'd get it from [his superiors] for mouthing off."

Despite his growing discomfort with military life, the weekends offered a respite for Don. He and the others would go exploring. Sometimes they would drive to San Diego, where they would park in the middle of a lime grove, mixing drinks and telling stories "until we were blitzed out of our minds," laughs Oelze.

Los Angeles also had its appeal—for a different reason. Stan Mason's mother had recently moved from Prescott to the city of Alhambra, located just east of downtown L.A. near Pasadena. At least one weekend a month, Don and the others would go with Stan to his mom's new house and help her fix it up. "We'd do certain projects, like paint the garage, for room and board for the weekend." At night they reverted to their high school habits of buying beer and driving from one end of Colorado Boulevard, Pasadena's main street, to the other. Then come Sunday, they'd return to the base.

The boys all returned to Prescott for Christmas in 1957. But while the others went to happy holiday homes, Don was confronted with yet another family crisis. On September 13, 1957, Frances Elizabeth Imus filed for divorce from her husband. On the papers filed in the Yavapai County court, Frances stated that no community property had been accumulated in Arizona.

Frances was represented by a local attorney named Jack L. Ogg, who requested she be awarded sole custody of the children. The lawyer also outlined his client's reason for requesting the dissolution:

> That the Defendant has been guilty of excesses and cruel treatment toward this Plaintiff in the following manner, to wit: That prior to the separation of the parties in March 1957, the Defendant was drinking intoxicating liquor to excess and was extremely abusive to Plaintiff. That Defendant's acts were without cause or justification and that as a result of Defendant's wrongful acts and his attitude toward this marriage, the Plaintiff has suffered great emotional distress and any continuation of this marriage would be a detriment to her health and welfare.

It took the process server nearly a month to find Don, Sr., and serve him with the dissolution papers. And it was from his efforts that Don discovered where his father was living.

On January 18, 1958, Judge W. H. Patterson ruled that "the Court finds that the Plaintiff has sustained all of the material allegations of her complaint by competent evidence," granting the divorce and awarding Frances custody of Fred. Her now ex-husband did not appear at the proceeding nor did an attorney on his behalf.

When Don returned to Camp Pendleton after the holiday break, he and his Prescott friends were finally split up. Now that their combat training was finished, it was time for them to be assigned their separate duty stations.

"Camp Pendleton is a large area and it has all these sub-camps in it," explains Oelze. "Bert went over to one camp with the 11th Marines, I went to Camp Margarita they call it, with the 5th Marine Regiment, and Don went to the artillery unit."

It was at this point, once he lost the daily contact and support of his friends, that Don's inability to cope finally broke the surface. Whether it was by design or not, the word that came back to Don's friends was that he simply hadn't been able to "cut the mustard, if you will, in the artillery unit, because it required somebody to be serious and have some skill in setting up cannons and driving vehicles and whatnot. He just wasn't able to cope with all of that."

Later Don's explanation was more pragmatic: "I wasn't no real marine. I didn't want to shoot nobody."

Whatever the reasons, Don asked for, and was granted, a transfer to the drum and bugle corps, which did little to improve his already questionable reputation. Fairly or not, the drum and bugle corps was for those recruits who were deemed unfit to cut it in other duty stations. In other words, it was a place for the otherwise unqualified to ride out their enlistment.

But to Don's friends his assignment to the drum and bugle corps was more amusing than insulting.

"We all kind of poked fun at that a bit because Don did have some physical coordination problems," Phil laughs at the memory. "When he marched, he didn't march like ordinary people. It's hard to describe, but he kind of had a hitch to his walk. And sometimes both arms would be swinging in the same direction at the same time. Let's put it this way, he's not much of a dancer. So when they said they'd put him in the drum and bugle corps, we pretty much guffawed at that."

"We did some weekends together," Phil says. "Don loved jazz, I like jazz. He called me one time and said, 'I'm going to pick you up and have you meet a friend.'"

Actually, cohort in mischief was more like it. Oelze describes how Don and his friend "borrowed" the license plate from a general's car and "mounted it on this marvelous old Buick, with the fenders hanging in shreds, that his companion was driving. As we drove through the gate, the sentries braced and saluted when they saw the general's insignia on the car. It was just another of Don's touches."

Imus took his friends to the Lighthouse, which was in Del Mar, a coastal community near San Diego. "It was a bar that sat on the end of a little pier out over the water and had awfully good music. So we spent the evening down there."

On other occasions Phil and Don would go to an occasional movie in town and even coordinated trips to Prescott, but, recalls Oelze, "Don did less and less of that as time went on."

Don lost track of his Prescott friends as the months slowly passed and he not so impatiently bided his time to get out of the service. What had started as a grand adventure had been brought to earth by the drudgery of daily military routine. However, there would be one more adventure on which Don would embark before his tour of duty was completed, this one of a highly personal and painful nature.

Shortly before he and the others from Prescott were scheduled to be released, Don called Phil Oelze and Bert Schenberger to ask them a favor. He needed to go to Los Angeles and wanted to know if they would go along. Besides needing a car, which Bert agreed to drive, Don also needed their moral support. The reason for the trip was as surprising as it was poignant—Don wanted to find his father, and it would turn into a day neither Bert nor Phil would ever forget and one that would be seared onto Don's psyche forever.

They drove in on a Saturday morning, and Don directed them to a seedy neighborhood in the heart of Los Angeles still known as Skid Row. Even the best areas of downtown L.A. on a weekend resemble metal and glass ghost towns because there are no real residential areas near the business district. The only people to be seen are those who make the street their homes and those who try to help them, mostly workers at the local mission.

As Bert drove slowly down the dilapidated streets of Skid Row, they saw men huddled in urine-stained doorways, using dirty pieces of cardboard as makeshift mats. Others sat in groups on the curb or nearby steps, many holding conspicuous brown paper bags with the familiar glass neck of a liquor bottle just peeking over the top. With the window open, the smell of the street blew past them in pungent wafts. Although the sky was a bright blue and lazily swaying palm trees were visible just off in the distance, the atmosphere on these forgotten streets of lost souls was gray and palpably dank.

When Don couldn't spot his father from the car, they started searching by foot. "It was a matter of sorting through the derelicts—asking and talking and looking," Phil recalls quietly. They finally found Don's father in a crumbling, long-neglected building, where he was "lying down in a very dimly lit room with several other men."

It was immediately obvious that Mr. Imus was in severely ill health. Phil recalls that even when Don's dad had been somewhat sober and on his feet, he had looked ravaged and worn from the years of drinking. Now, however, "he looked like a very, very old man. While Bert and I were busy running around trying to find some clean cloths or towels to wash his face and clean him up, Don held his father's head in his lap."

They stayed in the room for almost two hours, watching Don

trying to communicate with his barely conscious father, even though "he didn't seem to recognize Don was his son."

Finally Don signaled the others it was time to go. He said good-bye to his father, walked out the door, and never looked back. "There was nothing Don could do at that point," says Oelze. "And to my knowledge, that was the last time Don ever saw his dad alive."

Suddenly it became very clear to Bert and Phil why Don had never really been much of a drinker. Back in high school he had always shied away from the beer, preferring to drive instead. And even in the service, on those quiet weekend nights in the lime groves, Don had barely touched the drinks they had made using the freshly plucked fruit. It was no wonder Don didn't associate getting drunk with having a good time.

On the mostly silent ride home, the full impact of how devastating alcoholism could be, its far-reaching effects, and the tacit stigma attached to it permeated the car. Don's friends didn't know what to say, although he didn't invite or solicit any words of compassion anyway. Instead, he kept his thoughts mostly to himself and after that day he never talked about his father's problem in any kind of detail with any of them.

Phil and Bert had been witness to an intensely personal, private moment, but rather than create an even closer bond among the three, it seemed to generate a fissure that would never quite be fused back together. They had gotten too close, seen too much, and Don wasn't someone who liked being made vulnerable to others or who allowed the cracks in his emotional armor to show. He didn't need anyone else's compassion, and he surely loathed their perceived pity.

The biggest irony is that although he liked to think of himself as the strong, silent type who could take it on the chin without flinching, Don was unwittingly setting the stage to follow stride for stride in his father's tragic footsteps.

Chapter Four

IN JULY 1959 PHIL OELZE AND BERT SCHENBERGER WERE RELEASED from active duty and assigned to reserve status, meaning they were free to go home to Prescott. Don, however, was not with them. Because of misconduct, he was forced to serve additional time in the Marine Corps.

"I know we called him and said, 'Come on, we're going to school. We're off to college,' and he said, 'No, I can't make it with you guys.'" Oelze is admittedly vague when talking about the reason for Imus being detained in the service. "I have some reticence to talk about that aspect of it. He had some problems and didn't come home with us at that time. He had to stay at Pendleton another couple of months to make up time."

Like a summer-school detention? "Yeah. He was just not a military person," Phil sighs. "I could see how he might incur the wrath of some spit-and-polish officer who didn't have the time or the luxury of trying to understand Don and his behavior."

But Oelze is also quick to agree that the military isn't structured to be anyone's group therapy. "Well, that's true. That's why conformity is so damned important, because they need to have a machine. They don't have time for personalities."

Imus was finally released from active service in the early autumn of 1959, the once-great adventure ending with a relieved whimper. Back in Prescott, he reunited with his mother and Fred, who had just graduated from high school. But most of his old gang was gone. Phil and Bert were off at college in Phoenix; George, who had left the service for a time and then re-enlisted, was still in the marines, and the rest of the gang with whom Don had been less close had also moved on to college.

At home Frances had adjusted to life without father and continued to keep to herself, except for occasional visits with George's family, although in truth she had never developed any particular closeness with them. Both Don and Fred were acutely aware that it was up to them to care for their mother. What they didn't know was how they'd do it. There certainly wouldn't be any help from the Imus side. Their father had recently died and they'd been estranged from the rest of the clan for years.

The biggest question facing Don was what he was going to do now. Although he had left school prior to his senior year, he had earned his GED in the marines, which all the recruits who hadn't finished twelfth grade were encouraged to do. So college was an option, and in fact Don did attend the University of Arizona—for six days. The reality was, Don wasn't interested in more schooling or having to toil under any more authority figures. It didn't take him long to decide what he really wanted was to pick up where he had left off at the talent show. Don wanted to be a rock 'n' roll singer, and he certainly wasn't going to achieve that goal by hanging around Prescott. He needed to be in Los Angeles, but first he needed to make some money. And in his pursuit of music glory, Imus would take just about any job available.

"When I got out of the Marine Corps I had a number of different jobs," recalls Imus. "One of the jobs I had was working as the window display person in a department store in San Bernardino, California." That wasn't far from his hometown, Perris.

But in a foreshadowing of the future, Don would lose the job because of his unorthodox sense of decorum and the lack of an internal appropriateness detector. In this case, he shocked his supervisors by doing a mannequin striptease. "My job was to display clothes in the window," explains Imus, who instead "was undressing [the mannequins] in the windows in the morning and people were walking by on their way to work. They fired me for that."

In 1960 he headed to Hollywood to try his luck as a singer and songwriter. During his time in Los Angeles, Don continued to scramble for money while trying to make the necessary music industry contacts who would help him break into the business. But the record world was a close-knit community that didn't feel the need to welcome wanna-bes. And it was an industry in flux, undergoing a transition that was more revolution than evolution.

In just a few short years, leading popular music acts like Perry Como and the Mills Brothers were replaced by the new wave of pop stars like the homegrown Elvis Presley as well as the first stirrings of the eventual British invasion that would thrust the Beatles into the global spotlight. Rock 'n' roll was poised and ready to take over the radio airwaves and there was nothing the social and media gatekeepers of the time could do to stop this cultural tsunami.

As evidenced by his choice of tunes for the talent show, Don leaned toward music with a blue-eyed soul bent, and hoped to find his place as one of the new breed. But because of L.A.'s sheer size, it's a daunting place for anyone trying to establish themselves in any business, much less a struggling singer with no contacts, no credentials, no representation, and no demos. He tried to make some connections, and much-needed money, by finding odd jobs in recording studios but was unable to nudge the doors open even a crack. Soon enough, the jobs ran out and so did his cash.

"One thing led to another and I ran out of money and got evicted from my apartment. I wound up sleeping in abandoned cars and in a Laundromat on Vine Street in Hollywood. I would crawl behind the dryers and sleep there. Women would be doing their laundry and spot me and scream."

Despite his situation, which for anyone even slightly introspective was a little too close to his father's life for comfort, Imus claims he was never particularly worried that this was going to be his eventual lot in life. "I must have assumed something was going to happen," he says. "I wasn't in any great despair."

But life on the street does get old. His transience lasted a couple of months before he finally realized he needed to regroup. He wasn't giving up on his goal to be a professional singer; he was merely giving himself a chance to rethink his approach and to get some money back in his pocket. In 1961 Don hit the road and "hitchhiked back to Arizona to near the Grand Canyon, where I got a job at this uranium mine. I know, it sounds bizarre."

The area where Don found work as a miner is referred to as the Globe-Miami area, two adjacent towns known as mining centers. But his job in the uranium mine ended abruptly after Don broke his leg in an underground accident. However, as soon as he was healed enough, Don went back to mining, this time at a copper mine in Superior, Arizona, which is outside Phoenix.

"I worked a mile underground," Don recalls. "I was there about a year and a half. Made lots of money—a hundred, hundred fifty a day."

Although the pay was good, it was emotionally brutal. George Davis remembers going to visit his cousin "when he lived down there in Superior in this old hotel, little more than a flophouse, that was as bad as you can get and still have a roof over your head. You had to see it to appreciate it."

But George understood Don's primary goal was simply to fatten his bank account. "He saved his money, and then he got out of there," says Davis, who adds that being an entertainer was "always his ambition. And he really worked for it. He didn't have any help."

As he usually would, Fred eventually joined Don at the mines, and between the two they managed to save up enough money to start promoting themselves. For a while Fred and Don would go back and forth between Arizona and L.A. as they tried to lay the groundwork for a recording career. Phil remembers once getting a surprise call from the brothers while he was still in Scottsdale going to Arizona State. "They'd been grubstaked by working the mines up in Globe-Miami and stayed with us on their way back to Los Angeles."

Back in L.A., Don got a job pumping gas while he and Fred tried yet again to establish a recording career. At night Imus spent hours listening to black disc jockeys and in the process amassed a comprehensive mental catalogue of rhythm and blues, from classic titles to obscure "B" sides. The music inspired Don, who continued to write songs while Fred strummed tunes on his guitar. His appreciation for R&B, first apparent by his decision to perform Fats Domino back during his high school talent show, led Imus to develop a pointed contempt for white artists who would get rich by recording cover versions of songs first sung by black singers.

George Davis remembers visiting his cousins in Los Angeles, who did not exactly show him a night out on the town. "They were pretty livid about saving their money," he laughs. "Don was trying to cut a record and they used to do photo sessions and other promotional stuff, trying to get into the show business world."

And to a degree, they finally did. With Fred, Don had formed the duo JJ Imus and Freddy Ford, and together they cut a single, "I'm a Hot Rodder." Politely put, it was not the stuff of dreams. In retrospect, Imus offers two reasons for his failure to make it as a singer. "The records weren't good enough and I didn't have enough money to pay the deejays to play them."

The dirtiest non-secret of the music business was the payola involved with getting songs air play. If enough money changed hands, a deejay would agree to play an unknown's record. But without the cash the record would be tossed into the nearest garbage can—not that any amount of money could have helped "I'm a Hot Rodder."

By the mid-1960s, Don's performing career was in purgatory, on indefinite hold, going nowhere fast, and his contact with former friends in Prescott was next to nonexistent. And the loss of communication was mutual, with Bert, George, and Phil becoming busy with their own lives and burgeoning careers, with Oelze going into business, Bert becoming an airline pilot, and George still in the military. Amazingly, the last time George Davis recalls seeing Don was in 1965, shortly after he finished his second go-round in the service. For a while after, they corresponded but eventually that, too, stopped.

Ironically, after Don became famous, George admits he was more reticent to contact his cousin and old friend. "My stand on that and why I haven't really kept in touch with him is because you always have the feeling if you call, because they're a celebrity, they'll think you're looking for something.

"I'd do anything in the world for Don today. I'll back him until the last cow comes home. Don made it on his own without any help from anybody, and all I can say is thank God he made it."

But at the time it filled George with sadness that Don faded from his life. The reasons for Don drifting away were no doubt partly geographical and partly because his life had taken a couple of sharp turns. First, he and Fred had both gotten full-time jobs as brakemen on the Southern Pacific Railroad, which profoundly limited the time they could commit to their music careers.

"That was a good job," Imus says. "It was fourteen to fifteen hundred a month. I'd never made that kind of money except in the mines, and the mines were awful work. This was easy, it was like a country club."

Moreover, Don had become seriously involved with Harriet Ann Showalter, a mother of two little girls who had been recently divorced from her husband, John Salamone.

From the beginning of their relationship, Don was extremely close-mouthed about Harriet, a petite blonde, and continued to be throughout their tumultuous years together, so much so that he even refused to reveal her full name during interviews after his career took off, claiming he always called her "old what's-her-name." As far as her personal background, all he has said is that Harriet was a dancer when they met. Eventually, Harriet and Don were living together in a modest Hollywood apartment located at 1834 N. Harvard Street.

Even though she already had two daughters, Nadine, born in 1960, and Antoinette, called Toni, born in 1962, it wasn't long before Don and Harriet added to the brood. Elizabeth Ann Imus was born April 29, 1966, at Hollywood Presbyterian Hospital. Just twenty months later, on December 8, 1967, Ashleigh Suzanne Imus was born.

Considering his distaste for conformity, it's not too surprising that Don showed little interest in marrying Harriet, despite fathering two children with her. And as if money wasn't being stretched to the limit by his growing family, Don, along with Fred, was also taking care of their mom.

"After his father died, his mom kind of floated around with them for a while," Phil Oelze recalls. "I think she moved to Palm Springs because Don, the warm and fuzzy side of him that you don't see very often, actually took care of his mother. He's been kind of self-centered, but I don't think he ever missed a beat when it came to taking care of his mom. When he had a little bit of money and he was able, he looked after his mom. I think it's the mark of a good man who looks after his mother, and takes good care of her."

George Davis agrees on both counts. "I know that Don did everything he could to take care of his mother after he started making some money. He put her up over in Palm Springs, where I used to visit her once in a while. He and Freddie both did what they could to help her, whenever they could."

Unfortunately for Harriet, Don wasn't nearly as conscientious about his own role as a father. "Without going into all the gory details, I wasn't around much because I was working for the railroad in those days and I was gone all the time." Despite her relationship with Don, she was still, for all practical purposes, a single parent. At first glance, it may seem odd that Harriet would have been so acquiescent when it came to Don's lack of parental participation, but as many single mothers will attest, finding a suitor willing to take on the responsibility of another man's children is rare, so she may not have felt to be in any position to complain.

Raising children is an expensive proposition in itself, much less supporting a parent, too, so more often than not Don found himself financially stretched. Fortunately, working the railroads was a decent enough way to make a living.

But his job security was about to come to an abrupt end when he was injured in a train accident on the job. "I was switching boxcars down in Long Beach and the engineer had been drinking," Don remembers. "I was on engine with a fireman and they turned the engine over. It's a big forty-ton diesel engine and I hurt my neck pretty badly and some other things."

Whether accident prone or the victim of bad luck, yet again Don had suffered a serious injury while working, causing Fred to note with a smile, "It's his leg, his foot, and it's his back. That's just how it is."

The mishap did put a scare into Imus, who was aware how close he'd come to being an invalid or killed, and according to a friend, Don "decided he wasn't going to work in that kind of occupation anymore."

Before the railroad could let Don go, he sued.

"I thought it might be a good thing to sue them, which is what I did." Don was awarded a cash settlement. In later years he would deny that the injuries had been exaggerated simply to get money out of Southern Pacific. "I was really hurt," he says, adding, "My neck has hurt for the last forty years."

The settlement was modest but enough to give Don a chance to pursue his music from a new direction. While recuperating from his injuries, Don happened to hear an advertisement for the Don Martin School of Radio and Television Arts and Sciences, which at the time was the premiere broadcast school of its kind in Los Angeles, and an idea took root that had been floating in his mind for a while.

Having been thwarted in his previous efforts to get his record played on air because of the rampant expectation of payola, Don decided to get his music played by going in through the back door. "I had never thought about being a disc jockey, but we decided one of the easy ways to get our records played is if I were a disc jockey. My thinking was that I would get a job in radio and play my own records."

In retrospect, he would call the plan "an idiotic thing," but it was his incentive for enrolling at Don Martin and learning how to be a disc jockey.

"On the way up to work in Palmdale, I would listen to the local radio station, KUTY," Don would say later. "I figured I could do as well as those guys, but I was afraid to go into the station. I didn't know anything about radio. I didn't know how it worked. I'd never been to a radio station."

Getting into radio back in the 1960s, when AM radio was still king, was not nearly as easy as it is today. In the last thirty years there have been profound changes in the rules and regulations overseeing radio, and the government had greater restrictions on operating a radio station. For example, AM disc jockeys were required to have a first-class radio-telephone operator's license, and to get it, would-be deejays had to pass a highly technical test given by the FCC that concentrated heavily on electronics.

The reason deejays needed such technical proficiency was that the smaller stations, where people went to get their first jobs, couldn't or wouldn't pay to have a licensed engineer or announcer. So any deejay applying for a job had to be able to do both those jobs, which required the first-class license. Many times, according to students from the era, radio schools would offer a crash course in which they supplied students with as many past FCC tests as they could get their hands on, allowing the would-be jocks to cheat by just memorizing the answers.

But the Don Martin school expected its students to actually learn their stuff. Located in the heart of Hollywood at 1653 N. Cherokee, the school had an impeccable reputation and was proud of its standing in the radio community. Photos of famous Don Martin alumni adorned the walls, and the instructors maintained a no-nonsense approach to the work. Even though the equipment was starting to get a little outdated, it was still perfectly functional to give the students a well-rounded education.

"The curriculum was fascinating, very in-depth, and highly concentrated," says one former student. "I learned more sitting in a class taught by (then director) Steve Brown one night than I had in four months at the junior college I was attending. It was an impressive place—and years later it still carried a bit of status among alumni and those who had never attended but had heard of the place, and the instructors and the students were very serious."

One of Don's classmates was Roy Williams, who would eventually go on to run Silavardo Broadcasting. In 1967 he enrolled about a month after Don had already started his training, and the two of them quickly struck up a friendship. "We kind of helped each other through radio school," Roy says of the twelve-month course.

"The critical thing with Imus is that this school was a very traditional radio school in that the announcers were trained to be like NBC and CBS announcers," explains Williams. "They didn't play rock and roll, and the audition tapes they had the students put together were very much a middle-of-the-road type of tape, a very announcer-type tape."

Williams says that even in 1967, despite its obvious popularity, rock and roll was still very much considered an upstart among the old-school radio people. "It was mass appeal but yet it was a teenybopper format and not something that people who owned radio stations took seriously."

So at Don Martin's in the mid-1960s, students were still trained to be "the NBC big-voiced announcer," says Williams. "You read the copy and you played the Dean Martins and Perry Comos and those types of records in your audition tape. But Imus was the first to say, 'I'm not doing that. I'm doing a rock and roll one.' "

Although it may be hard to understand the enormity of Don's rebellion, it was literally earthshaking to the school powers-that-be. Besides always being one to buck the expectations of those around him in authority, Williams believes Don had an even stronger motive for breaking the mold—being relatively older than the other fresh-faced students, Imus felt the pressure of time crowding him.

"Later on, after we got our careers kind of going, he just admitted, 'Hey, I'm too old to have to do all this basic stuff. I need to do something that's going to make it work,' " recalls Roy. "That was his whole deal. He planned to be different so he could get there quicker. Then once *he* did it, of course, then everybody else who was younger and into the new music decided that's what *they* were going to do too."

Even though Don refused to be bound by format, Williams

remembers him as a "good student. He wanted to be a jock, as most of the guys there also wanted to be."

Unfortunately, Don's serious side was often waylaid by external factors. Although he was acutely interested in what the school had to offer, he was eventually thrown out prior to his graduation for being "uncooperative." According to Imus, "I didn't get my diploma because I still owed them $500. But I did have my first-class FCC license."

Imus never did pay the school the money he owed, even though it remained a venerable place of radio learning into the late seventies, when it finally began to fade, as colleges began offering state-of-the-art courses in broadcasting. The Don Martin School of Radio was eventually purchased by the Columbia School of Broadcasting, which had their own curriculum—and a very questionable reputation.

Perhaps the reason he didn't feel particularly pressured into paying up was that even before his would-be graduation, Don had succeeded in landing a part-time job. After completing enough of the course for him to feel confident he could handle the technical aspect of being a deejay, Don applied for a job at Palmdale's small station, KUTY. Art Furtado, the station manager, describes how "Imus walks in and says he wants to be a disc jockey. Well, he goes on the air and right away it was obvious he was a tremendous talent," marvels Furtado. "Just like that."

And just like that Don was hired part-time to work weekends, where he initially patterned himself after the big-time L.A. deejays of the day, such as the Real Don Steele, although L.A. disc jockey Brian Bierne, who's a longtime friend of Imus's, noted that Don "wanted to be between someone on the radio and Lenny Bruce, who he very much admired, mixed with another, Mort Sahl."

But before Don could even establish a style for himself, he was thrust into a more center stage when, "the morning man skipped town and I took over in June as Captain Don for $425 a month," the sobriquet an apparent personal in-joke relating to his less than fulfilling military experience.

Ironically, just as Don's career as a disc jockey began, his brother's ambition was waning. Although for many years after, Fred continued to compose songs in his spare time and had one tune that made the country charts, "I Don't Want to Have to Marry You," sung by Jim Ed Brown and Helen Cornelius. But even that coup wasn't enough to prod Fred into pursuing music full-time anymore.

"I probably don't have a lot of drive. I'm a lazy person," Fred says serenely, who estimates the ten to fifteen minutes he spends on the radio a week as part of his brother's show "is enough. You have to be really dedicated and I'm just sort of dedicated."

In the beginning Don didn't see himself as particularly dedicated either. "I didn't have an act when I started. What I was on the air was what I was—just a jerk with an aversion to authority. I had good timing and I was funny. But I didn't have any intention of staying in radio."

His intention was to fulfill his self-stated original master plan—become an important deejay, play his own records on the air, become a star, then leave spinning tunes behind for the bright lights of performing. But thanks to a set of circumstances awaiting him in Palmdale, Don would enjoy an unprecedented creative freedom that would allow him to transform the role of disc jockey from ad hoc record pusher and product promotions man into a performance art unto itself.

Chapter Five

BY THE TIME DON IMUS BECAME A FULL-TIME DISC JOCKEY, RADIO WAS in many ways still trying to redefine itself. In the Golden Age of Radio, the audio landscape was a primary source of national entertainment, filled with classic shows such as *Fibber McGee and Molly*, and the purveyor of stars, including Burns and Allen, Milton Berle, and Bob Hope. With the advent of television, however, radio abruptly shifted its focus to music. When rock and roll seduced a generation, the 45 rpm record became king and disc jockeys were there to play the hits and hawk products to earn the station some advertising money. While some deejays became known personalities, they were still limited, little more than glorified cheerleaders whose primary function remained selling the call letters, the promotions, the commercials, and the records.

But Imus was innately programmed to push those well-established, traditional boundaries, if for no other reason than to keep his own interest fresh. Plus, those years on the ranch were starting to percolate to the surface of his personality; he didn't want to be penned in and approached his time behind the microphone as a lone cowboy riding a solitary trail, determined to go whatever direction his impulses took him. And it would take only a couple of months before those impulses made Don the most notorious deejay in the history of Palmdale, a town of only eight to nine thousand people.

Ironically, once Don was finally in a position where he could have played his own records on the air, he realized he never would. 'Hey Jude' and some other records were out then and they were so much better than the ones we were doing, I began to understand why nobody played our records."

So Don's attention shifted to developing his skills behind the mike, and his impact on the small community's listening audience was almost immediate, remembers Tim Shaw, an Antelope Valley College student with his own radio aspirations. "He definitely influenced me as far as I said, 'I can do that!' He was probably the best thing that hit our little town, it was quite impressive. Although L.A. is just over the San Gabriel Mountains from Palmdale, and I grew up listening to stations like KRLA and KHJ, where you had much more professional announcers on the air, we still listened to our local station, KUTY."

Even before Shaw first heard Imus on the air, he and a couple of other students from the college, including senior class president Steve Buffalo, would occasionally stop by the station and meet the disc jockeys. Buffalo's initial interest was to promote events he was arranging at the college. "We went over there to kind of meet with those folks. We bought some advertising, then went in and packaged something for the deejays."

But after Imus went on the air, the visits took the form of social outings. "We did a couple of little interviews when we were having a concert or dance or something and we kind of got to know him. He was very friendly, very open. He'd invite you over and talk to you in between songs. We'd just kind of sit around and shoot the bull in between him spinning records.

"He just liked to talk. He always enjoyed talking to people about what was going on. He was a very good conversationalist and he was always interesting. He wasn't your typical deejay, you know, *Hey, what about this band or that band?* You could see he had some depth and was always somewhat politically aware. I don't think he knew a lot about radio back then, but I think he was looking to move up. I think that was maybe in the back of his mind.

"From what he told us, he felt that he kind of just stumbled into it. He used to joke that he hopped a freight train and accidentally fell off in Palmdale, where the tracks ran right near the radio station, walked over, and happened to get a job."

Despite downplaying his efforts to become a deejay, Don had hit the ground running, bringing with him an unorthodox approach to his job that made him an immediate personality, particularly among the station's teen and young adult listeners. And he had an innate sense of showmanship.

"He played well with the media in the area," says Buffalo. "He got a lot of coverage from the newspapers because he was always doing something outrageous. Don had a way of positioning himself to be noticed.

"I had always thought there was something special about Don because we had known deejays who had come through the system; they turn over so rapidly at the radio stations, and here was a guy who was really different. He was unique and you could see it then. I think a lot of the people in the community thought, *He's a different sort. He's got a different play on how he does stuff on the air.*

"Even different from L.A. You had a lot of kids up here listen to KRLA and KHJ, which were your two major rock stations at the time. But what happened was, when Don got on the air, a lot of people up here switched over and were listening locally to KUTY because he was so funny."

It wasn't so much that he was especially polished or had a commanding presence as he was simply new on the ears of listeners. Prior to Don's arrival, KUTY was broadcasting a typical but uninspired morning show that included mostly local news and music. Nor were the on-air personalities memorable.

"Before Don, you had really pretty mediocre deejays," says Buffalo, who describes the typical local disc jockey as a guy who "graduated from high school and thinks, *I want to be on the radio*, without any real formal training.

"Or maybe you got some guy who'd been in the business twenty years and he was really into the forties music scene and now he's playing rock. It's paying him a little money, so he's just kind of there. Then here comes a guy who's just totally different from that—he's got some things to say."

Deejay Brian Bierne agrees. "Most people's first impression back then was that Don wasn't very bright. He was an off-the-wall guy so you wouldn't think there was a lot of depth to Don."

Even in his earliest days, Don would sprinkle his show with political commentary, most of the time cloaked in humor, but occasionally he let the curtain drop to show glimpses of ideology such as when he found himself raging against the Vietnam War to his Palmdale listenership. "I wanted to burn down every building in the country," he says.

Beyond Imus's astute running commentary about what was going on in the world around him was his method of putting together a show, which was a relatively novel concept. "I remember Don would work on his program, not just kind of show up and talk. He had a concept and an idea. I remember we'd sit around the station and he'd say, 'Hey I'm thinking about running this contest, what do you guys think of that?'

"He was just so different from the guys who would just say something like *Here's the latest hot record from Creedence Clearwater Revival.* At a time when most disc jockeys were doing a lot of time and temperature stuff and one-liner-type comedy or content, Don did make comments about various people, like the station owner and other small town politicians in the town and stuff like that. Yeah, he took potshots at 'em and he had fun.

"His show, then, although on a much smaller scale, was very much like it is now. He was always either talking about someone or something. It wasn't just here's a record and let it roll, there was always something he wanted to talk about. Don was pretty down to earth and he had a charisma about him. It was pretty obvious he was going to go on and be a major player."

But first he concentrated on being a big fish in his little radio station pond and his notoriety came quickly. "He was pretty outrageous," laughs Tim Shaw. "You have to understand, he was in a very conservative community that was somewhat aerospace oriented, but still very based in agriculture, with a lot of alfalfa farms and stuff like that still in this area at that time."

While what Shaw characterized as "outrageous" would hardly elicit a raised eyebrow today—in 1968, Imus's verbal assaults on public figures and others he held in contempt were shocking. And, in many cases, very funny.

"His thrust, if you will, was being critical of politicians for being politicians, and living the good life at the taxpayers' expense," explains Shaw. "I don't want to say he was a conservative by any means, although I think some of the things he may have said would have been taken to be from a conservative point of view. But I don't think he really espoused any political agenda or ideology per se. He just got on their cases for being politicians.

"If there was any conservatism in his politics, it wouldn't be because one was successful economically. It would be the kind of conservatism that came from more of the grass roots, critical of the government intruding into our private lives and being too involved. He definitely has a disdain for authority figures, people trying to tell you what to do and how to live your life."

Despite his railings, Imus managed to avoid sounding preachy, as it were, because of the liberal doses of humor he injected into his observations. "Oh, he had an attitude, all right, but it wasn't a bad attitude," Shaw notes. "Don knew how you had to act as an entertainer. It was a persona he would have to have.

"He wasn't necessarily egotistical, but he knew he was very popular. And he had people talking."

Never more so than when he announced on the air one day that he was going to run for state congressman against Barry Goldwater, Jr. According to station manager Furtado, Don got the idea after "he found out that congressmen made forty thousand dollars a year. He said he was tired of working for forty dollars a week at this crummy outfit when he could be making forty thousand. He said he wanted to get on that *band*wagon. I can still almost quote him verbatim, it was so funny."

Running as an Independent, his campaign slogan was, appropriately, *Put Don Imus on the gravy train.* He also warned his potential voters not to call him in Washington if he won. "I think people thought it was a lot of fun," says Shaw.

Vern Lawson, who worked for the local paper, the *Antelope Valley Press,* for thirty-nine years, remembers the Imus campaign vividly. He had been at the paper only a few months when he was assigned to cover a press conference called by the upstart deejay. At the time, the only impression he had of Don was that he was "a renegade disc jockey on KUTY who made outrageous comments from time to time. I mean, I probably heard him on the air sometime but not regularly, although I could tell by listening to him that he was not an ordinary disc jockey."

Imus chose a vacant storefront right across the street from the *Ledger-Gazette* as the site for his press conference. When Vern and the handful of others arrived, nobody could figure out what Don was up to.

"We didn't know what he was going to announce, so there were only four or five people who actually came to the press conference. The area had two major papers—the *Antelope Valley Ledger-Gazette,* a five-day-a-week daily that has since folded, and our paper, the *Antelope Valley Press,* which was a weekly. And there were probably three or four radio stations in the area," recalls Lawson, who says the main reason he came was because "it was convenient, being right across the street."

The reporters huddled in a small room that had no chairs to sit in. Nor was there a dais. Vern says that they had been waiting only a few minutes, when Imus walked in. "He simply stood in the middle of the room and said, 'I'm going to run for Congress.' Somebody said, 'Are you kidding?' And he said, 'No, I'm serious.' And that was it."

The assembled reporters stared at Imus in disbelief, quickly pegging his announcement as a gimmick, if for no other reason than he was hardly the picture of the political establishment, even for 1968. "He had wavy hair and wore it about as long as he does today, and he dressed very casual. His face was less craggy than it is now, but of course he was a lot younger.

"I guess he filed the necessary paperwork, so we did run the story. But it was all self-promotion. I don't believe he ran any advertising except for when he was on the air."

Nor did the papers make a point of following up on Don's campaign announcement, explains Vern. "Back then, it was so competitive between the newspapers and the radio stations for advertising dollars that generally they tended not to acknowledge each other's existence. So the newspaper wasn't about to promote somebody on the local radio station."

Not that Don needed outside promotion or to buy any advertising time, because he had the radio show at his disposal and he managed to convince over eight hundred people to vote for him. "He did a big campaign, promoting it on the air," laughs Steve Buffalo. "But back then, especially in a small, little, family-owned station like that, no one would ever challenge the equal-time rules."

And Don wasn't above bending any and every rule he could get away with, even when the impulses flew in the face of established procedure, such as adhering to play lists. Occasionally, the deejays might freelance a bit and play some album cuts, but when Imus joined the station, KUTY followed a fairly straight Top 40's format, meaning if the song made it into the Top 40 on the Billboard chart, it got played, although, as Tim Shaw recalls, "I don't think Don was true to the format. He liked to break format. A Top 40 format usually meant you had a play list of records you had to play, and they needed to be played a certain number of times. But if he didn't like a record, it didn't get airtime with Don. He was not afraid to do things that would upset the apple cart, especially management."

Or if it did, Don would make his displeasure obvious. One song Shaw remembers Don found particularly bothersome was the cloying, pseudo-psychedelic wail of "Crimson and Clover" by Tommy James and the Shondells. "He hated the song. He detested it and he said, 'I have to play it because of the station and because everybody likes to hear it but I don't have to play it slowly.' So he just played it as fast as he could just to get it done," making it sound like the Chipmunks on acid. "Then he'd say, 'There it is. You heard it.' That would have probably been one of the first times anyone had pulled that stunt on the radio."

Because they were mostly a Top 40 station, KUTY's deejays shied away from heavy rock 'n' roll such as Iron Butterfly, but they played the Stones, Beatles, and Doors. However, as Shaw remembers, "It could even get as poppish as Andy Williams. Don was more rock 'n' roll oriented, though, which was in keeping with his blue collar image."

But that blue collar image didn't necessarily include the blue collar work ethic that the best way to get things done is to do it yourself, especially when the required work was dictated by supreme radio powers on high Broadcast Music Incorporated, better known as BMI.

In the days before computerization became a way of life for all technologies, there was a time when deejays were periodically required to manually write down the title of every song they played, along with the artist and composer. The log would have to be kept for two weeks running during a specified time of the year, and it was from these ledgers that BMI calculated the amount of royalties, which were determined by air play, they paid to the songwriters of these songs.

The bigger stations, like in L.A., had a taping system, and some secretary was required to sit there and write all that down. But out in the small markets, deejays were expected to do it themselves. Routinely, the jocks would write down their own information as the song played, or create a log when they were done if they didn't want to do it exactly as it was happening. However, Don refused to keep the log himself in any fashion. But because the station was legally obligated, it had to be done by someone. So Imus, who was hardly making enough money to support his family, hired a listener, Robin Hilborn, to do it for him.

"I was listening to that particular radio station, and Don said that he was doing the BMI, described what it would entail, and asked if anybody would like to come down and work. I thought, *This sounds really cool,* so I wandered on down there and he gave me the job. I know he paid me something, but whatever it was it was pitifully small."

Every weekday for two weeks Robin sat with Don during his shift and diligently wrote down all the songs he would play. For the most part, she says, they were the only ones there. "Occasionally, people would wander through, but it was just us. I don't even think there was anyone else in the other part of the office. I mean, it was a very small station. I'm sure he would be the first one to agree with you. He probably can't even remember what the call letters were," she laughs.

Robin guesses, though, that Don preferred the solitude, doubting he socialized with the other deejays because, she notes, "the two guys who were there at the time—one was really in love with himself and the other was kind of a jerk."

Just as the college kids did, Robin found Don to be immensely likable and open. "Oh, yeah, he was a very nice guy. We would make small talk and he was chewing his gum like he's chewing his gum now. I would have been probably eighteen or nineteen and he was like Big Brother, trying to get me set up on a date with Rick O'Connor, one of the other jocks there who was about my age. 'Well, this would be really cool if you guys went out.' Actually, it would have been a terrible idea," she laughs, but one that Don teased Robin about the entire time she was there with him.

It was the general consensus among his small group of friends and acquaintances that Don was simply really happy to be there and genuinely enjoyed what he was doing. He had a sense of freedom that would have been impossible to experience pumping gas or working on the railroad and he was, in a very large sense, finally doing what he had always dreamed about—performing for the masses.

"He flexed his creativity," comments Steve Buffalo. "It was fun for him, the commentary in between playing the songs or when somebody would phone in and talk to him and he'd take off on things. I think that's what hooked him, that he was able to do those things. Nobody told him, Oh, you can't do that on the air. So he did it on the air and got away with it. I don't remember him using profanity on the air, just some outrageous little characters he'd launch into."

Or insults he would hurl, such as those directed at the Lancaster Drive-in manager, Bernie Rawitch. "Bernie had a great sense of humor," says station manager Furtado. "Don would insult the hell out of him and Bernie would just laugh like crazy."

While most station owners would take a dim view of Don's list of sins—ignoring play lists, resisting the BMI log, ridiculing local and national politicians and businessmen, mocking evangelists—KUTY's proprietors, David and Kay Mende, were notoriously lax about such protocol. And as such, they were the perfect bosses for Don. In large part, had they not been as lenient as they were, Don might never have developed the style for which he would later become famous. They set the foundation for the on-air act that would take Don to the top of his profession.

"It wasn't a corporation deal," explains Buffalo. "KUTY was a small rock station, and there weren't a lot of controls placed on it. I know it used to drive Art Furtado kind of nuts, because he was kind of overseeing the thing for the Mendes."

According to Tim Shaw, it was David Mende who was particularly willing to let Don run verbally wild. "I remember Kay telling me that she would be shocked at some outrageous thing that Don would say on the air. She'd say, 'Did you hear what Don said this morning?' to her husband. And he'd say, 'That's all right, let him go. We don't want to stifle that creative impulse.' So they didn't put any reins on him."

What Don hadn't known when he approached KUTY for a job was that the Mendes were rather notorious around Palmdale for being, bluntly put, the town drunks.

"Yeah, they were both kind of alcoholics," Steve chuckles. "They were not really hands-on operators. He'd spend most of his time out drinking with the local folks at the bars and showing up once in a while. The few times I came across Mr. Mende, he'd had a few drinks. Obviously, he was not paying a lot of attention to what Don was doing on the air. And Don was doing a lot of crazy stuff."

Including making fun of the Mendes, alluding to their well-known drinking proclivities. "But that was common knowledge," says Shaw. "It wasn't like he was telling anything everybody didn't already know."

The Mendes, now both deceased, would later sell KUTY, and today the station is all Spanish-language, but while Imus was at the station, KUTY enjoyed its greatest popularity and highest listenership of the Mendes reign, bolstered mostly by the teens, college students, and young adults—all of whom were being influenced by the general atmosphere of 1968 and who became faithful followers. Don Imus was the perfect deejay for the counterculture revolution sweeping the nation. And he was probably also Art Furtado's worst nightmare when it came to selling advertising.

"Here he's trying to keep the station afloat," sympathizes Buffalo, "and you're dealing with owners who are detached from it and then you've got this deejay on the air, running wild. But the benefit of all that for Don was, he was working at a station for people without any awareness that he was doing things that maybe weren't kosher with the FCC. He could get away with a lot of things. And because it's a little radio station and nobody noticed, he was able to formulate what he was going to do in the future."

He was also able to get away with personally self-promoting stunts that at any other station would have gotten him dismissed, such as the time Don used his morning show as a week-long audition tape. Just as actors compile clips of television and film acting performances to use as a kind of visual résumé, deejays would compile what are called air checks, which are recordings of their shows, to send out to prospective radio station employers.

Air checks allow potential employers to listen to a one- or two-hour radio program in a matter of minutes. Job-hungry announcers record their programs as they are broadcast live, then they edit out the music and other nontalk elements. What's left is similar to a coming attractions trailer for a movie. Prospective employers can determine an applicant's on-air abilities and style in a matter of a few minutes just from listening to an air check. Don understood the importance of a good air check from the first moment he ever cracked open a microphone at broadcasting school. And according to longtime friend Terry

Nelson, Don was trying to move up the ladder from Palmdale almost from the day he arrived, even though "he was a total green kid. He didn't know squat about squat.

"So what he did was, he started doing an air check and every single day, he did the exact same show, the exact same bits, the exact same liners—everything at the exact same time," laughs Nelson. "And he did this for like a week or two. Then he took the best of all of those shows, spliced them all together, so he had a killer air check."

In other words, just as a director will shoot the same scene many times, then choose the best one to put in the movie, Don did the exact same show over and over so he could pick what he felt were his best done bits, then package it as if it were actually from just one show.

"Then he sent this air check out to a good medium market and they called him back and went, 'Wow, man, we got your tape and that was just great. Fuck, what're you doing in Palmdale?' Then they go, 'Send another tape, just send another tape but we gotta have it in two days.'"

Having no time to put together another "best of" air check, Don had to record his next show and use that as his next air check. The difference between the two tapes was significant. "They called him back and said, 'What the hell are you trying to pull?'"

What surprised a lot of people is that Don's appearance didn't necessarily match his on-air persona. "Most of the time when I saw Don, he had a western look about him," recalls Steve. "He wore boots. Was clean-shaven but had wild hair; a lot of it. And he was very thin."

"I do recall that he dressed simply," agrees Tim Shaw. "He had more of a blue collar look that I assumed came from working the railroad."

His look was also practical. For all his notoriety and popularity, Don was still making pitifully little money, considering his family situation. And as he would continue to do, Don seemed to go out of his way to keep his family life completely separate from his personal life. So much so that neither Tim nor Steve were even aware he was father of two children. However, Robin Hilborn met Harriet and the kids on a couple of occasions during her brief tenure as Imus's song-log girl.

"I remember having her come in with the kids a little bit before he was finished. They would sit over on the side of the studio and would just wait until they were done with his shift. The kids weren't running around because we were in the studio and they were really tiny then," Robin recalls, referring to Elizabeth and Ashleigh, who would have both been toddlers then.

While in Palmdale, Don and Harriet lived at the Hunter Apartments, which was located on a residential street in the downtown Palmdale area not far from the radio station. Tim Shaw, who was familiar with the complex, describes the building as "rinky-dink" and says all of the dozen or so units were very small.

Steve remembers Don driving a beat-up old car, "nothing that stood out. He didn't arrive in town with a lot. He didn't move stuff in a moving van; he may have had a couple of suitcases and that might have been it."

Prior to Palmdale, Don had blamed his frequent absences from home on his job with the railroad. But even though he was on air only four hours a day, Don was still out more than he was at home with Harriet and the girls. Ironically, he didn't have a reputation as Mr. Social, but he would spend hours at the radio station both before and after his shift, working on the next day's program and later began moonlighting at night as a local guest emcee, mostly at the college.

After Steve and Tim got to know Imus, they would frequently

ask him to be master of ceremonies at a number of functions they were in charge of organizing. Considering the town's size, Antelope Valley College still managed to attract major musical acts.

"We had Iron butterfly, Eric Burdon and the Animals, Rick Nelson did a show for us, and the Nitty Gritty Dirt Band," remembers Shaw. "Steve Martin, this was during his early days, was one of our openers. We did a pretty good job for a community college of bringing in some decent stuff."

Steve says that the incentive to Don was purely financial. "We'd give him twenty-five dollars to come over there and emcee a concert. Back then radio didn't pay real well, so people hustled to get money where they could. At that point in time, making a hundred bucks a week was doing good. He was out in a small market learning his trade, which is what you gotta do. You gotta go out and pay your dues. That's why he got tied into doing the college stuff because twenty-five bucks wasn't bad money back then.

"He also did some things out in the community because radio around here was very promotion-oriented, with deejays showing up for an opening or for some special celebration. Usually back then, people took care of the radio guys, who would get some free meals and this kind of thing, so Don got in to that."

In addition to the twenty-five dollars, Imus also got extra free tickets to the concerts. But it's telling that he never once brought Harriet along with him to any of the functions, showing up instead with associates from the radio station. Prior to the start of the concert or dance or show, Don would get up onstage and address the audience.

"I don't recall him attempting to be funny when introducing the band," says Shaw. "Usually, he would just welcome everybody and played it pretty straight." But Buffalo says that even when playing it apparently straight, Imus could get the crowd going. "He was a very funny guy. And he still has the same mannerisms and way of talking."

But what Don really wanted to do, still, was be a rock star. Even though his listeners believed he was born talking into a microphone, Don longed to be the one making the music, not the one playing it. So to get his rocker fix, he began promoting a local group called Rattlesnakes and Eggs, led by singer Marty Pru, whom he met during a performance at the college. In addition to hyping the band on air, a power he now controlled, Don would also occasionally perform with the group.

But their professional relationship was cut short by Don's blossoming career. After only eight months in Palmdale, Imus left for a larger market on the radio station ladder. And just like that, he was gone. But the mark he left for those who knew him has proven indelible, although as always when talking about Imus, the opinions are mixed. Some were surprised Don's style didn't self-destruct his fledgling career.

"He was here less than a year, and it wasn't obvious that Don was destined for greatness at that point," Vern Lawson believes. "We didn't realize that, and we kind of lost track of him until a few years later he made a big hit in New York."

But others, like Tim Shaw and his buddies, had no doubts Palmdale was merely a brief stop on a train ride to professional glory. "I was not surprised at how well he did, because I think we all knew he had the talent. As far as the trouble he stirred up, that wasn't a surprise either. He was just taking it a step further every time. Every time he moved up the ladder he became a little more outrageous."

But typically, once Don moved on, he didn't look back. Lawson recalls that once an *Antelope Valley Press* reporter tried to get an interview with Don when he made it to New York but he never even called him back. The fact was, sentimentality was simply not part of his nature. He couldn't afford it to be. So anyone expecting Don to keep in touch, or even pretend nostalgia, would have been stung with disappointment. Once Palmdale disappeared from sight in his rearview mirror, it also disappeared from his mind's eye. The only thing now in his field of vision was the next opportunity awaiting the Imus gravy train.

—————————— ▬▬▬▬ ——————————

Chapter Six

IT WASN'T UNTIL AFTER IMUS HAD LEFT KUTY THAT HE AND HARRIET finally got married. Typically, though, they didn't plan even a modest wedding, choosing instead to take their vows in front of a judge in the small town of Tracy, located outside of Stockton, where he was KJOI's new morning man.

Harriet and Don were married on June 25, 1969, by Judge Arthur S. Affonso. Because they knew nobody in the area, their witnesses, Stephanie Sullivan and Linda Ortega, were two clerks called into duty. In testament to the emotional ambivalence with which Don was entering this marriage, he married Harriet with one day to spare; they had applied for the marriage license back in Los Angeles on March 28, and it was set to expire June 26.

When Don finally exchanged vows with Harriet, it was somewhat anticlimactic considering what the couple had been through over the previous several years. Not only had Harriet come to the relationship with children from a former marriage, she had also come laden with the baggage of a vengeful ex-husband named John Joseph Salamone.

Since both Don and Harriet have consistently refused to talk about their early relationship and marriage in any detail, one can only speculate what drew them together in the first place. He was a struggling would-be performer stifled by his job on the railroad and she was a married mother of two very small children when they met. What is apparent is that Harriet seems to have shared Don's penchant for being intentionally vague and, in some cases, outright contradictory, about their pasts, using revisionist personal histories to reinvent themselves.

Harriet Showalter was born September 3, 1941, to Warren and Sara Showalter, both of whom were originally born in Pennsylvania. On her marriage certificate to Don, Harriet states she was born in California, but on both Elizabeth's and Ashleigh's birth certificates, she lists Pennsylvania as her home state. But then again, Don claimed to have completed two years of college on his marriage certificate, apparently deciding to count his years in the military equivalent to academic studies. And for reasons completely mysterious, the marriage certificate lists his address as his longtime 1834 N. Harvard Blvd. apartment but hers as 6315 Willoughby.

Most curious, however, is that Harriet claims her marriage to Don was her first. Again, she apparently justified the falsehood, which in California is a misdemeanor crime, by deciding that the question pertained only to marriages performed within the borders of the United States, because Harriet had indeed been married before.

Around 1959, when she was still a teenager, Harriet had met John Salamone, an ex-convict in his early thirties with a history of alcohol and trouble. As a younger man, Salamone had been dishonorably discharged from military service and had also served time at a prison in Georgia for criminal assault. Despite his questionable past, Harriet became involved with Salamone and soon found herself pregnant. Late into her second trimester, Harriet eloped with John, and on February 1, 1960, the couple were married just across the California border in Tijuana, Mexico, a one-time-favorite spot for couples wanting no-fuss, no-wait marriages. They returned to L.A. to set up house, and on May 17, 1960, their daughter Nadine was born. Less than two years later they had another baby, Antoinette, born January 2, 1962. But as most people could have no doubt predicted, the marriage was rocky from the start. John was a drinker who would turn mean when drunk and frequently used his fists on Harriet.

In May 1964, John was involved in a car accident on a freeway entrance ramp in which a truck driver was severely injured, and by February 1965 the couple found themselves defendants in a personal injury civil lawsuit, with the recuperating truck driver asking for a settlement well into the five figures. But by that time Harriet and John's relationship was as good as over, because she already had a new man in her life, a frustrated performer named Don Imus.

By the summer of 1965, Harriet had become pregnant by Don and he was now faced with the prospect of starting, and supporting, a family. For whatever kind of absentee father he would prove to be over the years on a physical or emotional level, Imus has never shirked financial duty, and he had every intention of supporting his child.

On October 18, 1965, Harriet and John got a quickie Mexican divorce back in Tijuana, then returned to Los Angeles. But obviously, Salamone harbored anger and resentment over Harriet's infidelity, because just five days later, on October 23, 1965, John picked up his two daughters and spirited them off, leaving no forwarding address.

Harriet was understandably frantic, especially in the first weeks when she didn't know where John had taken the girls. According to court documents, Harriet says she "expended substantial sums of money and time and effort to locate the defendant in attempt to recover custody." All Don could do was try to be supportive to the woman carrying his child and help her efforts to locate the little girls.

Eventually, Harriet found Salamone and the children in Anchorage, Alaska, where he had found work as a laborer. Even though she was approximately five months pregnant, Harriet arranged a trip to Alaska, and on December 13, 1965, she traveled to Anchorage and found John and their children living in a hotel called the Tiltin Hiltin, located at 832 A Street. The hotel, claiming to be "Anchorage's Newest!" also boasted saunas and steam baths.

According to an affidavit she filed later, Harriet claims she found her daughters living in deplorable conditions and accused her ex-husband of maintaining them "in a condition of filth and squalor without proper food, clothing, shelter, or parental supervision." Harriet demanded to take the children back to Los Angeles with her, but Salamone "refused to return the kids."

Once back in Los Angeles, Harriet continued her efforts to reason with Salamone, speaking to him by phone on several occasions. Finally, during a conversation on May 16, 1966 (which he had charged to her mother's phone bill), John agreed to return the children to her in Los Angeles. But according to an amended complaint for sole custody filed July 29, 1966, in Los Angeles Superior Court, Harriet was not reunited with her daughters until June 3, 1966. By that time Nadine and Toni had a new sister, Elizabeth, who had been born April 29.

But once the girls were back in Los Angeles, Salamone refused to leave his ex-wife and her new family in peace. Nor was there much Don could do to make John stay away, since at that point he still shared custody of the girls. But as the threats of violence increased and Salamone taunted Harriet about taking the girls back again, Harriet's only recourse was to seek exclusive custody of the girls. In February 1967, under the name Harriet Imus, despite not yet being married to Don, she once again went to court to try to secure sole custody of her daughters.

This time she told the family judge that Salamone was "a violent person" who had "on numerous occasions" not only threatened her life, but Don's, that of Harriet's mother, Sara W. Myers Gerke, who was now divorced from Harriet's father, and even baby Elizabeth's. Even more ominously, Harriet claimed that Salamone had told her he'd taken their daughters once and would do so again "to avoid the jurisdiction of this court" if she tried to obtain sole custody.

Finally, on June 9, 1967, Judge Martin Katz granted Harriet "sole, separate, and exclusive custody" of Nadine and Toni, who by this time were seven and five respectively. (Don legally adopted Nadine and Toni nine years later, on October 25, 1976.)

Now not only did Don have three children to support as his own, he and Harriet were also expecting another child. And despite their ever-increasing family, they were still living at the Capri Arms Apartments, located at 1834 N. Harvard Blvd., in a glamourless area east of Hollywood.

To help put food on the table, Harriet worked as a waitress for as long as her pregnancy allowed, but then quit as her due date approached. It's no wonder that when Don hurt his back and had the opportunity to go to Don Martin's school, he jumped at the chance—he was in serious danger of becoming trapped by his circumstances and settling for a dull but steadily paying job with little hope of advancement. So when Roy Williams, Don's school buddy, remembers Imus as being driven, he knows it was more than just personal ambition fueling his engine.

By the time Don was hired to be the KJOI morning man in Stockton, he and Harriet were raising four children whose ages ranged from Ashleigh's eighteen months to Nadine's nine years. Once again, to help support their brood, Harriet went to work as a waitress, this time at one of Stockton's nicer restaurants, while Don tried to make a name for himself at what was an important California radio market.

KJOI, which was 1280 on the AM dial, was the Heritage Radio station in Stockton and was considered "a big-time radio station," according to Roy Williams, who as it happened was working as a deejay in nearby Modesto at the time. "A lot of talent went through there," says Williams.

When Imus accepted the job in Stockton, KJOI was still playing what was called a middle-of-the-road format, but what he didn't know is that the station was planning to switch formats. Roy remembers getting a phone call from Don, who had just landed at the airport. "He wanted to know about this radio station in Stockton, and I told him I thought it was a good deal because I knew they were about to go Top 40, which was one reason they hired Imus."

In 1969 such a move was actually still considered a risk, explains Williams. "You have to consider, the only really big radio talents were at the more traditional radio stations, like middle-of-the-road. If you looked at Los Angeles then, the big guys were Lohman and Barkley at KFI. In San Francisco it was Don Sherwood at KSFO, and that was a middle-of-the-road station. These stations were not playing rock and roll until later."

In Stockton, one of KJOI's rivals, KSTN, was doing a kind of light rock, "or chicken rock, as they used to call it," laughs Williams, who adds that once KJOI switched formats, they "brought in a whole new staff and they took the ratings by storm in one book."

The radio station where Don worked was located inside the huge Stockton Hotel, a designated landmark, which is a full block long. At one time a functioning hotel, by the time Imus arrived in Stockton it had been converted into a business center, and in addition to the radio station, the county human resource offices were housed there.

"KJOI was in a fishbowl," describes Roy. "The station sat right in the corner of Webber and El Dorado, and there were floor-to-ceiling glass windows on two sides and the disc jockey sat in there. You had your little name plaque there, and cars would go by and honk and you had a speaker outside—I mean, you know, it was show biz."

And Don wasted no time marking his territory. It was at KJOI that he first began calling his show *Imus in the Morning*. Although he was working under a new moniker, having retired Captain Don, Imus simply picked up where he had left off in Palmdale. "Imus was totally uncontrollable," says Roy. "Don was his own person, had his own ideas. And he put a lot of time and effort into it. He spent a lot of time on his show—he always wrote his show every night, which was more than anybody was doing. As far as the radio community was concerned, everybody thought he was outrageous. He was doing all this stuff that everybody wished they could do but they were too afraid to do because it was still a very formatic period in radio."

The leading style was tailored after the so-called RKO format. RKO was the largest radio conglomerate at the time and its stations used a format where a morning deejay would play records, do the time and temperature and little else. RKO stations across the country had found great ratings success by allowing the music to be the star of the show. If you couldn't fit your personality over the first ten seconds of a song before the vocals started chiming, then you were too much a talker for this music-intensive format.

With Imus, Williams says, "you had a morning guy who was doing all kinds of stuff rather than just time and temperature. Everybody knew that he was different, and the jocks would all say, 'Jeez, did you hear what he said today?' "

One of the jocks fascinated with Imus's outrageousness was Terry Nelson, who became, for perhaps the first time in his life, a friend Don also considered a true peer. Nelson, who grew up in Modesto, had also just come to KJOI as part of the station's revamped format.

"I'd heard the guy on the radio doing the morning show, which was a good show, and he sounded really good. From the first time that I met the guy, he didn't look anything like he sounded. So I didn't know what to expect. But we just hit it off right away and became really good friends."

Nelson was working early evenings when he first arrived in Stockton, so he and Imus didn't cross paths much initially. "But every time we'd see each other we'd kind of click and say, 'Hey, let's get together.' Imus is one of those guys, to me, from the very first time I met the guy, he can just talk to me and I would just start falling out. I mean, he just has that effect on me. Like, he'd call me up and as soon as I'd hear his voice, he'd say 'Nelson' in his clipped tone, I'd start laughing."

Terry and his wife, Maria, were two of the few people who spent a lot of time with both Don and Harriet, who rented a house in North Stockton, which was an unassuming, middle-class part of town. "Harriet was a very attractive lady," recalls Terry, who said she told him she used to be a model. "She's just a sweetheart lady and was totally supportive of Don. They even had the same mannerisms. They just struck you as a good couple, which is why we became such tight friends. Most of the time they were at our house."

Although he was making twice the salary he had earned in Palmdale, Don still wasn't making an awful lot of money, so the family was forced to live modestly. And Don was forced to drive an old, beat-up 1960 powder-blue Ford. "It was just a piece of junk," laughs Nelson. "And it didn't have reverse in it. I remember every time he came over, he would park across the street purposely so nobody would be in front of him. Or when we were downtown running around, because every time somebody would park in front of him, we'd have to push the sucker backwards so it could get back far enough so he could pull out and drive away."

For whatever Terry and Don didn't have financially, they made up for in good times at the radio station. "It really was a lot of fun. Everybody was always laughing and joking and doing stuff." Even though there was less leeway as far as format was concerned, Terry says the overall atmosphere of the station was "a lot looser than it is today."

With none so loose as Don. Not only was Don a unique on-air personality, his off-mike eccentricities also earned him a notoriety of a different kind. Nelson remembers that above all other things, Don was a complete slob who left the control room constantly littered with his stuff. "When I'd see Imus in the mornings, I'd walk in there and the studio was always a total mess. He always had his coffeepot in there because he drank coffee and smoked cigarettes like crazy.

"Now, just out of courtesy, when you get ready to get off the air, you clean it up before the next guy comes in. But Don always left the place a total mess. The guy who followed Don was Mike Wynn, who was just a crazy mother. One morning Mike told Don, 'When I come here tomorrow, if this studio is like this, I'm just dumping all this shit, I'm just throwing it all on the floor, man.' And Imus is going 'Yeah, fuck you.' But in a good way," laughs Terry.

So the next morning, Nelson recounts, Wynn came in to find the control room just as slovenly as ever. "Imus signs off and he's got his coffeepot, all of his papers, junk everywhere, with food and garbage lying around and Wynn walked in there and with a clean sweep wiped all that shit off on the floor. It went flying everywhere.

"And Imus was just blown away. He calls me up, going, 'Nelson, you won't believe what Wynn just did. He came in and just wiped all my shit, my coffeepot, knocked it all off everywhere.' And I said, 'Well, he told you he was going to do that, didn't he?' And Don goes, 'And the stains were just all over that control room for the longest time.' "

Interestingly, though, there were no hard feelings between Wynn and Imus, and in fact, Mike would later brainstorm with Don and help him come up with some comic bits.

When Don left the station, he would usually head home to

spend the afternoon writing, regularly sitting at his typewriter for up to five hours, methodically pecking away, putting down ideas for bits to use on his show the next day. Frequently, he would ask Terry to critique his work.

"He'd say, 'What do you think about this?' and he'd read it off. Most of it was pretty bad and I'd tell him so. And Don would say, 'Yeah, it is.' "

Nelson says that one of the most important lessons he learned from Don was the value of honesty. He recalls the day they were immersed in shop talk, discussing their mutual radio gigs, and "he said, 'You know, let's do a thing here. I won't ever lie to you about something I hear you doing and you ask me about and you've never lied to me so don't ever lie to me. Whatever we do, wherever we go, when we talk, let's talk and don't tell me something sounds good on the radio if it doesn't. And I'll do the same for you because if we're not honest with each other, like we're honest with ourselves, neither one of us will grow and go anywhere or do anything.'

"I found that so refreshing and from that day forward we just had a terrific understanding. He'd call and say what do you think about this. And if I liked it or liked part of it, I'd say this was good or that sucks or I don't get it and he would do similar things to me. It really, really helped us both out, the fact that we were so honest with each other about everything that we talked about."

Imus also encouraged Terry to start writing because, according to Don, it was the only way to get better. "And that was true," concedes Terry. "It really got his juices flowing and it really helped him grow and expand. I saw a big change come over his talent from the time he came to Stockton and the time he left, and I believe it was because he was diligent about writing every day."

Don was also equally diligent about laying the groundwork for moving up in radio. Roy Williams comments that for all the talk about his tendency to break the deejay mold and his never-before-heard-of outrageousness, "the thing Don did the best in the early years of Don Imus was he really promoted himself. Every time there was a news clipping, anytime he was mentioned doing anything, he always made sure it got into the trade publications. And it looked good on a résumé when you sent it out. That's what he did best."

While most of his bits merely raised eyebrows or elicited a few surprised gasps, a couple of his on-air stunts in Stockton left a much stronger ripple in their wake and eventually led to him being fired. The most well-known gag was when he initiated an Eldridge Cleaver look-alike contest. Cleaver at the time was a fugitive member of the feared militant Black Panther organization and was listed by J. Edgar Hoover as one of the FBI's Most Wanted Men in America. The first prize was a $5,000 fine and ten years in jail.

Many years later Don would reflect back on his mind set in suggesting the contest. "My position, my thesis was that J. Edgar Hoover and Richard Nixon simply wanted to arrest any black and would accept any black person as Cleaver. Their mentality, in my mind, was 'Well, they all look alike, so let's just get one.' So it was a quick way for someone to get some money."

According to Terry Nelson, the stunt "just scared the hell out of the boss, the general manager, and the program director. Oh, man, it just freaked them all out."

Roy Williams adds that "he was doing stuff he thought was funny and probably in a larger market would have been okay, but you have to remember the time. Eldridge Cleaver and the Black Panthers were serious stuff. The war was going and you have to understand, Stockton is a very, very conservative town," he notes, which helps explain why one of Don's first run-ins with management came over his refusal to wear a tie to work.

"And the owner of the radio station, Ort Lofthus, was Mr. Stockton. He knew everybody in town, so every time Don would do something, he would get a call from a friend or a buddy and Don was always in trouble."

But contrary to the oft-repeated conventional wisdom, the Cleaver contest did not directly result in Don getting fired, although, as Roy notes, it would have been a "good enough reason. But the Cleaver thing wasn't that big a deal. The station didn't make any big thing out of it. It wasn't until after Don left that he even paid any attention to it."

The true final straw that led to his dismissal was a stunt he did for Halloween. According to Terry Nelson, "There was a Holiday Inn in town and a sign on it said something like HAPPY HALLOWEEN, HAPPY SPOOK DAY and that's what got Don rolling on it.

"On the air he started talking about spooks, this is in 1969, and Stockton just wasn't ready for that. Businesses, advertisers, started complaining. You don't get on the air and do that kind of stuff—not on their radio station, man, not KJOI."

Adds Williams: "And you have to look at the fact you have an owner here who is very much involved in the community, a program director, Don Hoffman, who came from Salinas, which is not all that big, and they had this guy who they couldn't control. They saw him as a bad thing, not as a good thing. If he would have been a good thing, they would have stuck with him. But they saw him as somebody they just couldn't control and finally he said something that he shouldn't and the owner said He's out of here."

Although Terry Nelson also maintains that the average listeners understood the joke. "Don did well when he was on the air doing crazy things with people. But that was shock radio back then. When he started that stuff, people just couldn't believe it. They'd listen in every day just to see what he was going to do or what he was going to say, and then when he did the Eldridge

Cleaver thing or the spook day thing, they'd just go nuts. They'd call and laugh and talk and thought it was great, thought it was funny."

Unfortunately for Imus, management didn't. So it was really the one-two punch of the Eldridge Cleaver look-alike contest, then his spook comments that finally caused management to say "enough." Although one would have thought that Don knew full well he was almost daring management, according to Nelson he was genuinely shocked when they came in and told him he was being fired.

"I remember the day he got fired. I was sound asleep and he called me up that morning. 'Nelson, I just got fired.' And I go, 'Yeah, okay man. You woke me up to tell me this.' And he goes, 'No, I really did, man. I really got fired.' And again he was just blown away. 'They really fired me. Can you believe they fired me?' I said, 'Of course,' although I was blown away myself. I woke up when I realized he was telling me the truth, that it wasn't just some jive little thing."

Don had been in Stockton only ten months. With suddenly no job and no prospects and certainly no savings, Don spent the next few weeks getting his bearings. The first priority was finding work. "I was working weekends at KJOI when he got fired, and the thing is, he didn't have any tape, he didn't have anything to send out," recalls Roy Williams. "He probably doesn't remember this, but he did a couple of overnight shifts at KFIV down in Modesto just so he could put a tape together to send out. He was married with a bunch of kids. He and his wife were all-involved with radio. That was his life."

It was also his lot in life to be misunderstood, believes Nelson, who dismisses any notion that the two incidents that got him fired justify painting Don as a racist, especially considering Imus has said he supported Eldridge Cleaver and yippie Jerry Rubin in the presidential election of 1968.

"The thing about Don, he's really one of the most caring,

concerned people in the world that I've ever met. He's one of those guys, you can listen to him and think he's gruff or think whatever you want to think, but he's just a real pussycat. But yet at the same time," Terry acknowledges, "he can look you right in the face, maybe having met you maybe thirty seconds before, and say, 'Go fuck yourself.' I remember him doing that to people. Then he'd walk away, look at me, and give me that shit-eating grin. They'd all be offended and back off, afraid to approach him again, but if they only knew they could go 'Hey, wait a minute, asshole,' then he'd fall out laughing. He'd do a lot of that stuff just to get people's reaction.

"Don was just real talented and was just trying to find himself."

Not everybody, though, shared Nelson's foresight. More people shared Williams's view that "nobody knew who Don Imus was going to be. He was just another jock. There was always something that you knew he was going to do or say that would get him in trouble." And that after Imus left "there wasn't any more thought about it. The market was too small and Don wasn't there long enough to really build up a following. It wasn't like, Oh, man, you're letting a great jock go. Or, Oh, man, the audience is just going to be up in arms. Hey, the next day there was a different guy there and two or three days later they didn't even remember who Don Imus was. You gotta remember, jocks come and go."

However, Williams does believe that today, many in town appreciate the curious legacy Imus left Stockton on his way to radio prominence. "The one thing about Don I think maybe people look at it in a negative way but I always looked at as very positive was he didn't have to mention KJOI, and he didn't have to mention he got fired from there, but he always did. And I look at that as kind of neat because he always mentioned and kind of paid tribute to the radio station. People at least knew he worked in Stockton."

And now Imus needed to find work elsewhere—immediately. So while Don's on-air persona quickly faded from the collective consciousness of Stockton, he sat at home, waiting for a job he couldn't find. "Then I was told there was a guy in Sacramento who was probably the only man in America who would hire me."

Then for the third time in two years, Don and his family loaded their few belongings into his beat-up Ford and went to start yet another new life.

Chapter Seven

WHETHER OR NOT JACK G. THAYER WAS TRULY THE ONLY MAN IN America willing to give Imus a job, he would prove to be the right man to hire Don. More than anybody else Imus would work for in his career, Thayer was the mentor Don sorely needed. Although Don may not have lacked for confidence— his brother Fred noted that "you could have told Don in 1970, 'You know, I don't think you're ever going to make it in radio,' and he wouldn't have known what you were talking about"— Don was still professionally raw and unfocused. He had the ingredients but didn't know how to harness what he had.

Perhaps Thayer saw a bit of himself in Imus, because throughout his career Jack had been an innovator and had spent his working life looking for new ways to approach the radio business and helped establish and make commonplace then-novel practices such as Top 10 record countdowns, all-talk ra-dio, and "underground" stations.

Thayer was born in Chicago, but later his family moved to Minnesota and he graduated from high school in St. Paul. After attending college in Nebraska, Thayer got a job as a deejay in Rapid City, South Dakota. In the mid-1940s he moved to WLOL in Minneapolis, where he started a feature he called *Top Tunes of the Week*. In addition to teaching at the Beck School of Radio, Thayer also dabbled in music-related television through two local shows. The first, *Jack's Corner Drug*, was an afternoon teenage dance show that featured lip-synching. The other was a Saturday night program called *Top Ten Records*.

In the 1950s Thayer went to WDGY-AM, which at the time was in a "cash giveaway war" with rival WCCO. Thayer became the city's top-rated morning deejay and ended up running the station when he was made general manager in 1956.

"He had the highest level of vitality I've ever known," said Bob Montgomery, known as Bob White at WCCO-AM in the 1950s. "He had innovation and creativity."

His reputation as a visionary was occasionally rivaled by his willingness to be outrageous. In the 1960s, when he was general manager at WHK-AM in Cleveland, Thayer made the national news when he invited the leader of the Soviet Union to a sock hop. Eventually, he moved to California, where his trailblazing continued. He turned KLAC-AM into one of the first all-day-talk-show stations, and made KMET-FM the first full-time commercial underground station that played unreleased album cuts in addition to hit singles.

At the time he was working at KXOA as the general manager, however, Thayer was struggling to overcome some personal problems. According to Les Thompson, who worked under Thayer, "Jack was recovering. He had gone through a divorce and he ended up in Sacramento because he had fallen off the wagon."

And because the station owners wanted him to turn around KXOA, which was being bled dry by San Francisco's powerhouse station, KFRC. "They didn't have all these diversified stations with everybody playing something different," explains Thompson. "It was either rock and roll, country-western, or news."

So Thayer's assignment was to find a way to make the residents of Sacramento tune back to their local station. However, not everyone who worked at the station liked the way Thayer worked. "Be on the air and cut all the promos," says Les. "The station was going through changes, and Jack Thayer was a manager who wanted to stick his nose into everybody's business. Jack Thayer and I didn't get along very well."

But Thayer's keen sense of what worked over the air was still finely honed. "Jack was an entrepreneur," observes Thompson. "He could spot talent. He found Don and took him. I was the program director at the time, so I received the audition tape and all the information from where he was working down in Stockton and found out he got fired down there because he was a wild man."

But Thayer was intrigued, and despite Don's dismissal in Stockton, Jack hired him to be KXOA's new morning man. Don's friend Terry Nelson believes it was Thayer who is responsible for Don learning to channel his creativity in a more satiric way.

"He's the one who really shaped and molded Don and got him to be more focused and not going in a thousand directions at one time," recalls Nelson, who by sheer coincidence followed Don to Sacramento, when he was offered a job at KROY. "He told Don that a less controversial way to satirize current events was through the use of characters."

What Thayer was suggesting was something Don had honed to perfection in high school, during those nights spent driving up and down the main strip of Prescott, listening to the preachers selling their wares.

"He thought it was a good way to say stuff and somehow people would perceive when they listened to the radio that it wasn't really you," explains Imus. By having the fictional characters be the ones to say outrageous things, Don would be better shielded from criticism. "They might *know* it was, but it took some of the onus off me."

Thayer insisted Don spend a minimum four to five hours a day at his typewriter seriously working to develop specific characters to act as channels for his humor and the discipline quickly brought a new dimension to Don's show. His first fully defined character was Crazy Bob, who recited skewed versions of familiar children's stories and classic fairy tales:

> Hi, boys and girls. Today's story is one I like to call "Goldilocks and the Three Bears." But Baby Bear didn't say "Somebody's been sleeping in my bed and there she is." He simply said, "Good night, everybody."

In another story, Crazy Bob gives his revisionist twist to "Little Red Riding Hood."

> One Saturday morning, Little Red Riding Hood decided to take a walk through the forest to Grandma's house. . . . However, having read the story, Little Red Riding Hood decided to skip going to Grandma's house and instead went directly to the forest ranger's place. Little Red Riding Hood told the forest ranger that there was trouble at Grandma's house but neglected to tell him about the wolf. So the forest ranger dashed off, saying, I'll be back in an hour. And sure enough, about an hour later, the forest ranger returned, and Little Red Riding Hood anxiously asked him what happened. The forest ranger smiled and said, "Who would have thought that a dog like your grandmother would be such a wild wolf in the sack?"

Then there was also Judge Hangin', for whom police brutality is "the fun part of law enforcement" and whose professional life started as a highway patrolman.

> One day I trooped into court with about a pound and a half of bugs all matted up in my hair and I noticed this old judge sitting up there with this wooden hammer, just raking it in. Well, that's when I decided that I wanted the law to be my

friend. And the law *is* my friend. Anyone who hurts my friend should be beaten senseless.

Through the Judge, Don would take swipes at both law enforcement and elected officials of all kinds.

You may be asking yourself, well, Judge Hangin', what should I do if some sadistic cop caves my head in with ten-graded number-nine garden hose while I'm walking down the street minding my own business? My fellow Americans, life has its own way of evening the score. I mean, there's probably a time when you may have gone a little soon on a green light. Or perhaps went seventy when the speed limit was sixty-five. And you didn't get caught.

But if politicians were his primary target of contempt, evangelists were his primary source of satire, as channeled through the Reverend Billy Sol Hargis, who would try to sell virtually anything—from sin insurance to inflatable plastic pulpits to tasty sacred chickens—by invoking the name of God.

As you know from time to time, Billy Sol Hargis, on behalf of the Good and Discount House of Worship, offers tremendous opportunities for you to cash in on your faith. Say Hallelujah. As you know, Billy Sol Hargis is the owner and operator of the world's only truly religious amusement park, Holy Land, located right here in Del Rio, Texas.

You may order Billy Sol's *Holy Land Cookbook* for that religious meal Mom just can't seeeem to get together. Say Hallelujah! What a way to stretch the food budget, Mom. With Billy Sol Hargis's *Holy Land Cookbook* and a little ingenuity, you can take two of Mrs. Paul's fish sticks and five loaves of real Jewish rye and feed up to five thousand unexpected drop-in guests.

Terry Nelson remembers how Thayer's tutelage was allowing Don to finally fulfill his potential. "I first saw those traces of greatness when we were in Sacramento together, because all of a sudden he got his direction and self-belief and the confidence that he was going. He was working hard."

There were also other factors at work in the professional maturing of Imus, who now, more so than at his prior jobs, was beginning to adopt the western style that would become another of his trademarks—wearing cowboy boots, fringe jackets, and sporting long sideburns. In the late 1960s Imus discovered Paul Krassner's brilliantly lunatic counterculture journal *The Realist*.

Krassner was a wild and clever writer, who, like Imus, never missed a chance to rail against those in positions of power. Often uneven and outlandish, the magazine enraged conservative types, who regarded it as a "filthy avant-garde left-wing rag." Conversely, *The Realist* became a darling of radicals everywhere. Imus says he ordered every back issue of *The Realist*, and in later years subscribed when the magazine resurfaced in 1985 after stopping production for eleven years.

Besides Krassner, Imus studied the routines of Mort Sahl and the monologues of Lenny Bruce. It might be telling that one of Imus's favorite Bruce bits is when the comedian keeps repeating a derogatory term for blacks, his point being that even the most hated and insulting racial slur can be neutralized and robbed of its power if we stop giving it power over us.

"Lenny Bruce, you gotta remember," comments Imus, "was brilliant, you know what I'm saying?"

Perhaps the routine had particular meaning to Imus, who had already been dogged by charges he was racist because of his Eldridge Cleaver and spook gags. But the accusations seemed to genuinely surprise him. "I'm not a racist. I'm not bigoted. There are just funny things about everybody."

And he also acknowledged that there were lines he wouldn't

cross. "Jokes about lynching aren't funny. Jews being exterminated isn't funny."

But just about everyone else was fair game, and Imus wasted little time letting his listening audience know that. He would take calls from women on the air and ask them, "Are you naked?" which became one of his trademark lines and which would eventually be picked up by other jocks around the country.

The radio station itself was brand new but small and sterile, the owners having torn down the old one, which former employees remember as being huge and a lot of fun to work at. The format Don was expected to follow was called Boss radio at KXOA, meaning *one hit after the other* which at that time included songs like "Bridge over Troubled Waters," Brook Benton's "Rainy Night in Georgia," "Kentucky Rain" by Elvis Presley, and others performed by the Jackson Five, Creedence Clearwater, and Led Zeppelin.

"The Boss radio format came out of Los Angeles, KHJ. You'd play hits, then hit-bound sounds, then you'd play an oldie," Thompson says, describing the song rotation. "You'd go by a wheel, do certain breaks at certain times. We had 20–20 news, which meant you did news at twenty after the hour and twenty till the hour. Then we'd come out of that with a hot oldie. We gave away cars and other promotions, you have to do that with Top 40 records. The jocks had to be fast and it was shotgun jingles. It was formatted completely."

Which, of course, meant very little to Don. He was much more consumed with the daily show he was putting on. He found a kindred soul in the KXOA newsman, Brian Bierne, who would go on to become a well-known Los Angeles disc jockey in the 1970s and who is still on the air at K-Earth in L.A.

"He was called Giant Frog," says Thompson. "And they used to go out and do stunts. There was a *Sacramento Union* reporter, I can't think of his name, they faked a kidnap of him and it was all over the news. It was a stunt we did for some promotion.

"There was also the superman costume gag, where he'd call up a cleaners, claiming to be a Mr. Kent looking for his suit. When they can't find it and he winds up saying, 'You can't miss it. There's a big S on the front. My name is Kent. Clark Kent.' Then, *Bam,* he hangs up the phone and goes to music.

"The telephone calls were important, he'd get people out of bed . . . he had quite an effect on listeners."

He was also having an effect on the station executives, who were not comfortable with his daily antics. At one point Thayer found out that his bosses were thinking of letting Don go.

"He took a real chance with me, you know," Imus says of Thayer. "He laid his job on the line for me. They wanted to fire me in Sacramento 'cause they thought I was crazy. He told them if they fired me, they'd have to fire him."

For as much faith as Thayer had in Imus, others, including program director Thompson, weren't always so sure. "He was just crazy all the time. He was great in preparation, but I could care less at that point in time because the station was going through ownership change and nobody knew where the hell they were going to be from one day to the next. Imus was a crazy man and everybody knew he was a self-contained bomb just ready to go off—but with talent. And that's what happened."

For the first time in his career, Don was about to come under the scrutiny of the Federal Communications Commission over a live phone stunt that became one of his most famous and infamous. Posing as an "International Guard" officer, Don called a local McDonald's to place a bogus order for the amusement of his listeners. The employee who had the misfortune of picking up the phone just happened to be there, cleaning.

"McDonald's hamburgers?"

"Yes, it is."

"This is Sergeant Kirkland of the International Guard, and I'd like to get some lunches to go if I possibly could."

"We're not open for another two hours, sir."

"Well, I wondered if I could give you the order now. I need quite a few and I'd stop by this afternoon and pick them up. I'd like to get, if I could, twelve hundred hamburgers."

"Twelve . . . pardon me, sir?"

"Twelve hundred hamburgers is what we'd like to get. We have a troop movement scheduled at one of the local colleges and we'd like to get some lunches to go."

"Just a moment, I'm going to have to ask my—could you hold on, Sergeant, a moment?"

In the background, as you hear the assistant manager, who sounds like a teenager, asking someone what he should do, you can also hear Imus laughing at the confusion he's causing.

"Well, we don't have enough meat or buns for twelve hundred hamburgers."

"Well, can't you get some from the other stores? This is the government, you know."

"Yes, sir! I'll have to do that."

"Why don't you just take the order and get 'em as soon as you can, then I'll call you back in an hour. Now, listen, on three hundred of those I want you to hold the mustard but put on plenty of mayonnaise and lettuce. Don't want any onions on those. On two hundred, make that two hundred and one, I want you to hold the mayo but lay on the mustard. . . ."

Imus spends the next minute barking out a mind-numbing combination of order until finally, the McDonald's employee apparently just hangs up. Afterward, Don thought nothing more about the gag. Neither did management. "We got a couple of letters, but nothing happened," Thompson says. "He never crossed the line far enough to get bothered by the FCC. Although another jock, Bill Whitman, did, because he used to fart on the air."

However, even though Don himself escaped personal scrutiny, his McDonald's gag did later cause the FCC to institute a new radio broadcast rule in May 1970 titled Broadcast of Telephone Conversations, and numbered 73.1206:

> Before recording a telephone conversation for broadcast, or broadcasting such a conversation simultaneously with its occurrence, a licensee shall inform any party to the call of the licensee's intention to broadcast the conversation, except where such party is aware, or may be presumed to be aware from the circumstances of the conversation that it is being or likely will be broadcast. Such awareness is presumed to exist only when the other party to the call is associated with the station (such as an employee or part-time reporter) or where the other party originates the call and it is obvious that it is in connection with a program in which the station customarily broadcasts telephone conversations.

In other words, this was the beginning of deejays around the country picking up the phone and immediately saying, *You're on the air!* But for whatever headaches Don had given the FCC, he was giving his bosses reason to celebrate. Five months after joining KXOA, the station was number one in Sacramento.

"We beat the living daylights out of KROY," gloats Les.

And also while in Sacramento, Imus won the 1969 Billboard award for Top deejay in a medium market. But according to Terry Nelson, for all his professional achievements, he was still hesitant.

"He was measuring his success but at the same time Don was very insecure. He needed to talk to his friends who were his friends, not just groupies and hangers-on, people he'd talk to and open up to. *What do you think about this. Do you think this is working? Do you think I'm doing the right thing?* And then he made up his mind. What he believed is the way he went."

Not had Don yet begun to benefit financially. "We weren't paying him anything," acknowledges Thompson. "Grand a month. It was nothing. He didn't have any money and drove some old beat-up thing."

At KXOA, Imus was making a thousand dollars a month and although that was twice as much as he'd made in Palmdale, according to Brian Bierne, there was "never enough money raising four children. My first visit to his house, I went in and his children were sleeping in the drawers because they didn't have any beds."

According to Terry Nelson, Don tried to be an attentive father although "Don was a workaholic and was really heavy into his work. But still, they spent time together and they would do things together with the kids."

Don's style of parenting, though, was decidedly hands-off. "He treated them, like Harriet did, like adults, like people. Whatever he and Harriet would do, however they would talk, then the children should be allowed the same freedoms to do it as well. They were very much parents. They tried to raise them as important individuals and at the same time they had rights, too, as long as the kids kept it in line.

"If he was going to stay up all night, he'd say, 'Hey, the kids ought to be able to stay up all night,' providing everything else was cool with them. 'If I want to stay up all night Saturday night, they can stay up all Saturday night. If I have an opinion on something I do, then they should have an opinion on what they do. Hey, if I say fuck, they ought to be able to say fuck.'

"He loved his family a great deal."

But others who worked with Don say that his marriage had begun to show signs of strain in Sacramento. And as Don would find out in years to come, children need not only parameters and clearly marked boundaries, they crave it as a sign of parental care and interest. But back in 1969, Don believed that the thing they needed him most for was to provide for them materially. So to help supplement his income, Don did outside appearance work but still made time for radio station promotions. "We got a national award signed by President Nixon for a public service thing we did involving drug rehab. We ran a big campaign to get money that Don and the whole station was involved with," says Thompson. "We did something every month."

Other than work-related activities, though, Don didn't socialize with many people at the station, says Lee. "He and Brian were close, but Don hung out mostly with himself."

Nor would Don get much of a chance to broaden his social horizons in Sacramento. Just six months into his run, the new owners came in and cleaned house.

"They made the station Candy KNDE instead of KXOA and everybody got fired," says Thompson, "Giant Frog, the news guy, said in his last broadcast, 'No news is good news, so goodbye.' And I was let go after being a program director for years and years, then saying I wouldn't understand the format—they went from Boss radio to some dope-smoking format."

But for once Don didn't have to scramble for his next job. Thayer, who had been aware the ax was probably going to fall as soon as the sale of the station was complete, quickly found employment at Cleveland's powerhouse AM station WGAR, and when he left Sacramento for the Midwest, he took Don with him. It was an opportunity Don would make the most of.

Chapter Eight

I N THE RADIO UNIVERSE, CLEVELAND MIGHT NOT EXACTLY BE THE
promised land, but compared to the markets Imus had
worked so far, it was at the very least a golden calf. With
Thayer as his general manager, Imus was virtually guaranteed
free rein on the airwaves, and he wasted no time taking full
advantage of his creative license.

When Imus arrived, WGAR, 1220 on the AM dial, was undergoing a dramatic overhaul because, according to deejay Chuck
Collier, it had become "a fifty-kilowatt AM dead horse." While
the rest of the radio industry was embracing the back beats of
rock, WGAR had clung tenaciously to the old line, playing the
mellow sounds of crooners like Steve Lawrence and Dean Martin.

Even the station, which was housed in downtown Cleveland
in the penthouse of the old Statler Hilton Hotel, was a throw-
back to a different time. The console sat forlornly in the middle
of a huge air studio that had originally been designed during
the days when there were still radio orchestras.

Intent on revitalizing and modernizing the station, the owners had brought in Thayer, who once again exerted his visionary management skills by opting for what was then a unique,
and risky, format.

"We were the first major market to put an oldies format on
the air," says Collier. "WCBS in New York did it but not until
1972. We were the first."

The reason such a concept seemed so radical is that in 1970 rock and roll had been a specific music form for less than fifteen years. Elvis had burst on the scene only in 1956, a year after Bill Haley's *Rock Around the Clock* signaled that a new musical era was being born, so prior to 1970 there really wasn't enough music to support a play list for a full-time oldies format.

"Back in the sixties, say 1965, you would have only eight or nine years to play with, so maybe you'd play one oldie an hour," notes Collier. "Most of those would be from the sixties and you'd occasionally go back to the late fifties, and play Chuck Berry and others like that."

But now it was going to be all oldies, all the time, and Thayer set about building the team of deejays who would give the station a much-needed personality and attitude adjustment. In addition to Don, Thayer's other major on-air hire was Chuck Collier.

"I just got out of college and was working in Cincinnati at WSAI, which was a Top 40 station. I sent tapes out to the bigger markets in Ohio and luckily, Jack Thayer brought me up and interviewed me, along with program director John Lund."

For all the notoriety Imus had garnered during his California career, he was an unknown commodity in Cleveland. All Collier and the other deejays knew about Don is that he had worked with Thayer previously in Sacramento. "He never heard of me and I never heard of him."

But Collier realized quickly that Don was a different breed of radio man. On their first day of work, Don hung around the station after his show and invited Chuck to join him in the hotel coffee shop. Imus sat comfortably chatting while Collier was fighting the butterflies. "I did two to six, the afternoon show, so I remember it was about one o'clock. I felt like saying, *Don, I can't do this, I've got to be on the air in an hour. You've done your show.* I was just a nervous wreck, ready to go on in an hour. But Don never lacked for any self-confidence."

Imus was coming of professional age in the new era of Top 40 radio, which was centered around the personality of the deejay. So even though Imus has frequently been referred to as "the original shock jock" because he was the first to fuse risqué insult humor with his music spinning, perhaps a better title might be the Pioneer of Personality Radio.

Bill Scott, former program director at New York's WINS, notes that Imus came on the scene just as "public perception of what information was. You began to get more media comment on public figures. Imus was in the early ranks of those who did it with a highly developed irreverence that some people took offense to. I did not ever put him in the category of shock jock. There are others who fall into that category because they would be using language or relying on, not only sexual innuendo, but fairly blatant discussions of sex.

"Imus was not, is not, a shock jock, at least in the accepted understanding of that term." Scott admits, however, that "when he came in, because he was so different, there was a certain sense of shock. But the shock was more because he was so irreverent. The difference was, he was irreverent with a tremendous sense of humor and a very good eye for the political scene and trends. He was irreverent *and* insightful, which made him significantly different from those who were merely irreverent.

"The difference between a real, professional talent and someone who may do well but is doing so strictly by shock or using certain language or strictly concentrating on sex is enormous. On the one hand, you have a real pro, and on the other, you have people who aspire to be real pros, but while they may become reasonably successful, in fact, [they] are not."

More simply put, one critic noted that Imus's combinations of humor and commentary were particularly successful because Imus was on in the morning, and his antics helped wake people up.

Cleveland got its first morning dose when the new format kicked off on Wednesday, September 9, 1970, and listeners who tuned in to WGAR expecting the stylings of Como or Sinatra were caught up short. "All of a sudden we're playing Jammy Jack and the twist and going, *The time is 9:21, mama.* It was like, *What in the world . . . ?*" laughs Collier, then jokes, "Don and I hit the airwaves the same day and that's where the similarities end. He hit the air running. The rest of us were on playing Elvis records and he was crazy. Don just left Cleveland on its ear; hit 'em right between the eyes with his crazy sense of humor.

"It was just a general off-the-wall craziness. He would have characters, he would have prepared bits. He put more thought and preparation into his show, which was unheard of at that time. Today it's nothing, with the zoos and everything, you have two and three people, but back in 1970 it was innovative."

Don's cast of characters kept growing and now included Hy from Hollywood, a lisping gay caricature who would tell tales from Tinseltown as read from the fictitious *Screen Slime* magazine; a David Brinkley sound-alike who delivered that day's news, and Brother Love, who talked suggestively to the women of his congregations.

Callers to the show never knew what Don might say to them, just as the station management never knew what public figure Don would skewer next, and it made them understandably nervous.

"It was under the heading of unheard-of, what he was doing, talking about people, making fun of them, and it was new and people didn't know how to take it," Collier explains.

So much so that the owners of the station strongly urged Thayer to dump Imus. And for the second time Jack Thayer laid his job on the line for Don.

"They thought I was crazy and they wanted to fire me," Imus recalls. "I was on the radio screaming about Jesus and I was a little dirtier than I am now. He told them if they fired me, they'd have to fire him. So that was pretty admirable. Of course, he had no other choice, I don't think, I mean, there was no way to make it other than with me."

Thayer refused, and within two months, by Christmas 1970, WGAR was number one. "So, of course, when the management saw the fall book, any fears were allayed," Collier notes wryly. "After they saw the numbers of a dying horse, that horse getting up and ready to run a race again, it was Hey!"

Don's grab-'em-by-the-throat assault on listeners and the new format succeeded far beyond anyone's wild imaginings and resulted in a dramatic turnaround for the station within a single one book, or ratings period. "In sixty-three days, took an old, crummy, stupid station playing old, stupid records and turned it completely around," Imus snorts.

Braggadocio notwithstanding, it was lucky for Don that the station's fortunes had indeed changed so spectacularly. Because although he had always managed to get away with just about any insult he cared to hurl, Imus finally picked on the wrong man.

Bob Zames, a meteorologist, had been a local weatherman on WEWS-TV, Cleveland's channel five, for ten years. On November 2, 1970, Imus put Zames in his sights and on the air, claimed he'd been with Zames at a San Diego Chargers football game and that the weatherman was "crocked" and basically incapable of controlling himself.

Then, on November 23, Imus took Zames on again. According to the lawsuit Zames filed over the broadcast, Don told listeners the weatherman was "crocked, smashed, bombed, and otherwise not in control of himself." Then Don really got on a roll and said that Zames "proceeded to draw cloud formations on the anatomy of a fat lady in a green dress who was seated at the table; that the fat lady struck the plaintiff over the head with a wine bottle; that if the plaintiff failed to show up for his weather broadcast that night, it would not be 'because of the old sore-throat gag,' but the reason would be a hangover or effects of the wine bottle."

On December 12, 1970, Zames sued WGAR and Imus for libel and slander. After asserting that he was a respected member of the American Meteorological Society, which "requires its members to maintain the highest standards of profession, character, reputation, and efficiency," Zames claimed Imus's insults had damaged his reputation and had damaged his earning potential, not to mention caused him the requisite "personal humiliation and mental anguish." Zames, who was making $16,000 a year, sued for $200,000 in compensatory damages and $400,000 for punitive damages.

WGAR quickly worked out a settlement with Zames, and Don never missed an on-air beat. Nor did he ever apologize to either Zames or the owners of the station. He didn't care that he had just cost management substantial cash; all he cared about was his show and those who were listening.

And Imus played up that take-this-job-and-shove-it defiance whenever he could. "A lot of hip people dig my act because they think I'm crazy like they are," Don once noted. "But my gig is really aimed at the average blue collar working guy who scratches his way up from nothing, lives in a big house, and drives a Mark IV, and at the same time tells his bosses to buzz off. I got more guts than talent."

And while he also may have had more fans than detractors scrutinizing him, the media heat was more steamy in Cleveland than it ever had been in California. One columnist for the *Cleveland Plain Dealer* was so outraged by Imus's antics, he began urging the public to send their policies back to Nationwide Insurance, the company that owned WGAR.

But the band played on. In 1970, *Billboard* magazine named Imus top deejay of the year in a major market. Don was the station's undisputed top deejay and was the center of their promotional campaign. One billboard simply had the phrase IMUS

IN THE MORNING printed on it, then had crossed out the IN and replaced it with a handwritten IS.

Among his coworkers, Don was generally well liked, although he never developed any close or long-lasting friendships in Cleveland. "He would walk around WGAR with a leather vest on and a western outfit and some Wranglers and some cowboy boots," recalls Collier. "Don and all of us, we hung around the station and got crazy, but we just didn't go out or get too personal. But he got along with everyone. Don was a good guy, just an off-the-wall funny guy with tongue-in-cheek humor, sarcastic humor. I enjoyed him."

One reason the jocks at WGAR didn't socialize much outside the station was that the deejays weren't in much demand for promotional events. "Back in those days we didn't do a lot of work," Collier says. "There were not a lot of remotes, there was not a lot of emceeing because of being so new and being oldies. Now oldie shows are a dime a dozen, but because we were trailblazers with the format, promoters had not caught up with it. There was just nothing like that going on." So the WGAR crew was overlooked.

The local Cleveland businesses and organizations might not have been interested in having Don promote their wares and causes, but he was nevertheless now recognized as a major player in radio, known by reputation throughout the industry. And that was both good and bad. On the plus side, he had improved the ratings of every station where he had worked; he was innovative and undeniably talented, and, above all, he was unique.

However, the downside was troubling. Imus was a loose cannon who refused to be restrained by format or good taste; he went out of his way to antagonize management and, most significantly, he had started missing work. Where once he had been the first to arrive and would stay long after his shift was over, Don left the station scrambling several times when he either showed up late or not at all.

Because he had no close friends at WGAR, his coworkers could only wonder what was behind the sudden change in his attitude. And there were times when it seemed as if Don himself was unsure how he felt about where he was going. As he often said, he'd never intended to be a disc jockey, but now he was one and he had little choice but to ride it out and see where it led.

"Sometimes it seems strange doing my show, sitting in there, talking to nobody but the microphone. I guess I play to the telephones, they're my audience," he once mused. "I really like to hear somebody call and say I'm doing a dynamite show. When I'm going good, those lines are lit up all the time. Of course, even when I'm not, the phones light up anyway, so I guess you really never know, except inside yourself. I'm a fatalist anyway, prepared for things to fail. Knowing, you can handle that."

Journalist Martha Sherrill believes Don's fatalism is an integral part of his success. "I think part of his appeal is that he didn't care about being a deejay. He cared and he didn't care in that he was willing to leave it at any moment and go off and do something else. And that gave him a kind of power."

And a certain dark appeal. There's something fascinating about anyone who so willingly walked the edge. The question loomed, was it simple creative genius or plain self-destruction lurking underneath? Whatever it was, it brought more ears to the radio, and at WNBC in New York, that was their most pressing mandate. So in late 1971, after fifteen months in Ohio, Don was offered a job at WNBC in New York City, the Mecca of broadcast.

"We were all shocked," Collier admits. "We went, 'God, Don, man, you gotta be kidding!' It was the same thing again; WNBC had become a staid, stodgy radio station, so they probably looked at what Don had done in Cleveland and said, 'Hey, let's give it a try.' "

Like others he'd worked with, Don left a trail of mixed emotions in his wake. The *Plain Dealer* took a cue from the *New York Post* and printed a headline that screamed GARBAGE MOUTH GOES TO GOTHAM. And while most agreed Imus had a unique talent, many thought his style would eventually self-destruct and implode. "Nobody, not even he, in those early days thought it would ever be what it is today," notes Collier, who goes on to say that Don Imus might never have become Don Imus if it weren't for the support of his mentor, Jack Thayer.

"If that had not of happened, who knows? He might have made it later, he might have made it on his own, you never know, but it was definitely Jack Thayer who saw his talent."

WGAR as it existed during the Imus reign is gone. It's now an FM country station. As many AM-FM stations did once the ratings started to slip, they sold their AM station and kept the FM counterpart. Although Don couldn't have known it when he arrived in New York, he was about to be one of the last great AM disc jockeys, because within fifteen years FM radio would nearly destroy the AM market. But at the time the idea that AM could be dethroned seemed absurd, especially when looking over the New York radio landscape that Imus was about to enter.

Because it was the home of radio broadcasting, New York City had more powerhouse AM stations than any single city in the country, although like the music business itself, these stations were undergoing a transformation. Some still formatted their programming strictly around the music, the old RKO way, while others believed that deejays were now the center of the on-air universe.

WNEW, for example, had been the premiere station in the 1960s, but over the following decade, according to Bill Scott, "it fell completely out of step and seemed very self-centered. Although NEW had a personality sense with deejays like William B Williams, the Milkman, and an extremely funny, extremely clever morning drive team, Claven and Finch, the station was not progressive in its thinking and it began to slip."

The station appealed to an older crowd, a much different demographic than WABC or WNBC. And just as in television today, advertisers were more interested in the younger demographics and paid more in advertising rates to the stations that got the biggest share of the eighteen to thirty-four listening audience.

Another aging station was WOR, the home of John Gambling, who for years had been one of the city's most popular jocks. Although its audience was completely different from WNEW's, the station shared the same problems with advertisers.

"WOR's audience was primarily white, suburban, middle/upper-middle income, and that's what their programming played to," explains Scott. "And it did that very successfully for many, many years, but it maintained that audience many years after it should have. That station was a giant, but it began to wear down, and as times changed, it did not. But it was so strong that it took a long time for it to really sink. In the industry it was clear it should have been sinking faster, but they had a loyal if quite a bit older audience. As radio itself got more varied and the whole entertainment and information world became more charged, WOR did not move to be anything that would appeal to a new audience necessary to replace the audience it was beginning to lose, if only through attrition."

WMCA was the little station who could. A small, five-thousand-watt operation, MCA gained notoriety thanks to its Good Guys, which included deejays Dandy Dan Daniel and Ed Baer. What it lacked in power it made up for with marketing ingenuity, giving away thousands of gold-colored souvenir sweatshirts adorned with a smiley face. But between WABC's might and the burgeoning FM market, by 1969, MCA's broadcast day was divided between music and talk and would eventually change format completely.

In 1971, WABC was clearly the station to beat. They had the star lineup and the best-known personalities in the business, including Dan Ingram, Murray the K, who called himself the fifth Beatle, Harry Harrison, and Cousin Brucie Morrow.

"It was a very tightly, very brilliantly formatted station for what they did," Scott says. "Rick Sklar was the program director and planned his broadcast day virtually minute by minute as well as record by record, and was very successful with that."

It was WNBC's desire to overtake WABC that led the station to look for strong personalities who would give WNBC an instantly recognizable, distinct brand. Which is why in addition to Imus, management had brought in Wolfman Jack.

"And it was certainly a different type of personality who came in to NBC. By different type I mean far more involvement on the air of the personality than you had at ABC and other places, which were more tightly formatted as far as how much someone could say, the amount of time they had to talk.

"Sometimes stations would bring in somebody who had been successful elsewhere, then put them into a format where they really couldn't shine. That, of course, is crazy," Scott points out. "With the arrival of Wolfman, you had people who had tremendous talent coming into the market who also were given a platform to use that talent.

"The difference with Imus at NBC was the amount of territory he was allowed to cover. That was a function of two things. One, that was their plan, and two, they said, here's a guy who can cover the territory, so let's let him do it within whatever limitations we want to place."

Whereas a legend like Murray the K had "an outstanding knowledge of the music industry and a great feel for the music and was a great personality, it was all in that music vein and in that role as top deejay who knew his music and knew his personalities."

The same was true of Wolfman Jack, whose growling vocal delivery made him the quintessential night disc jockey and a favorite of teenagers and young adults. In fact, Wolfman would have been the kind of disc jockey Don and his high school friends would have listened to while out cruising late on Saturday nights. Interestingly, Wolfman Jack actually started his career at the Mexican radio station XERF-AM, a 250,000 behemoth that pumped out five times more power than was legal in the United States at the time and could be heard over a good portion of the Southwest, especially late at night. And in fact, it's quite possible that Don had heard Wolfman's show in the early 1960s, with the trademark howl echoing through the expansive dark nights of the Southwest as he played records ranging from blues to bluegrass.

Wolfman Jack, who was born in Brooklyn as Robert Smith, came up in radio when the trend was to have a nom de plume, so he decided on his radio stage name because he was a big fan of horror films and because it fit his voice, full of snarl and sandpaper. He believes that voice brought him his success.

"I've got that nice, raspy sound. It's kept meat and potatoes on the table for years for Wolfman and Wolfwoman," he once said. "A couple of shots of whiskey helps it."

It's also worth noting that while it's true that Imus developed a style all his own, there are some curious similarities between Wolfman's early shtick and Don's later on-air gags, such as how the Wolfman hawked plastic Jesus figures, inspirational literature, and even coffins. Then there was his trademark *Get yo'self nekkid* that he would bark into the microphone.

Although he would later become a celebrity deejay thanks to his appearance as himself in George Lucas's 1973 classic *American Graffiti,* and then as the host with the most on the *Midnight Special* for the NBC Television Network in 1970, Wolfman Jack was simply another star New York deejay with a great personality who focused on the music. He wasn't interested in social/political commentary or satire and irreverence.

Imus, on the other hand, "was not known for his playing of music," Scott laughs. "Never has been, never will be. Music was sort of a break time in there. I don't know of anybody who listened to him or talked about him who was even aware there was music."

Although Don was an unknown commodity to most of the New York radio community, he was known by reputation, and Scott remembers his hiring was met with a mixture of curiosity and wariness. "In the business there was talk that this guy was pretty wild and does some pretty wild things. So there was a certain anticipation that there was something of a difference coming in, and that to a degree, NBC was taking a chance, maybe staking out new territory in the market in that style. But had they brought in someone who was just, for want of a better word, dirty, that would not have worked. What they did was, they brought in an entertainer.

"Imus brought into the market a certain level of irreverence that was not there before. Beyond his ability on the air and his voice and sense of humor and such, he came across as an extremely sharp, intelligent guy who could spot and sense what was going on in the world, particularly in the market, and would weave that in with a kind of everyman approach so that listeners could identify with him when he tweaked the noses of officials. They could identify with him when he went after the high and mighty with humor. They could identify with him when he was sympathetic toward someone who the public could feel good about. He had that ability."

Ironically, it would turn out that the real question wasn't whether Don Imus would thrive and prosper in New York, but whether Don Imus would be able to survive himself.

Chapter Nine

ALTHOUGH WOLFMAN JACK HAD BEEN HIRED FIRST, HAD THE MORE established career, and was generally considered one of the top deejays in the country, the fact was his night shift simply wasn't as important to the economics and ratings of WNBC as the morning show was. Which is why when then-station manager Perry Bascom, who had been hired two years prior to Imus and was charged with improving ratings, scoured the country for a new morning man. And why after he hired Imus, Bascom changed the rest of the station personnel to center around Imus. "As the morning goes, so goes the station," Bascom said. "Morning is when you grab the big nuggets."

Imus did his first New York broadcast in December 1971. The next day he didn't show up and missed work. "The second day I was out. I overslept. Isn't that awful?" he asked, not sounding as if he felt awful about it at all. But as he freely admitted, "I didn't care whether they liked it or not. I just didn't care. But from day one, I liked New York."

In that first two-day time span, Imus had thrown down the gauntlet and made it clear to management that if they wanted his ratings, they had to let him play by different rules. But the problem was, Don seemed to have no rules, constraints, or boundaries, either on air or off. During his show he repeatedly referred to station manager Bascom as Mr. Vicious and the program manager, Pat Whitley, as Mr. Numb. He insulted a fellow deejay by saying he was at "the twilight of a mediocre career."

The studio setup at the station was similar in concept to the current one used by *The Today Show*—there was a glass enclosure through which passersby could stop and watch a deejay at work, where they might have heard Don, wearing his cowboy hat and boots, tell his listeners: "If you're on your way into the city, watch out! The Negroes are out in force."

One listener remembers driving into town, and as Imus's words came over the radio, several cars swerved out of spontaneous shock. What nobody could say for sure was whether Imus was poking fun at an irrational "white fear" or a bigot in a sheep's satiric clothing.

Nor were the stations cash cows, the advertisers, exempt. In fact, Imus seemed to save some of his most caustic comments for them, such as when he quipped that on Irish Airlines "Protestants have to ride coach." WNBC subsequently lost the account. But there were always others waiting to buy the time.

"Some advertisers were scared to death of him, others just loved Don," comments Bob Pittman, a former WNBC executive who would later go on to create MTV. "Certain advertisers loved it that Don tortured them on the air. While the stunts at the time were shocking, Don always had a very ironic twist to him."

Such as when he would sharpen his teeth to bite the hand feeding him.

> Fifty years of radio and this is what NBC has come to: foul-mouthed disc jockeys and dope-oriented records.

Whether listeners appreciated Imus's take on the world, or were turned off by the relentlessness of his verbal assault, the most important thing was that Don's show created a strong word-of-mouth response. Bill Scott remembers hearing people on the street saying, "Did you hear this" or "I heard this." Maybe in some cases he crossed the line, but not very often.

What he did, very cleverly, was give people routines they could talk about to their friends. Ultimately, that's the winning formula. It did not take long for the buzz to start, and then it built fairly quickly as the word got around.

"But I think there was more talk about Imus than there was about his ratings for a while."

And in fact, when Imus started, listeners inundated NBC with protesting letters and angry phone calls. Some from people who didn't like his signature tag line at the end of the show:

See you tomorrow, and, remember, if you get a chance, eat it.

And some from people who thought his humor reflected personal bias.

The Gay Liberation Front has failed in its efforts to have the post office honor them with a commemorative stamp, and a spokesman for the group now says plans are in the works to have the Treasury Department salute them with a three-dollar bill.

"For NBC that was a big cultural change," notes Bill Scott, referring to the station's previous image of mainstream white bread programming. "But while NBC corporate may well have been uncomfortable with some of the things Imus did, they could live with that because he wasn't the classic shock jock, and his talent prevailed."

Indeed, the only response the station management really cared about was the one reflected in the ratings. And in the all-important eighteen-to-thirty-four demographic, NBC was up almost fifty percent and WNBC had risen from seventh to fifth within months of Imus going on the air.

"People said I couldn't bring my act to New York. Well, I've taken this town over," Imus boasted at the time. "I *knew* I was going to take over New York."

For the most part, most of Don's superiors encouraged that kind of egomaniacal attitude because it only benefited the station. Occasionally, though, Don encountered people who weren't quite so willing to immediately play into his I-am-king-of-the-radio-world megalomania. Charles Scimeca ran an advertising agency and recalls when WNBC approached him about buying time on *Imus in the Morning* not long after Don had gone on the air. Scimeca knew about Imus but as a negotiating ploy suggested they participate in a little test to see just what Don's public appeal was.

"I said, 'Let's have Don appear at the opening day of a movie.' And they agreed." Charles picked a Thursday afternoon in Long Island at a theater located near a local university. He told them it would be terrific because it would attract all the college kids. Then when they went out there to the theater, maybe twenty people showed up.

"We went to lunch after that at a restaurant in Roosevelt Field. So I turn to the general manager and say, 'So this is the hotshot you tell me is going to change New York radio? That's the kind of draw he pulls?' Imus turns to me and says, 'Fuck you!'"

Unfazed, Charles told Imus he could do the same to himself in return, then Scimeca went ahead and agreed on a price per spot for the next year. Later, Charles invited Imus out to smooth things over.

"We ended up going out drinking and I told Imus, 'I set you up. The middle of a Thursday afternoon is the worst day to draw a crowd because all the colleges are very busy and it's the worst day for kids to be off. There was no way you could win.' To prove it to him, I arranged another premiere on a Thursday night in Manhattan at a theater on Thirty-fourth Street two weeks later and the lines were around the block."

It was one of the last times anyone would get one over on Imus or successfully use him as a negotiating ploy for their own benefit. But the experience had proven something—that New Yorkers were embracing him as one of their own. Don's friend from Sacramento, Brian "Giant Frog" Bierne, believes New York and Imus were symbiotically meant for each other. "I think New Yorkers really accepted Don. He was tailor made for that audience and that lifestyle with the *ahh,-it's-a-gloomy-day* chip-on-your-shoulder sort of attitude. So I think he fit right in."

Actually, while Don's show might have fit in, Imus himself seemed to be increasingly on the outside looking in, a visitor to his own life. In 1972 Imus was asked to present the 1972 deejay awards at the *Billboard* magazine convention held in Los Angeles. On the trip he was shadowed by a reporter who was researching a profile on him for a national magazine. The resulting picture was of a man being subtly swept away by his desire for success and validation and his disdain of those who wanted to give it.

While in L.A., Don did a tour of his former haunts. He stopped by the Don Martin school, still not paying them the money he owed. He drove up to Palmdale to visit his brother Fred, whom he was trying to get a job as a disc jockey in New York. "Fred is funny as hell on the air. He's gotta get that job, even if I have to pay his salary," Don declared, despite the fact that Fred had no interest in such a move.

Back in L.A., a dinner had been planned for Don. But at the cocktail party held prior to the event, which was being dubbed *Whatever Happened to Don Imus?* the guest of honor stalked out.

"Ain't no way I'm going to that dinner now," he raged to the reporter. "I don't care what anybody thinks of me. First thing at the cocktail party people start downing me, saying I was weak on the air, playing the wrong records. They can all buzz off."

Then, in a rare display of vulnerability, he added, "Hell, that really hurt."

But Don had his armor back on for the *Billboard* ceremony, and emceed the entire event in character as the Reverend Billy Sol Hargis. His manic presence, coupled by his refusal to let any of the winners say anything by keeping the mike firmly in his own control, made many in the audience shift uncomfortably in their seats. "They never saw anything like this before at one of these ripoffs," he said with a kind of grim satisfaction.

It was the last time *Billboard* asked him to host the event. Not that Don cared, because he was on top of the world, ruling his musical island fiefdom with no eye toward the future. But Don's success came with some casualties, most notably Malcolm John "Big" Wilson.

As often happens in the entertainment business, many performers are pure products of their time and are unable to reinvent themselves as styles and mores change. Such was the case with Big Wilson, who had been WNBC's morning man. He had worked at the station since 1962 and was probably best remembered for playing his piano on air. Prior to Don's arrival, Wilson was moved to middays and replaced by interim morning host Joe O'Brien.

"He was a personality I'd liken to Willard Scott," Bill Scott recalls, referring to the affable *Today Show* weatherman and resident goodwill ambassador. "He was an entertainer with a very warm feeling about him, very friendly, intelligent, but again, probably more in the WOR vein in music than Imus. He was obviously very capable, but NBC made a decision they were going to concentrate on certain kinds of personalities."

Big Wilson accepted the unenviable job of following Imus at ten A.M. but didn't last there very long. It was clear to both him and management that he no longer fit into an environment that catered to a Don Imus, who was almost single-handedly changing the station's image by the sheer force of his talent, or, as

Scott sums up, "a fortunate coming together of planning and talent." So Big Wilson left WNBC without any fanfare, taking over the morning shift at WHN. But he never again regained the prominence he once held and a year later moved to Miami and WIOD.

Of course there were some at WNBC who might have thought Big got out just in time, because even his coworkers never knew exactly what to expect from Don and many lived in fear of becoming the butt of an Imus on-air attack. In fact, you only had to work in the same building to be a target, as Meredith Hollaus found out.

Hollaus, who eventually became 66 WNBC's news director, was a news reporter when Imus joined the station and the only woman working on the floor, as news at that time was essentially a men's club. "It was totally the ol' boy club, but they needed a woman," she explains. "NBC needed a woman. All the stations did, so they got their token woman. I was the token woman. And I was very happy to be the token woman, let me tell you."

And although she never worked Imus's show, she was a frequent target of his satire, primarily because Don had such an eye for the ladies, and by all accounts, Meredith was a stunning blonde with a brain, the kind of woman, says a former news writer, "who could turn Imus's head on a dime."

Single at the time, Hollaus was horrified over one encounter with Don's brand of humor. While the standard practice among deejays was to keep hallway conversations limited to the hallway, Imus would crack open the mike and let his audience in and think nothing of making a coworker the brunt of an extremely personal joke.

"One day I was out because I had a doctor's appointment," Meredith recalls. "Somehow Imus found out I had a doctor's appointment and he went on the air the next day and asked Charles, 'Did the rabbit die?'

"Imus used that to get a laugh because I just happened to be handy. Anybody who was handy he made fun of. Anybody was fair game. He picked on me a lot."

Even so, Hollaus and Don did manage to forge an amicable relationship, and on at least one occasion she agreed to accompany him to dinner. But what she didn't know was that Don's advertising exec friend Charles Scimeca, along with another buddy, Peter Arabella, were setting Don up for the hot seat.

"Don and I were having lunch one day at a restaurant next to CBS, which is now a parking lot. But we went there one day and a friend of ours, Peter, was managing the place and Don kept talking about this woman named Meredith Hollaus, about what a looker she was and all. So he was going to bring her to dinner that night.

"Well, that night he does walk in with an exceptional-looking blonde. We order dinner and the waiter comes out with her dinner in a covered plate. When he takes off the top, all that was sitting there was a can of Alpo dog food. Peter Arabella says to Don, 'Well, you said that's what she eats.' "

Scimeca wasn't sure who was more stunned, Hollaus or Imus, as he and Peter kept after Don unmercifully. " 'Was this the woman you said was such a dog?' Finally, Imus said, 'That's it, you've had it.' He'd had enough and we knew when to stop."

Charles knew that Meredith probably wasn't sure whether Don really *had* called her a dog or not, because he had made a career out of insulting people, so he made sure she knew they had just been having fun at Don's expense and that he in fact had only ever raved about how she looked.

Interestingly, at least in his earlier years in New York, Hollaus says that away from the microphone "Imus was very quiet." Nor did he socialize much with others at WNBC with one significant exception—news writer Charles McCord. Many, including Imus himself, credit McCord with being an integral part of Don's success from New York to the present.

McCord, who hailed from Springfield, Missouri, was the straightest of arrows and at first glance the most unlikely of candidates to befriend Imus. But what most of his office mates didn't realize was that one of the things Imus respected most was intelligence, and he found that in McCord. Along with a twisted sense of humor that lies hidden under a carefully modulated demeanor.

"I've only ever been able to make him laugh once," Imus has joked about the man he's called a friend for over twenty-five years.

McCord recalls his first recollection of the outlaw deejay. "I saw this man with a pageboy, carefully coiffed, smooth hair. I thought, *Oh my God what have we got here?* Soon, I was to find out."

Charles wryly says that Don wasn't always the most thoughtful of coworkers. "None of the rest of us was making much money then. And he had this lovely little habit of walking through the lobby, pulling out a huge wad of bills, breaking the paper bands, tearing them off, and tossing them casually to the floor." Of course, even though Imus used to brag he was making $100,000 a year, his coworkers might have felt marginally better knowing his yearly salary was really "only" $80,000.

But what initially drew the two together can be described only as a meeting of the minds. "Early on McCord and Imus became very friendly and they worked well together," describes Hollaus. "There was a certain repartee between them. They could bounce off each other. Not only was McCord one of the finest news writers in terms of being able to tell a story, Charles was a very gifted, creative comedy writer. He wrote with Imus and also wrote a lot of Imus's material himself. Just like *The Tonight Show*, they were putting on a show every day. You couldn't do that with just one person. It was very easy for

McCord to write for Imus, because they were both gifted and worked so well together and had that same sense of humor, the type of humor that meshed.

"So after McCord finished his news shift in the morning, they would work together. Charles and Imus would write the comedy bits, then they would go into the studio and it would be recorded for the next day's show."

Some of Imus's most famous gags were developed by Mc-Cord, such as Moby Worm, the Great Destroyer. "We would have investment bankers calling up and asking Moby Worm to eat their office tower," McCord laughs.

Even though his characters were popular and had become a trademark of his show, it was still the social and political commentary where Imus used his satire to best effect. Which is why he presented the news differently from most deejays, who would normally just turn the news portion of the program over to someone else. But Don had the news interwoven into his show so he could comment on the day's events as it was being read. Although it's not unusual today for music radio shows to deemphasize news, it was still a relatively new approach in the early 1970s and one that disturbed many news people.

"Don's program wasn't designed for people looking for news," Bill Scott notes. "They were looking to be current but with his slant on what was going on. As a result, the news on the Imus show was of secondary or tertiary interest to the Imus listeners. It was the news he told them, in his satire as well as his perceptions, that they were interested in."

It didn't take long for Don's on-air performance to open up other opportunities. He collaborated with investors and opened a restaurant carrying his name, Imus's. In 1973 he recorded the album, *Imus in the Morning: One Sacred Chicken to Go*. He also received offers to do stand-up and appeared a few times at the Bitter End on his own, receiving positive reviews, such as Ian Dove's in *The New York Times*.

Sacrilegious and scurrilous, Mr. Imus peoples his make-believe revival tent and environs with misfits and ogres who sound as if they come out only at night. It is funny and perceptive and also has the genuine cutting slash of satire.

Imus also appeared at the Bottom Line with comic-author/ all-around-raconteur Kinky Friedman and his band, the Texas Jewboys. Kinky, whose real name is Richard, is a Jewish Texas good ol' boy with a ten-gallon wit that appealed to Imus and a home-on-the-range sensibility that made him feel at home. Friedman loved his cowboy hat and cigar as much as he did being clever. A few years down the road, a critic would refer to him as a "Jewish Will Rogers," which would prompt Friedman to respond, "Nah. I think of myself more like an ill Mark Twain."

However he saw himself, Kinky's material was the antithesis of politically correct and was received with far less critical acclaim. "He played my routines on the air," recalls Friedman, who still makes appearances on Imus's show today. "A number of deejays had gotten fired for doing that."

And for what many people would have probably agreed were for understandable reasons. Consider the lyrics of his song "They Ain't Making Jews Like Jesus Anymore":

Niggers, Jews, and Sigma Nus, all they ever do is breed
Wops and micks and slopes and spooks
are all on the list
And there's a little hebe from the heart of Texas
Is there anyone I missed?
Oh, they ain't making Jews like Jesus anymore.

"I was politically incorrect long before it was fashionable," he explains. But the Kinkster, as he refers to himself, was also the sort of guy you'd want around in an emergency. One time

Friedman witnessed a robbery at an enclosed automatic teller machine in New York's Greenwich Village. Rather than stand and watch along with the large crowd who had gathered, Kinky intervened and apprehended the would-be thief and held him for the police. One subsequent headline read: "Country Singer Plucks Victim from Mugger."

Even though Imus never lacked for company, he didn't have a lot of real friends in New York, much less close friends. So most of the time when he was out, he donned his public persona of big bad important radio guy, resenting everyone who was impressed with that. After one public appearance where several hundred fans had stood waiting to see him, Don snidely commented, "I don't understand that. I wouldn't walk across the street to see nobody."

Except, perhaps, for his friend Terry Nelson. Through another quirk of fate, Nelson had been hired to host the morning show at 99X-FM in New York, which was the sister station of WOR-AM. 99X—or WXLO-WOR FM—according to Nelson, was "the first lettered Top 40 rock and roll FM radio station east of the Mississippi."

It probably would have surprised many people who worked with Don at NBC to learn that on Nelson's first day on the air, he says "Imus had his engineer record my entire show for me, unbeknownst to me, for a souvenir. He called me up at the end of my show and said, 'Hey, man, I've had my engineer record your whole show because I thought you might want to keep it.'"

For Terry, New York was a bit overwhelming—"I mean, Sacramento is the biggest market I've worked"—and he was grateful to have a friend who could show him around. Although, he admits, he had no idea what a tour of the city with Imus really meant.

"When I first got there, Imus took us around and showed us the city. Literally wined us and dined us, my lady and me. I remember the very first time he took us he said, 'Hey, let's all go into town and have dinner.' So we came on in and we walk into this club and all of a sudden thousands of flashbulbs start going off. All the paparazzi were there taking pictures and going crazy and I'm going, 'Wow,' and looking behind me and all around going, 'Who's here?' I look at Imus and go, 'Who the fuck is here?' And he gave me that shit-eatin' grin and all of a sudden these people start converging on us, because it was *Imus* who had just walked into this club.

"I looked at him and I was totally shocked. To me, this was still old Don. I helped you push your old sixty-four to get it started. But he was a big star now. I was totally shocked. And every club we went into was like that. Not only flashbulbs going off but owners coming up. It just totally blew me away."

But if Nelson was taken aback by Don's social status, he was about to experience Don's power on the airwaves. It was still Terry's first week on the air, and he was admittedly still nervous and frightened over being the new morning guy in town, when that town happened to be New York City.

"We had a big experimental phone bank in the studio that had like one hundred different request lines. At that time we had board op engineers in the next studio who ran all your stuff for you. You just cued them when to do what.

"So I'm sitting there on the air and all of a sudden every one of my phone lines lit up. And I thought, *What the hell did I do wrong now? Did I leave my mike on and say something?* So I punch up one of the lines.

"Hi, is this Terry Nelson?
Yeah.
Where you from, where's your hometown?
Modesto.
Okay. Bye.

"I punch up the next line.

"Hi, is this Terry Nelson.
Where you from?
Modesto.
Okay, bye.

"I'm buzzing through these lines and they're all asking me the same thing. So I'm sitting there thinking, *Well, that's really weird.* Anyway, about another fifteen minutes later, all of a sudden the lines all light up again. And this time everyone asks

"What's your middle name?
Don.
Oh, okay, Bye.

"And I went through the whole number again. Then about fifteen, twenty minutes later, all the lines lit up again. They're going 'Where do you live, man?' All of a sudden I look up at my board op across from me and he's just rolling, just laughing his ass off. And he's a big Imus fan and he's monitoring Imus while he's doing my show."

And what the board op heard was Don making Nelson the topic of the day on WNBC. "He's on the radio, he is doing a whole show on me and introducing me to his whole market. That was just unheard of and just blew my mind.

"This was all in my first week. What an introduction."

However, it wouldn't be the last time Don would make Terry a part of *Imus in the Morning.* "Maybe a month later, I'm sitting on the air and Imus calls up on the hotline. I'd given him my hotline and I had his in case we needed to talk to each other in a hurry. He calls up and I'm busy, I'm giving my board op instructions and trying to get my bits out on the air and he goes,

'Nelson, do you want to win $10,000?' 'Sure man,' but I'm really not paying attention.

"He's going, 'All right, here's what you got to do. I want you to repeat after me, I listen to Imus first thing in the morning on 66 WNBC. Got it?'

"They're doing this contest called *The Phrase That Pays*. So, he says, go. 'Hi, I listen to Don Imus. I think he's the greatest, and I listen to him on NBC.'

"He stops. 'Nelson, that's not what I told you to say. Write it down. "I listen to Imus first thing in the morning on 66 WNBC." You want the $10,000?'

"Okay, man. 'I like Don Imus and I listen to him first thing on 66 WNBC.'

"There's another pause. 'Nelson, do you want the $10,000?'

"I'm thinking, *Please man* but say, *Sure*.

" 'Then repeat after me'—and he gives me the same spiel again. 'You got it? Yeah, man.'

" 'Hi, this is Imus.' And I get it wrong again and after a long pause he goes, 'Nelson, you stupid mother, you just blew ten thousand dollars.' Click.

"About this time, I look up again and there's my board operator just falling all over the place. Because he'd had our whole conversation on the air, running it on NBC. To me, that was the damnedest thing."

While Nelson's bosses could only be thrilled with the exposure for their fledgling FM station, NBC management were less amused. "That wasn't done, especially in major markets. He's with NBC and I'm with RKO, which at the time was the largest radio company in the world. You might call a jock across the country and talk to him about something, but not right there in your own front yard. If I'd of done that, RKO would have blown me right out the door. And if it had been anybody else but Imus . . . I know they gave him a lot of grief, but he just told them to go fuck themselves. That was literally his response for everything.''

As abrasive and dismissive as he was to his superiors at WNBC, and authority in general, for that matter, Don was the most generous of friends, both on a personal level and professionally. Nelson says sometimes Don's attentiveness bordered on the embarrassing.

''When he got his restaurant, it was a really nice place with linens at tables and it was always packed. So Don had given standing orders anytime Maria and I walked in the door, they were to bring a table out for us and set it up right up front. At times, we thought, *Oh, we'll just slip in* because we didn't want to take advantage of that, but he had people who recognized us and every single time, it was, 'Mr. Nelson, right this way' and a table was brought out for us. He's just that kind of a friend.''

Terry also credits Don with helping him become one of New York's higher profile deejays during his tenure there because of Imus's making a point to introduce Nelson to the town's movers and shakers.

''He introduced me to everybody in the world that you could imagine, media people, businesspeople. He told them I was a very important person and they should take the time to know me and I was just a green kid from Sacramento. 'Yeah, this is my good friend Terry Nelson and he's doing mornings at 99X opposite me.'

''All the introductions and attention he brought to me, on top of everything I did with RKO, helped a great deal. So it got to the point if there were things going on in New York and they needed people to come and sit and sign autographs, or they wanted personalities at a car show in Atlantic City, they'd pick the top three disc jockeys and it would usually be me, Imus, and maybe Dan Ingram from ABC, who was a living legend there, or Cousin Brucie.''

Just as in the smaller radio markets, deejays could pick up

substantial extra cash doing personal appearances. However, in New York, the money was better and the perks more lavish.

"I remember them sending limousines to pick us up and they'd pay me huge money to go and sign autographs for two hours. Then after I got finished, it would be Imus's shift and they'd pay him even *more* money—twice as much as they paid me," laughs Nelson. "He'd sit there and sign autographs and hand out junk."

Suddenly, it seemed as if Imus was everywhere and that his potential was limited only by there being too few hours in the day. He was in demand, he knew it, and he reveled in it. But in the process of working his way to the top of his profession, Imus had begun to lose himself in the process. He was living a lie that would ultimately reveal an ugly truth—that like his father before him, Don had become an alcoholic and was rapidly losing control of his life.

Chapter Ten

IN 1972 DON TOLD A REPORTER, "I'VE GOT IT ALL TOGETHER NOW. Hell, I'm a star now. I'm recognized everywhere I go now. I know what I am. I didn't get to be numero uno by being a dummy. I don't drink or smoke dope or screw around. I don't want nothing messing up my head. I'm too close to the line anyway."

The comments weren't merely self-serving, they were also not true. While Don had previously indeed reserved his wild ways for his radio show, after arriving in New York he had turned into a loose cannon both on and off the air. There's an old adage that says that while some people can swim in alcohol, others merely drown in it. The sobering fact was, by the mid-1970s, Don Imus was a man in desperate need of a life jacket.

When looking back at the beginnings of his addiction, Imus says initially, alcohol was simply a shot of courage. "I think I drank initially because it made me more comfortable to be around people. I was very uncomfortable around people, very insecure. If I had a couple of drinks, it made me feel better.

"I had been in radio only a couple of years when I came to New York and I'd gone for a long period of time and didn't drink because my father drank a lot, I mean, although he wasn't a falling-down drunk, I thought, *Why go down that road?*"

But once in New York, Don says, "I immediately started drinking 'cause you'd have to go out and hang out with Murray the K and Cousin Brucie. And I was required to meet clients, have lunch. I always felt more comfortable if I had a drink, because basically, I'm a shy person.

"It took me a number of years to notice that every time I drank, I got drunk. I mean, I never just had a couple of drinks, ever, ever. What I discovered, unfortunately, was that once I had a drink, I couldn't stop drinking until I got drunk."

However, that bit of self-knowledge would be a while in coming. Although he had shied away from drinking for the first thirty years of his life, from high school to the marines and well into adulthood, once Don began drinking, he dove in enthusiastically. Unlike some who take years to start suffering from the effects of drink, Imus's fall was almost immediate. In 1973 alone, Don missed one hundred days of work. The guys in the WNBC newsroom dealt with Imus's absenteeism with typical black, gallows journalistic humor—there was an ongoing betting pool going, where for a dollar you could bet on when Imus wouldn't show up for work.

For years Imus downplayed his truancy, offering flimsy excuses that were as illogical as they were unbelievable. "I tried to do a good job for two or three years," he said in an interview from the early 1970s. "I didn't do fine after a while because I wouldn't work. I was busy. I had a lot of stuff to do, you know. Got into photography, had this big, fancy apartment over on Beekman Place, put in some pinball machines, jukebox, and stuff. And you know, you'd be in the darkroom working until three or four in the morning. Come five, you're too tired to go to work. Just doing this morning show began to cause problems with my other activities.

"I've been working like hell for five years, with no vacations."

It was an interesting whine, because Imus was in fact spreading himself thinner every day. In addition to the stand-up appearances, he was also developing a pilot for ABC and was writing another comedy album. Such a load would have been manageable for the pre–New York Imus, who had always impressed people with his work ethic. But the drinking and drug use was taking too much physical and mental energy.

In an attempt to improve his attendance, Imus bought himself a black Mark IV, about which he noted, "I used to dream about having a car like this." And to eliminate the need for a daily commute from Connecticut, where he and Harriet had a house, Don rented an apartment in Manhattan on Astor Place. The station also paid for a personal car service to chauffeur their AWOL deejay. Nothing worked.

"They still had trouble getting him to come in in the morning," says Martha Sherrill. "They sent producers to his house, they sobered him up, they sent cars. The whole car service for Don was all about his not coming in, his drinking, his not being able to drive."

Even when Don did show up, he was often ragged, his puffy and worn face a self-portrait of hard living and excess.

"You could see it in his face," Meredith Hollaus remembers. "But his drinking and drug use never came across on the air. He always managed to pull it together. It was incredible. I don't think there was anyone else who could have done it. But you could definitely see it in his face. Staff members would find empty vodka bottles in his office."

"He was in terrible shape," agrees Charlie McCord. "He was drinking all the time. I'd take my grease pencil and mark the bottles to judge how much, the way family members do. I was very concerned."

Program manager Pat Whitley, who Imus called *Mr. Numb* on the air, also expressed concern at the time about Don's lifestyle. "That he likes to ridicule authority doesn't bother me. What really worries me now is the pacing of his life. He's got to take care of himself so he can be up for his show. It's getting pretty rough."

"This is the most crucial time of his career." Perry Bascom

told *Life* magazine. "He could destroy everything right here, right now. Too much has happened to him too fast. The reason he gets away with so much on the air is that he has always been so straight off the air. But if he gets into any kind of personal jam and blows his show here, regardless of what else he thinks he has going, nobody will want to touch him.

"We were aware of his absences and tardiness in Cleveland and we know it's a real hang-up for him. But Cleveland isn't New York. I've got guts too. We've been nice but we will crack down, hurt him in his pocketbook if we have to."

The hard line drawn by management simply exacerbated Don's already well-established disdain for corporate authority. From the very beginning of his tenure at WNBC, Imus had frequently turned his satiric eye at executives of all types, as reflected by an early routine about a busing program between NBC vice presidents and car-wash employees.

> The busing plan was initiated to provide the black employees of the Clean As a Mother car wash an opportunity for greater job satisfaction, while at the same time giving the NBC executives a chance to familiarize themselves with one of the realities of everyday living.
>
> It was announced the plan was working well and that the NBC vice presidents, while having some difficulty learning to operate chamois, soap machines, and buffers, were nevertheless expected to adjust well. The one-time car washers reported they had little difficulty in adjusting to a three-hour lunch.

But whether it was a sign of the times or a damning indictment on the priorities of corporate America, nobody in a position of authority officially intervened even though it was obvious to those he worked with that Don was floundering into self-destruction. As long as he held it together on the air, his personal problems were, in the end, left for Don to deal with alone. Even though his drinking and the resulting behavior was having a definite fallout effect on his coworkers.

"When he drank, there was more of a nastiness, a harder edge to him on and off the air," says Hollaus, recalling how careful all the staffers would be around Imus, fearful of saying anything to set him off. "He could bluster. He could be very nice. He could be funny. You never knew what mood he would be in. He was mercurial. You just never knew in those days. So people were very careful about what they said about Imus because he had a lot of power because of that microphone, and he used it.

"Imus had a wild temper. He definitely had an underlying mean streak, and because he was mercurial you never knew when it was going to surface. And it would be as cutting as it could be. It would be like a machete going through a field. And there was no way to top him. And furthermore, even if you could, or thought you could, he could always get back at you the next day on the air.

"Now, mind you, that mean streak was not always evident. It wasn't surfacing every day or every moment. I would say it was only when he was on the drugs or the booze. The drugs and alcohol did not make him a pussycat."

Occasionally, some of Don's associates did try to corral him in, notably Michael Lynn. "My lawyer said for me to stop acting like a child," Don once admitted.

But even when he wasn't drunk or hung over, Imus was developing a sharpness that was more cutting than satiric. Hollaus remembers the time he made her the butt of an on-air prank that went too far. At the time, Meredith had been promoted to news director.

"Imus had me having an affair with another manager at the station, who was married. I had had lunch with this manager a couple of times and this was Imus's bit for the week. I was single at the time, so they had me paired up with everybody. On Friday he announced he *was going to reveal who that married manager was.* It was a total joke on his part. He would make these things up. Not just about me, but everybody.

"The general manager was hysterical, and I was none too pleased either. But behind the scenes, NBC management was crazed because they thought they were going to have a lawsuit on their hands because I was having an affair and this whole thing was going to blow up on the air on Friday. And I had to convince them that I was not having an affair, so I led everybody to believe that I was going to get married and that I had a boyfriend and that I would sue if Imus gave another manager's name because that was libelous.

"He never did give the other person's name because NBC talked to Imus and talked him out of it, but that was at the point of, I would say, going over the line, if he had given a name.

"But there was always a lot going on behind the scenes because of what he was saying on the air, or threatened to say. One was never sure whether he was going to follow through on his threats. But he made so much money for the station, he put them on the map, and WNBC, like any other station, would bend over backward for him."

Although management kept their blinders firmly in place, Imus was a frequent topic of conversation among the rank and file. "There was hallway talk that he was a heavy partier," recalls Bill Scott. "There was a certain sense that as a result, he could be unreliable because of the partying; whether he was drinking or whatever, there was a question of his being ready to perform on some occasions."

Even though his personal problems weren't playing out on his show, occasionally he let slip small signs that perhaps he wasn't as together as he presented himself. Terry Nelson recalls the morning Don broke a cardinal rule of broadcasting.

Although Nelson worked the same shift as Don and couldn't

really listen to his show, he was able to tune in for a few minutes every morning. "Because I'm from California, I had to have my own car and drive to work. I would park next to the Times Building, which was a half a block from Times Square. And we had off-side-of-the-street parking, which is where you could only park for an hour before you had to move your vehicle to the other side of the street."

During a long song set that was followed by a news break, Terry would run down to his car and move it, and while in the car he'd check out Imus and the other morning jocks.

"This was maybe the first week I'd been there and I'm driving around the corner and I punch up Imus and he's doing his Imus fairy tale corner. He's got this lilting music in the background, innocent-sounding *tinkle tinkle tinkle* and he's doing his rhyme. The tag line should have been, *And somebody stole my hubcaps in the Bronx.* But what he said was *And somebody stole my fucking hubcaps in the Bronx.*

"I had never heard anyone use a four-letter word like that on the air. It just didn't happen. I went 'Holy shit!' and I smoked it over there and parked my car and ran back and called him up.

"Don, do you know what you just said on the radio?"

"What do you mean?"

"You were doing your fairy tale thing and you said *fuck.*"

"Well, yeah, I might have. Well, yeah, I did. So what?"

While colorful language is more common on the air today, that particular expletive is still *verboten,* one of the unspeakable seven words made famous by George Carlin. Although most people who heard Imus that morning no doubt thought he was simply being more outrageous than usual, it was actually a telltale clue that the alcohol was affecting his judgment.

Although Imus avoids much of any introspection regarding his surrender to alcohol, claiming it was merely a way to feel more social that got out of hand, others believe his fall from

grace was more emotionally complicated and tragically familiar. As Don's attorney, Michael Lynn, notes, "It's not something
unprecedented in our industry where someone becomes so concentrated with being the focus of media attention and the darling of the press and of audiences; it's very hard to be prepared
for how to deal with that."

Don once addressed the question of whether he was beginning to believe his own press clippings. "I guess I really am on
a star trip. That's really a solitary trip. It's a whole big ego thing,
all I think about. People always saying things about how it
changes you and all. I don't see how I've changed much, but
maybe I have."

Others saw it clearly. "Absolutely," Charles Scimeca says.
"Every time we went out, he had to put on. He'd be such a
different person. He felt as if he had to be *onstage*. When we
were out by ourselves, he never acted that way. But as soon as
someone came over to the table, he'd turn into the other Don. It
was obvious he was uptight."

Even his mother noticed a change. "Don used to call two or
three times a week," she said in an interview a few years into
Don's time at WNBC. "Now I'm lucky if it's once in two weeks.
He is so aloof and preoccupied these days, it's not like him."

Terry Nelson agrees that Don was simply overwhelmed by
the success and all the trappings that came with it. "He came
from a very poor family. When he got into the biz, man, he just
played it by ear and had fun with it. When Don got very successful, he was a crazy man for a while and it's kind of a natural
transition where people will do that. All of a sudden you find
yourself in the middle of high rollers, parties, and everybody
wants to be your friend, 'Hey, what d'you want? You got it.'
and 'Here, I just brought this for you' and you get caught up in
good old rock and roll."

While the hedonistic temptations offered by alcohol and,
later, cocaine, undoubtedly played a significant role in the

transformation of Imus from single-minded workaholic to hung-over party animal, his binges weren't simply about temporal pleasures. Addictions seldom are. Some suspected the demons sitting on Don's shoulder were born out of more complicated issues.

"He has a great deal of anger in him. I don't think he would deny that," Charles McCord noted, an observation that could have been said of Don from the time his family began falling apart as a child. Anger against a loved father who fell by the wayside, anger against a fragile mother who perhaps wasn't as strong as her children needed her to be, anger against the faceless government bureaucracies that taxed and foreclosed his family into poverty, anger against all those who felt Imus was somehow less valuable as a person because of his refusal to conform. Ironically, the same anger that had propelled him to succeed was now threatening to destroy all he had achieved.

Another view is offered by journalist Martha Sherrill, who believes Don was always looking for respect, not just from others, but from himself as well. "Part of that was, I think, his frustration at being a deejay. He had always had these dreams of being a performer and being somebody different. I don't think spinning pop records and golden oldies was his idea of a dignified or meaningful career. And I think he sort of hated himself."

Compounding Imus's problems at work was his deteriorating home life. It was ironic that for the first time, Don had finally been able to afford a nice house for his wife and family, a spacious home in the upscale community of Greenwich, Connecticut, only to have the marriage start falling apart.

"She could not deal with his persona," observes Charles Scimeca. "She knew him as the quiet, sensitive person he was underneath it all. But his act became so much a part of his personality that it really tore her up. She was not happy." Charles also admits that Harriet viewed him and Don's other drinking buddies as bad influences on her husband, so he wasn't exactly welcome. "No, I never went over to the house for dinner. We would just meet and go out in town. He kept a place in the city so he could stay in town."

And the reality was, Don was going out nearly all the time. "He was a nonparticipatory resident of the household," says McCord.

"They loved each other," maintains Brian Bierne. "But there was always the constant friction at that point. And again, you know, Don was gone a lot as his success began to accelerate."

At one point, their relationship became so fractious that Harriet moved into a nearby house with the children. The move was largely symbolic, because Don was seldom home anyway. While he had never been a particularly involved, hands-on father, now he was almost invisible, physically and emotionally, to his children.

"He never spoke much about the kids," Scimeca says. "If I asked him something about them, he would answer but never really volunteered the information. He was out of touch as a parent. Like so many parents who are successful, they think what they're giving the kid is fine and it's really not. He'd say, 'What does she have to be upset about?' "

Unfortunately for his daughters, Imus would never be as involved with their lives as they might have needed and wanted him to be, a fact he acknowledges today. "You know, I wasn't there much. There were years I was drunk all the time, and they knew I was on drugs for years, but I never abused them."

Which was no small blessing, all things considered. Especially when considering Don would become aggressive and mean when drinking. "Don was a nasty drunk," admits Scimeca. "We'd go out and he'd have six or eight drinks over lunch and he'd get into confrontations, all you needed to do was look at him. One day, some guy came out of the elevator and asked Don a question and Don punched him in the mouth. That was not fun to be around after a while."

It was also becoming increasingly difficult to work with. And it eventually reached a critical point where management was losing patience. And in a bit of poetic, Shakespearean irony that even Don had to appreciate, his demise at WNBC came at the hands of the very man who had helped Imus become the top rated deejay in the first place.

After Don left WGAR in Cleveland to go to New York, Jack Thayer had gone on to become president of Nationwide Communications, a company in Columbus, Ohio, that operated several radio and TV stations. For some reason, it was assumed by many that Thayer had brought Imus to New York, but as Don pointed out, "They all get confused. I was here three years before he came."

Actually, Don was there a year before Thayer was made president of NBC radio in 1972, a position he would hold until 1978. And during that period he was still introducing innovations, such as a twenty-four-hour news network called News and Information Service.

The framework for Imus being let go was set in place when Charlie Warner became general manager and brought in Bob Pittman, another creative executive who would later go on to start MTV. Just as Perry Bascom had been charged with changing WNBC from the player of elevator music. The new regime was also looking to go in a new direction.

"They were pretty certain when they came in what they were going to do," says Meredith Hollaus. "They were going to change WNBC. They were going to do a different type of radio, and they were not looking for stars." In fact, over the next several years, Meredith notes, Warner and Pittman would have "a revolving door of disc jockeys."

Although the change in radio philosophy gave the new management team a ready-to-wear official party line excuse to give when explaining their decision to release Imus—*there was going to be a change in format because the current format wasn't making any money,* wrote *Newsday*—the reality was that Don was being fired because he was out of control.

"Something had to be done," Pittman states. "Don was spiraling down. He was probably the most talented man ever on the radio that certainly I've ever worked with and he didn't give a damn about his radio show."

According to Hollaus, though, "it was never any one person who was making the decision." It was just obvious to all concerned that Don was too much trouble. "Pittman was the one who had to do the firing."

In 1977, after seven years at WNBC, the Imus era came to an ignoble end. (What is less frequently remembered is that it was also the end of Bruce Morrow's time at that station, as Cousin Brucie was also let go during the management changeover.) But rather than being stunned into self-reflection, the chip on Don's shoulder simply grew.

"I didn't care I got fired. I remember Warner said, 'What do you want us to tell people?' And I said, 'What do you mean?'

" 'Well, I mean, do you want us to say we couldn't reach a contract?'

" 'No, no, no. You tell them you fired me.'

"The perception was I was difficult to work with. So after they fired me, they asked me to stay on the air for another month, which I did. I was supposed to leave the air September 3, 1977, but they took me off two or three days ahead of time— really a sleazy deal—thinking I was going to say something. I hadn't said anything for a month and a half other than I had played a jingle, *You're fired!* But I didn't complain about it or put the station down or anything. So they used me for over a month."

Don was most disturbed by what he considered Jack Thayer's

cowardice and lack of respect, and he found himself deeply disappointed in his former mentor, even years later.

"When they fired me, his actions didn't speak very well for him at that time. He should have fired me himself or he should have been in the room when Charlie Warner fired me. He shouldn't have had some lightweight like Warner, who I did not know, fire me. Not that I shouldn't have been fired. He shouldn't have saved my job, he just should have been in the room."

While he later came to understand that he deserved to be fired, his initial reaction was completely in keeping with an alcoholic's denial. "When I got fired, I thought what a terrible mistake they're making. I figured I could get another job tomorrow. I couldn't. I found that out later, but that day I didn't know that."

Perhaps the most surprising reaction to Don getting released came from the coworkers he had so often mercilessly made miserable.

"The people at the station were terribly upset," admits Hollaus. "We weren't told ahead of time that Imus was being let go. There was no warning. The announcement was *Imus was let go.* That's how we found out.

"People admired Imus's talent. I would say the majority were willing to put up with anything to do with Imus because people admired him, even though he could be an SOB and had a mean streak. Instead, people at WNBC resented Bob Pittman and Charlie Warner for firing Imus."

Hollaus spoke for most of her coworkers when she says, "I didn't always like Imus. I didn't always appreciate what he was saying about me. I still get calls from people who tell me he's still talking about me from time to time. I wasn't the only one, you can be sure of that. As I told you, everybody is fair game. But I have a lot of respect for Don Imus."

Most people at WNBC believed that the firing signaled Don's

last hurrah. Like Moses, he had been to the mountaintop and seen the glory that might have been his save for his own fundamental weaknesses. Worse yet, he was stubbornly unrepentant, maintaining a steadfast denial about his drinking.

"I always thought I just drank too much," Imus says now. "I know it sounds idiotic, but I didn't think I was a drunk or an alcoholic." That's because in Don's defensive mind, alcoholics were people living on the streets of Skid Row in Los Angeles, dying among strangers on the floor of a flophouse. But at that point in his life, it was futile to try to make Don see an accurate reflection in the mirror. As he always had, the more he felt the outcast, the more he dug in his heels, assuming a me-against-the-world posture.

When looking back now on his first experience in New York, Imus is just as brutally honest when assessing himself as he is dissecting others. "I went through a period in the seventies where I was enormously successful in New York. I had been in radio only a couple of years and I was in *Life* magazine and I was a big deal. Then I got fired for being a complete jerk, a drunk."

And while Imus would prove to be professionally resilient thanks to his vibrant talent, his personal demons would continue to put his inner redemption and salvation in serious jeopardy and doubt.

Chapter Eleven

_____ ▬▬▬ _____

GETTING FIRED IS A SURREAL EXPERIENCE, NOT TO MENTION ONE IN personal rejection. Some people react with tears, others with overt anger. Don's initial reaction to being let go was typical and instinctual; just as he had when the other kids had labeled him unworthy as a teenager, Imus immediately erected a chip on his shoulder to ward off the hurt of not being accepted. Adopting a "me-against-the-world" attitude also helped obscure the need for self-reflection. He initially saw his firing as a situation where he was a victim at the hands of others, as opposed to the result of his own actions.

Because he had been such a high-profile personality, and in New York no less, Imus assumed that his unemployment would be an annoying but brief time-out from the limelight. And there was some interest in him, and Imus was offered a couple of radio gigs but "for no money," he says. Plus, the proposed jobs were nowhere near the A-list quality positions he had expected.

Finding radio a suddenly closed door, Don agreed to do a syndicated talk show for Metromedia called *Imus Plus*. Mercifully, it was canceled quickly. "Did you see my show? It was the worst TV show ever done," he says now bluntly. "You know, it's like Cheryl Ladd shouldn't make record albums and I shouldn't be on television."

As his bank account began to dwindle and the spotlight of public attention began to turn its glare elsewhere, Imus thought back to what his lawyer, Michael Lynn, had told him after NBC had let Don go. "He was one of the few people who was straight with me. When I got fired, he said, 'I don't really think you have the guts to straighten yourself out. I think you're fucked up.' Everybody else told me I'd be okay." But as the realization that nobody was interested in working with him crystallized, and it became apparent to Don that he might not be able to find any work in New York, he said, "It began to be clear to me that I got fired because it was my fault as opposed to their fault."

He had come full circle. Through the example set by Krassner in *The Realist,* Imus had, in the early 1970s, "used it [outrageous behavior] as a barometer of how far you could go." He saw now he had gone too far. After nearly a year of being without work, Imus was finally offered a job—back in Cleveland at WHK-AM, which was country at that time. It was the ultimate karma.

"The idea of going back to Cleveland was humiliating," Imus admits. "But I had to do it. I needed to make some money and get my act together."

He was also ready for some penance. "I mean, from a personal standpoint, to pay whatever price it took to get back here. You know, you can never determine what the price is going to be on these things. You have to decide if you're willing to do it or not, and even if you are, it doesn't always mean you're going to be successful."

But typically, even though he'd been humbled, Imus didn't want to give the impression that he'd been made vulnerable, so he downplayed the financial hit he had taken and would later say that his job at WHK had paid him "big money, you know, almost as much as I made [in New York]." However, that has to be seen as merely a face-saving claim. In reality, Imus's salary in Cleveland afforded only a modest lifestyle and was a pointed visual reminder on the turn his life had taken. Don's comedown wasn't painful only for him, but uncomfortable for his friends.

Larry "Ratso" Sloman, who had made appearances on Imus's WNBC show as an ad hoc sports correspondent, recounts going to see Don in Cleveland while Sloman was on a book tour. "I remember driving through the snow to the most mundane subdivision imaginable. I see him standing in the door. He goes, 'It's a long way from Sutton Place, huh, Rats?' "

Even if his lifestyle had been brought down a notch or two on the glamour scale, Chuck Collier notes that Imus's personal feelings of humiliation aside, working at WHK wasn't the equivalent to banishment to Siberia. "It was not an obscure station when Imus came back. Five thousand watts at 1420 on the dial, it was very high-profile and very much personality oriented and very highly rated. It was number one in a lot of areas. Don fit right in.

"Yes, Cleveland is a smaller market than New York City, but it was not going back to Cleveland in exile."

Although he was back in radio, there was no *Imus in the Morning* show this time around. Gone also was much of his former rantings, railings, and innuendo-laced chatter. Instead, Don worked the afternoon shift and worked on cleaning up his act and changing the focal point. He also had to rely on himself, not having his writing partner and comedic soul mate, Charlie McCord, there to inspire him.

"The main thing is I started to sound good on the air," he says. "I wasn't being dirty and I wasn't being negative and I wasn't making the listeners' problems mine or my problems the listeners'."

Surprisingly, though, Imus says the subtle change in tone was easy. "I never liked being dirty," he would claim in 1981. "I never liked doing that. I was never comfortable doing that anyway. It was just an easy way to be funny and sleazy. The idea in those days was to talk dirty and play the hits. And that was really what it was. We were playing fourteen records an hour, and if you could think of something filthy to say over the intro for seven or eight seconds, good."

Imus admits that the inspiration for his early-career innuendo had come from "the guys who preceded me, like Wolfman Jack. When he was on XERF out of Del Rio, Texas, the station had a Mexican transmitter, so it wasn't licensed by this government and he was the guy who I first heard talk filthy to women on the telephone.

"He was subtle—*Are your peaches fuzzy, baby?* Or he'd have them sit on the radio and he'd kiss the microphone, stuff like that. It impressed me, sitting on a ranch listening with a little battery-operated radio. So later, I thought, *Gee, that seems like a good idea, we'll just tailor it down.*"

But as he tried to take stock of his life and career, Imus came to the conclusion that he'd "rather not do stuff on the radio now that people have to be embarrassed about. So I feel much better about what I do."

If Imus had become a victim of his own self-creation, then toning down his act was a step toward, if not expiation, then at least improved self-esteem.

"I think that might have contributed to the way I felt too; that I knew I was doing stuff on the radio that was just cheap. It was just a cheap way to be funny, to say something to shock people and then be successful as a result of it. You know you shouldn't be; you know it's not right."

There was another more practical reason that Imus felt he could afford to turn down his act a few degrees. By the time he got back to Cleveland in 1978, nearly every market in the country had an Imus-type deejay. "The morning man at WHK was a guy named Gary Dee," recalls Collier, "who was just really more outspoken and wilder than Don."

Outrageousness was no longer unique. In fact, others had taken it to the level of what was being coined *shock jocks*—they would say anything they could get away with for shock value but usually neglected to give equal consideration to creativity, wit, and humor. So in that way Imus was still a unique radio talent, and if he were to stand out in the crowd, it would be by exploiting those things he did best.

All of his adjustments, both professional and in attitude, weren't so much the result of new self-awareness as they were the means through which he could achieve retribution and prove to the world he still belonged in New York. "My goal was to come back here to NBC, not to any other station," he explained. "Once I was successful in Cleveland, I stopped acting like a lunatic and I was offered a couple of other slots in New York but I didn't want to do that. I wanted to come back here."

So he waited and kept himself on the straight and narrow, returning to a lifestyle more in keeping with his early days in radio. Brian Bierne, who had worked with Don in Sacramento, remembers that Imus "was running and getting himself in shape. Eating right, sleeping more, trying to rebuild himself so there was a real different Don Imus than there had been a few years before."

Those who kept in touch with Don believed he had truly turned a corner. Although he wasn't as newsworthy his second time around in Cleveland—there were no outcries by newspaper columnists denouncing his show, nor did he provide WHK with a miraculous turnaround in ratings—within the industry word spread that Imus had pulled himself together. It was a buzz that held particular interest for his former employers at WNBC.

After Imus left, the morning slot was taken over by the duo of Brink & Belzer. (The latter of the team, Richard Belzer, would go on to a successful stand-up and acting career, most notably as a detective in NBC-TV's *Homicide*.) But without Imus, WNBC's morning ratings had plummeted and the station had suffered an overall fall in listenership. In the revolving-door world of radio management walked a new general manager,

Robert Sherman. This time it was his turn to improve the fortunes of the station, and the question lingered, if Imus worked miracles once, could he do it again?

Sherman instructed Bob Pittman to go to Cleveland to meet with Don and make an assessment as to how he was doing. And to hear firsthand how Imus was sounding on the radio.

"I got on a plane and went to Cleveland," Pittman says. "And as I sat at the airport, I turned on the radio so I could listen to Don. And you know what? Don sounded great."

That's because Don had made sure he would. Someone back in New York had tipped Imus off that Pittman was coming into town unannounced. He called the airlines, and as he suspected, Pittman would arrive while Don was on the air, so Imus "pulled out everything good I ever did that year."

When Pittman and Imus met face-to-face, Don was determined not to let old anger and resentments ruin his chances for a second shot at New York. "I still thought they were assholes, but I wasn't going to go out of my way to tell them that."

The restraint worked. A short time later, Imus says, "Sherman called me and asked if I wanted to come back here."

But this time Don would be packing alone. As if foreseeing where his second chance would eventually lead, Harriet decided she'd had enough. She and Don had become little more than roommates who tolerated each other. So she and the children would stay in Cleveland, at least for then. Plus, there was no guarantee Don was going to last in New York, and uprooting the children was difficult on them, especially now that the two youngest were teenagers.

Don agreed to terms with WNBC for $150,000, although once again his fudging over money would come into play. In interviews given after his return, he indicated he'd been offered $200,000 and even then would add, "I'm not making enough money, that's for sure. I'll tell you that. I'm going to make more. If you want me to be truthful about that, I don't care. I mean, I think they ought to pay me a lot of money because they're making a lot of money."

Years later, when he would reinvent himself as a talk show host/borderline journalist, Imus would finally stop feeling the need to pad his financial stats. But at this point in his career he seemed to regard the dollar figure a company was willing to pay as a reflection of his personal self-worth. Even though the impression he gave was that he had stopped drinking and partying, Don knew it was merely a facade. "I stopped drinking for a while and stopped doing drugs for a while. For *a while,* that's all." But he kept it in check long enough to give NBC a reason to bring him back. Although management might have taken the stance that Don was being given another chance, his former coworkers understood the real reason *Imus in the Morning* was making a return engagement.

"They *had* to rehire Imus," explains Meredith Hollaus. "And the reason they brought him back was money. It's always money." In other words, their loss of advertising revenue hurt more than the thought of taking a chance with Imus.

So on September 3, 1979, Imus returned to the air on WNBC. The station was filled with equal parts excitement and tension, especially on the part of the green, newly named nineteen-year-old producer of *Imus in the Morning*, Lyndon Abell. Lyndon had heard enough war stories from the others to have serious concerns about meeting Don. "I was prepared to bail out as soon as it looked bad."

But his fears, at least initially, were unfounded. As the mike opened, Imus read a short monologue written by Charles McCord, who was once again by Don's side. The bit began with a gospel chorus of angels. . . .

> And on the third day of the ninth month in the second year since he spoke unto them, he said, lo, he arose once more to issue forth.

Then the voice of the Reverend Billy Sol Hargis boomed over New York.

> Send me to Cleveland? You can't do that. . . . God's only chosen, re-rosen disc jockey has returned!

Ad sales went up almost overnight. Although Imus was still outrageous and still populated his show with his array of characters and skits, he did not exude the same aura of professional immortality he had his first tour of New York radio duty. He now knew what he had to lose and didn't want to suffer that humiliation again. And for a while that memory of having been to the mountaintop only to free-fall to the rocks below kept Don focused on his work instead of on his after-hours social life.

"I was successful young and I failed," he would admit bluntly. "But I think I deserve success this time, as opposed to last time. I mean, I'd only been in radio a couple of years and I don't think that I ever thought that I'd paid any dues, and I hadn't; not any radio dues or performer dues. There wasn't time. I think most people who have problems dealing with success don't think they deserve it. They think they're either lucky or . . . When people cheat to be successful or they're dishonest or deceitful or do something bad to people or they don't think they deserve it, there's a tendency, I think, to have problems dealing with success. But I didn't do anything bad to anybody this time."

More than ever, his gags incorporated the political climate of the day, such as one of his first stunts back, the Search for Idi Amin, the despotic former ruler of Uganda. Pittman points to it as vintage Imus. "Every day he's on the phone calling around the world looking for Idi Amin. Then one time he called Libya, and someone on the other end said something about, 'Mr. Imus we know who you are.' I've never seen Don go straighter and probably paler than he did at that moment."

As he had before, Charles McCord was an integral part of Imus's show, but now McCord's influence was even greater because of the increased political content of the show. "McCord began to play a bigger role after Imus returned to NBC and his participation in that program was very important in Don's comeback," asserts Bill Scott, the former general manager of WINS. "After he was let go, the Imus who we know today, and people have known for a number of years, is more the Imus who came back. The Imus before he went away was not as insightful as the Imus who came back.

"Imus evolved over a period of time—he became more attuned to the political scene and more attuned to talking to some of the big names in politics and government and this is where McCord, with his news background, played a significant role."

Don's radio audience was as loyal as ever, says Scott, because Imus needled the powers-that-be. "The public loved it. Here was their guy, Imus, sometimes twisting their ears. As in any field and certainly in broadcasting entertainment, there are stars and there are others who are really very good. Imus is a star."

For his part, Don maintained that one of the differences in his show was that he was no longer channeling through his characters. "They don't represent how I feel or what I'm thinking. In the past they always did. They spoke for me. Now they speak for themselves. They're on their own. I'm serious."

Once he had settled in, Don also tried to make amends to some of the people who might have suffered the fallout of his previous behavior, even as they remained comic targets. "When he sobered up, he was apologetic," recalls Hollaus. "Imus and I talked a couple of times alone. He took me aside. We'd go off into a studio and talk and Imus would say to me, 'Don't pay any attention to what I say about you on the air. You know it's my routine. Because, remember, I have daughters. I love my daughters and respect them. And I do think a lot of you. But what I do on the air is a different story.' I felt his apologies were absolutely genuine."

And as longtime friends of Don would attest, when sober Don was not a mean or vindictive person. "People who know him know what he's like," says Terry Nelson. "I think people who don't really know him may not have that insight. I don't think that very many people know Don is just a pussycat and a very dedicated person."

Imus himself says he has looked inside himself and believes he's "nice to people, kind, honest, decent—you know, do unto others as I would have them do unto me. I really do try to live that way. I like people. I get angry, but I try to be honest in dealing with everybody, as honest as I can possibly be."

His brother Fred describes his sibling this way: "Don's the only person I ever met that if you want an honest answer, he'll give it to you. You always know where he's coming from."

Nelson agrees. "Don is one of the most honest people I've ever met in my entire life and he's like that all the time. He believes in his convictions. Don was like that, and still is like that, with everybody. If you do ask him, he'll tell you what he thinks. You can put that in the bank. Right or wrong and he will stand by those convictions. He always said if he was going to go talk in front of whomever or to whomever, he wasn't going to change his attitude from what he did on his radio show to what he would do in that particular situation. He wasn't going to sell out to anybody for any reason. Don was always like that, which I found to be an admirable trait. And he's been like that always, regardless of whether he was talking to the boss or a client or his own family. I think that's wonderful, he's really a man of his convictions.

"He never intentionally hurts anybody. He's brutally honest."

And it was the brutality of his honesty that was still at the heart of the criticism against him. It wasn't so much his honesty, but the way he would use honesty as a weapon that offended some and brought charges of racism and misogyny.

Although he has always steadfastly denied being racist, Don did at one point admit to experiencing a change of attitude toward women. "I think I like women better. I like them a lot. It must have been something I've done subconsciously. I have lots of women friends who I don't try to insult.

"You know, it's difficult for men to have women friends. I mean, do you know many men who have women friends who don't feel intimidated that they have to go to bed with them?"

Now that he was essentially a bachelor even though he and Harriet remained married, Don started dating again but stayed clear of any serious relationships lest it interfere with his work. He lived alone, and even preferred to clean up after himself. "I don't want a housekeeper. There's a certain therapy in doing that yourself. I go to bed at ten or eleven and get anywhere from four to six hours sleep a night. I get up at four, make some coffee, stare out the window, see the tugs go by on the Hudson. If there's somebody there, I try not to wake them up, and if they aren't awake I pin a note to their blouse so they can get home," he jokes, referring to his tendency to date women quite a bit younger than himself.

In one interview Don joked that "one of my kids is coming to live with me. She's fifteen. She'll be able to relate well with some of the girls who I go out with. They're about the same age. They can all play dolls together," he said, then added more seriously, "I *am* looking for an older woman."

But he wasn't looking too hard. For the most part, his day revolved around work instead of social activities. After his broadcast was over, he and McCord would spend the afternoon on any number of projects, not always involving radio, such as when they were reworking a script for Paramount. In 1981, Simon & Schuster published the novel *God's Other Son*. Although Don was the listed author, he openly credits that McCord served as rewriter and editor. The book is the fictional biography of Don's most famous creation, the Reverend Dr. Billy Sol Hargis, the younger brother of Jesus. From his Discount House of Worship in Del Rio, Texas, Billy Sol expounds the commercial side of God's word.

> I don't care if it rains or freezes as long as I have my plastic Jesus, riding on the dashboard of my car. I can go a hundred miles an hour long as I've got the almighty power, glued up there by my pair of fuzzy dice. . . .
> Fall down on your knees and praise Jesus with me. A plastic Jesus from our automotive novelties division for you to affix to the dashboard of your own personal automobile. Turn that thing from a Chrysler into a Christ-ler.

The paperback also included a full color poster of Don Imus. Like his radio show, the book brought forth conflicted critics, who laughed even though they thought they shouldn't. As *People* magazine noted: "The author of this novel is an early-morning deejay on New York's WNBC who operates in high hysteria, right on the edge of FCC-outlawed obscenity. . . . *God's Other Son* is rude, crude, gross, scatological, sacrilegious and racist. But it's packed with laughs for readers who can stifle their outrage at the sheer tastelessness of it."

Imus's own assessment is less reflective but more to the point. "The book's not William Faulkner, but it's not shit either."

So by 1981 Imus seemed to have made a complete comeback. Even though *God's Other Son* didn't make anyone's best seller list the first time it was published (the book would be reissued in 1994 to significantly greater success), he and McCord were considering doing another book, but, as Imus said, "We haven't made a deal on it yet, because we want a little more up-front money."

Don Imus won first in his high school talent assembly, singing to the accompaniment of combo members Bob Baller, left, and George Davis, right. Not shown are Gene Neil, saxophone, and Richard Franks, piano.

Bob Will, old man; Joann Gruedel, young girl; Don Imus, soldier; Jim Custer, priest; Linda McMillan, angel; Rene Beshear, king; Lynette Despain, rich woman; Anthony Kraps, rich man; acolyte; and Stella Wallace, Holgar: cast of high school Christmas play, *Why the Chimes Rang.*

Members of the cast take time out from rehearsal to pose for the photographer. Don, first row (seated), third from left.

Don's high school teacher, and director of the high school play, Ethel Tyson.

Photo: John E. ▌

"Ratpack" (left, Don) & "Sixpack" (right, Fred) were nicknames given them in high school in Prescott, Arizona.

Fred Imus

Don's high school friend, Phil Oelze, second from left, as class president, 1957.

Don's cousin George Davis, 1957.

Don's friend Bert Schenberger, 1957.

The Don Martin School, which no longer exists, was formerly housed among the group of buildings in a Hollywood complex on Cherokee Avenue.

Don and Harriet were living in this modest Hollywood apartment with their four young daughters while Don struggled to make ends meet as a train brakeman.

After failing to make it as a singer in Hollywood, Don became homeless and was forced to sleep in Hollywood laundromats such as this one. He would sleep behind the dryer for warmth.

Don Imus and Governor Lowell Weicker of Connecticut at the Volvo Tennis Tournament.

Imus and Mike Francesca (sports commentator at WFAN) at the Special Olympics.

Imus as governor of Connecticut. *Left to right:* Charles McCord (WFAN newscaster), Imus, and Rob Bartlett (WFAN comedian and writer).

The WFAN cast, *from left to right:* Mike Breen (sports news), Rob Bartlett, Lou Rufino (engineer), Jane Gennaro (impressionist), Jeff Shade (engineer/producer), Larry Kenney (impersonator), cardboard Imus, Bernard McGuirk (producer), Charles McCord (newscaster), Laura Nembuch (public relations contact), 1991.

Left to right: Vince McMahon, Imus, Mike Lupica, Rob Bartlett at Yale University.

Portrait of Imus, 1991.

Imus at home in South Port, Connecticut, 1991.

As it would turn out, the sales for *God's Other Son* were tepid and plans for a follow-up dissolved with each box of returned books. Imus felt that the publisher had not promoted the book properly and for many years would carry a resentment against the publishing world in general. When it became clear that Simon & Schuster had lost interest in another Imus novel, he let it roll off his back. "We have lots of stuff to do." Including working on material for Imus's occasional stand-up gigs.

Although Don claimed, "I'm not one of those guys who wants to be in the womb and stuff. I don't have a beard or wear dark glasses or want to hide from anybody or any of that stuff at all." At the same time, he preferred working in the solitary confinement of a radio studio to a stage in front of a live audience.

"On the radio I know people are out there laughing even if I can't see them. I don't want to be a nightclub comic. I only do it now because I get so much money. I charge ten thousand a night. That's why I do it. So you don't get many people who want to pay you that, but they're around."

More than anything, Imus seemed intent on keeping his current success in perspective. "I went out to Cleveland and did what I had to do and it was terribly humiliating and I hated it. I did not want to do it but I did do it and I did come back here and I have worked hard. I've never been late in two years. Never come close to being late. So I don't take it all seriously. I don't think I'm any big deal. It's just that I am a big deal, but that's fine. There are lots of people who are big deals in things they do that don't get any public attention.

"I'm not a millionaire or anything. I mean, I probably am a millionaire but I don't have a million dollars. I will have, but I don't care. I can do what I want to do. It's more important to do what you like though. I really mean that, corny as it sounds. It's better if you can do something that you want, and one of the benefits is that you're not independently wealthy. If you're in a position where you have to work, it's better to be doing something that you like. I know enough to make a million dollars a year. Now, what else do I have to know?"

Don claimed that another indication he was back in fighting form was his decreased reliance on sunglasses. "See, I used to wear dark glasses. I was trying to cover up a lot of stuff in those days. I used to have four or five different shade densities so that some of them you could see my eyes through. I'd wear those when I talked to someone I liked. The less I liked someone, the darker the glasses were. And," he adds pointedly, "when I would talk to any executive, I would wear mirror glasses."

Against all odds, Imus hadn't just gotten a second chance in New York; if anything, he was actually more popular the second time around. To the point where even non-fans knew who he was. He once related that on his way to work in the early 1980s, he'd have the cab stop to get the morning papers, "which is always an interesting experience because all the hookers are there on the corner. They all recognize me—I know it's not because they've ever heard me but they see me on the bus ads and on television."

Lightning had struck twice, but Imus seemed aware that he had yet to answer the unspoken expectation that he was a time bomb. "I'm not failing this time and I'm much more successful now than I ever was," he said at the time, then added matter-of-factly, "I'm not surprised or anything. I know that it requires a tremendous amount of work. It's not an easy job. It's ten to twelve hours every single day.

"I like being successful. It's better than being unsuccessful. But," he added in a 1981 interview, "it's tough to handle."

Trying to help Don was McCord, who seemed to spend more time with Imus than his own family. "After the show, McCord and I would work on the next day's show up until four or five o'clock," Imus says. Then they would go eat, often at a Mexican restaurant on Seventieth and Columbus, although Imus says the tequila was off limits. "McCord screamed at me and wouldn't let me drink."

But the fact was, Don hadn't given up drinking; he had merely gotten better about keeping it out of the view of his coworkers. Nor was he any more open about his personal problems. Few at the station, for example, were aware of the family crisis involving his daughter who had come to stay with him.

"Like so many parents who are successful, they think what they're giving the kid is fine and it's really not," notes Charles Scimeca, Don's advertising friend. Imus would occasionally talk to Charles when any one of his daughters would be angry with him. "He'd say, 'what does she have to be upset about?' "

An ironic comment, considering Don's own upset at his family situation growing up. Like other fathers in his situation, even though he might not have been a hands-on parent, Imus had provided well for them in the end, with his daughters enjoying a private school education and, now that he was back in New York, relative financial security. But with children, saying it with a check isn't always the care that's needed.

Scimeca remembers the night that truth was brought home to Don. "I called him, and he was just coming back from the hospital because he'd come home to find that his daughter had shaved her head and slashed her wrists."

Once she had recovered enough to travel, Don flew her back to Cleveland, and after that traumatic experience, Charles says, "he never spoke much about the kids. If I asked him something about them, he would answer but never really volunteered the information. He was out of touch as a parent."

It was the first indication to Scimeca that perhaps not all was as well with Don's world as it appeared from the outside looking in. As everyone in Don's sphere would soon learn, though, we can see only what people are willing to show us. And as Imus's addictions started once again to take hold, it became harder to keep the curtains over his private hell closed. Once they fell open, his friends and peers were confronted with the frightening, and potentially lethal, visage of alcoholism.

Chapter Twelve

―――――――――――― ▬▬▬ ――――――――――――

WHEN RECOVERING ALCOHOLICS AND DRUG ADDICTS TALK ABOUT having been in denial, they're not talking only about a refusal to acknowledge they have a disease; just as difficult to accept is the realization that there's no such thing as ever being able to drink *just a little.* No amount of self-control can temper alcohol's lure to an alcoholic, so the only solution is to stop forever. But for many, that reality is simply not an option until their lives are almost in ruins. For some drinkers, such as Don's father and others like him, not even the indignity of living out their lives in a stupor on the streets of Skid Row or huddled on the floor in a flophouse is enough of a reason to seek help. Because by the time they have fallen that far, the alcohol has robbed its victim of both hope and self-worth, replacing it with resignation and self-loathing.

One of the more insidious aspects of alcoholism is how it gradually takes over control of the drinker's body and soul, until one day they're confronted with the frightening realization that they couldn't stop drinking even if they wanted to. For a long time Don Imus didn't want to stop, and for a while he fooled himself into believing he could handle his drinking and drug use. Others who had witnessed his previous professional implosion were dismayed to learn that Don was still flirting with distilled disaster, but because he was able to work and show up for work, Don believed he had the situation under control and his demeanor didn't invite concern. "I'm not the kind of person you can come talk to about anything," he admits. "I was a very typical story. I was never able to just take a couple of drinks. Every time I drank I got drunk, but I didn't see anything wrong with that."

In the early 1980s, Don started doing cocaine again. "It was just that everybody was doing cocaine," he says. "At least, everybody I knew. It was available. The first two lines are great, as I remember it, I think, and then the next ten years are a nightmare."

The second time around, Imus says, "I did cocaine for three or four years, I guess. I was an episodic cocaine user." But he managed to stop on his own in June 1983. "I just got sick and tired of being sick and tired. The payback got to be too much, coming off cocaine just got to be too horrendous, the shakes—just hideous. But my drinking escalated after I stopped doing cocaine, and I had a tough time stopping drinking. It would take years."

In the beginning, Don usually managed to rouse himself for his show. "I could work but it was tough," he says. But even when Imus had an edge to him on the air from the residual effects of drugs or drink, listeners took it to be Imus just being cranky, a trait that many found appealing. "There are those of us who wake up feeling foul and we want to hear somebody who's in just as bad a mood as we are," notes journalist Martha Sherrill.

Bob Pittman believes Don's drinking stemmed from basic insecurity. "Don doesn't think he's as talented as people think he is." Or perhaps it might have been more accurate to say Don hadn't yet found personal and professional validation yet.

Imus, when reflecting on it years later, would admit, "Insecurity, fear of success—I think all of that."

Plus, the early 1980s saw Imus go through a difficult period both on and off the air. On June 7, 1982, Harriet finally filed for divorce, accusing Don in the court papers of "acts of gross neglect of duty and extreme cruelty." She also claims he "threatened to cut off all support," so in addition to requesting custody of their minor children, Elizabeth and Ashleigh, Harriet also asked the court for child support, alimony, and that Don pay for the legal fees.

The court documents also reflect how Don and Harriet had both continued to live right at their means. According to financial statements, Harriet's yearly nut to run the house in Shaker Heights, Ohio, was $75,046, which included hefty tuition costs for Elizabeth to attend private school and Ashleigh the Cleveland Institute of Music. He in turn was living in the penthouse at One Astor Place, which cost $1,945 a month. Neither were insignificant amounts in 1982.

In papers required by the court, Imus's salary history with WNBC was laid bare, showing he had earned $150,000 his first year back (1979–80), $250,000 for 1980–81, and would be paid at a rate of $350,000 in 1982, although Harriet believed his actual total income with personal-appearance fees and other earnings was closer to $500,000.

On September 21, 1982, Don and Harriet agreed to the terms of divorce: He agreed to pay for the house (maintenance, mortgage, utilities, taxes), the car (insurance and repairs costs), medical and dental expenses, private school tuition and room and board away from home, and $300 a week in spousal support. Which tended to lend credence to Imus's retort to Harriet's claim that he threatened to cut her and the children off financially.

"I was never one of those guys who leaves and stops sending money. I just shouldn't have been married in the first place. The marriage was a horrible mistake. I think she would agree."

In the years following the divorce, Harriet stayed in Ohio for several years, then spent some time in North Carolina before moving back to California in the late 1980s. She currently lives with her third husband, Maurice Cook, in Tustin, a community located south of Los Angeles in Orange County. Not only has Imus never publicly revealed any details about their marriage or divorce, Harriet has likewise remained silent.

When asked now to comment on her years with Don, she will only say that "he lies a lot. If I decide to write a book and publish something, I'll do so. In the meantime . . . I'm not interested."

Around the same time his divorce from Harriet was becoming final, a new marriage was taking place at WNBC. General Manager Robert Sherman had hired a brash, ambitious, and undeniably crude disc jockey named Howard Stern, who had most recently been working in Washington at DC-101. Although the station hierarchy saw the Imus-Stern combo a winning one-two punch because both had a reputation for being outrageous, in most regards the two men were glaringly dissimilar in both style and substance—a fact that would become a flash point of professional enmity over the years as both their careers took off in markedly different trajectories.

The irony is, Howard Stern existed in large part due to the barriers Imus had broken at every step of his career. Stern was reaping the benefits of Don's trailblazing. To put it in perspective, when Imus first came to New York glory in 1971, a thirty-one-year-old father of four, Stern was still in high school. Equally ironic is that just as Imus was scaling back the sexual innuendo on his show, Stern was making a name for himself in large part because of his constant patter on all matters sexual. In the end, theirs would be an uneasy personal mix that would see Stern resentful of Imus's status with management and Imus put out at having to team up with anyone for promotions sake.

From his first moments at NBC, Stern felt as if he were being treated with less respect than he deserved, especially when compared to Imus. The first insult was when they initially refused to let him bring along his DC-101 sidekick, Robin Quivers.

"We wanted Howard without his aides-de-camp," explains Sherman, "so he'd be as naked and vulnerable as possible to good management."

In other words, they already had their hands full with Imus, so they wanted to make sure Stern was as compliant as they could force him to be. In the end, however, they acquiesced and hired Quivers, although it did little to sate Stern, because by that time his resentment was welling over.

"The bastards made us take the subway," Stern recalled in his autobiography, *Private Parts.* "They wouldn't even give us a damn car to use. I was begging them to help us because we were making personal appearances after each show. Meanwhile, vodka-breath Imus had a twenty-four-hour company-paid limo. Robin said he was the only guy who looked as if he was being limoed to a park bench."

More insulting to Stern, though, was the suggestion by management that he tailor his show to be more in keeping with the Imus style. "They kept telling me that I should develop characters for my show just the way Mr. Imus had. They sat me down every day and forced me to listen to tapes of Imus's show while they cooed how brilliant and creative Mr. Imus was.

"It was amazing the way everyone at that station was kissing Imus's ass. And he was doing a lame, tame show with characters who were older than me. He had his Reverend Hargis bits and this stupid Moby Worm routine, which was just his voice put through a synthesizer.

"No real conversation, nothing innovative, just the same stupid bits over and over. Lazy radio. I didn't get it, but Mr. Imus the genius did characters, so they wanted me to create characters for my show. I told them a hundred times, I don't do characters."

In counterpoint, Imus was mostly oblivious to Stern or anybody else, because by 1983 his drinking, and to a lesser extent his drug use, was once again overtaking his life. "His drug of choice was more alcohol than anything else," comments Mc-Cord. "It was devastating. It was horrible to watch."

Bernard McGuirk, who would become Don's longtime producer for *Imus in the Morning*, recalls, "My first day on the job in 1983 at NBC, I mean he was there in boxer shorts, running up and down the hallways at the radio station in his underwear, screaming at people. That was my first impression of him. I didn't know what to think; here's this middle-aged guy staggering down the hallways of an office building yelling and screaming at no one for no apparent reason."

McGurik's introduction to Imus occurred on the same day of the notorious phone booth incident, where Don decided to relieve himself at the nearest possible location.

For a long time, nobody, not even Fred, could convince Don he needed professional help to stop drinking. "He was supportive but there's not much you can do with a drunk," Imus notes. "Particularly a drunk as I was, an episodic drunk; didn't drink all the time but when I did drink, I'd be drunk for a week or so and then lie about it. Particularly when I did cocaine."

Perhaps it might have been different if Fred had been in closer physical contact with Don. But in 1983 Fred had relocated to Texas. After floating through a series of small-market radio jobs, the younger Imus came to El Paso to work as a disc jockey on a country and western station. When the station shut down, he gave up broadcasting completely to restore classic '57 Chevys full-time. That passion led to Fred delivering paint to body shops. "I was sick of moving around and El Paso is an easy place to live. If you want to get lost, come here. You can make a nice living delivering paint, but it's never enough."

As usual, Don was supportive of his brother's choice. "I love Fred and like him more than any other person in the world. I love him to death. He's a very likable guy, whereas half the people in the audience think I'm an asshole."

So did a few of his coworkers at the time. Ironically, Meredith

Hollaus was of the opinion that compared to Imus at the height of his meltdown, "Howard Stern was just the opposite. Howard was a loose cannon on the air, but the nicest person off the air, a total gentleman."

Finally, it was once again his attorney, Michael Lynn, who forced Don to confront the truth. Just as he had challenged him after he had been fired in 1977, Lynn was intent on forcing Don to see the truth—he was an alcoholic. "It hurt me to see him being hurt that way and I told him exactly what I felt about it and that I thought he needed to get help. And, in fact, he did go for help."

Imus stopped doing cocaine, which by that time had been costing him $3000 to $4000 a week and began going to Alcoholics Anonymous meetings. Remembering the experience with his father all those years before, Don's conception of the "typical" alcoholic was colored with false expectations.

Looking back now, he says: "I remember the first AA meeting I went to was here in Manhattan over at Citicorp and I expected to walk in and see a bunch of guys in raincoats. Instead, I walk in and the room is full of Ally McBeals. I'm serious. Young women and men. Some people you knew. I was shocked."

The meetings seemed to help, and Don was able to quit cocaine for good and also stopped drinking for a while. Once again his friends and coworkers prayed Imus was finally getting the help he needed and that this time it would work. Because he was consumed with his own life crisis, the last thing Imus wanted was any professional annoyances. Since Stern's arrival, Don had paid little overt attention to the station's afternoon man—until the new general manager, Randall Bongarten, decided that WNBC needed to incorporate some new advertising and promotional strategy by pairing Imus with Stern for a television ad campaign.

"There could only be one position for the radio station: We

needed them to be together," Bongarten would say later. "It just had to be."

The station hired the Penchina, Selkowitz Inc. ad agency, and their mandate in part was to let viewers know that Stern was his own unique talent separate from Imus, even if they did share a reputation for being unpredictable. It's interesting to note that for all his problems off mike, it was Stern's job that listeners believed might be hanging by a thread. "The real reason that a lot of people listened to Howard was that they wanted to be listening when he was yanked off the air," Steve Penchina, the creative director, remembered about the research they gathered.

(Just as television compiles ratings based on the thousand or so Nielsen families, who keep track of their viewing habits, radio used Arbitron ratings diaries to discern demographic information.)

But what was most surprising to the admen was that Stern had a significant female listenership, although few wanted to admit it. While acknowledging in their diaries they had tuned into Howard's show, when contacted directly most women denied they enjoyed the show. "We concluded that the women were lying to us," Penchina says. "They were closet listeners who sat and loyally listened to this raunchy show every day."

Their findings led to the tag line, *If we weren't so bad, we wouldn't be so good.* Coming up with the slogan had been the easy part. Now they had to convince Imus to share the stage with Stern, a prospect he did more than balk at.

"On the day of the commercial, Don didn't show up for several hours," remembers Bongarten. "When he did finally show up, he didn't want to make the commercial."

Imus actually left the studio for several hours and was convinced to return only after Bongarten had told Michael Lynn that the ad agency was prepared to shoot the spot without him.

"Eventually he came back and eventually we shot the commercial. I think we did something like thirty takes. Don was absolutely terrific once he finally got involved with it."

In the spot, Bongarten, flanked by Imus and Stern, is reading a letter of apology from the management as the bad boys are forced to sit and listen.

> Because of certain indiscreet remarks by Don Imus and Howard Stern, WNBC radio apologizes to the following: the National Organization for Women, Governor Cuomo, the New York Jets, the United States Congress—both houses . . .

The commercial was a huge hit, and did much more for Stern than Imus, who was already a New York institution. Suddenly, Howard was as publicly recognizable as Imus. Because of this increased public awareness, Bongarten hired a car so Stern could be driven to and from work from his home in Queens as a "security precaution."

Although Imus had finally come through for the television spot, the ad agency and station management had learned their lesson. For the next television spot of the campaign, Don and Howard were photographed separately and their shots reprinted together on a poster. In the commercial, the poster is being vandalized by people walking by.

Suddenly, Imus was no longer the station's crown jewel. Over the course of 1984, Stern's ratings, which in the beginning had been more than modest, suddenly started an energized climb up. In the spring book, he recorded a 3.8 share of the audience; in the autumn it had risen to 4.6, a twenty-one-percent increase. Stern was not above trumpeting his rising profile. "I'm a hero! Yeeessss! . . . I'm the greatest radio personality that ever lived!"

Stern's success was a pointed indicator of just how much times had changed. His on-air ruminations did indeed make

Imus's long-ago crack 'Are you naked?' seem as innocent as a mom and pop store. Even a comment such as 'I couldn't wait for the hostage crisis to be over to speculate on how many bonus miles they'd earned' seemed gentle when, by comparison, now WNBC had to deal with a disc jockey who wanted to offer a gag called Bestiality Dial-a-Date, where he would play matchmaker to a man and a woman who had had sex with animals—an idea that never made the air after station management ordered Howard not to go forward.

Despite the apparent tension between the two, Imus refused to chastise Stern. "Honestly, I have no particularly personal feelings about what he does."

During the time that Stern was solidifying his position on WNBC, Imus's ratings started to flounder. They weren't merely flat and static, they were actually starting to sag; in one twelve month period, he dropped from sixth to fourteenth. Part of the decline was the transition radio itself was undergoing, with the powerful FM stations starting to assert themselves. And part of it was no doubt simple familiarity. What Don needed was a shot of professional adrenaline, and the opportunity was provided by the relatively new medium of cable television.

After his dreadful experience on *Imus Talks*, Don had said, "I don't want to be on television, really. I love radio. I don't think I would ever be good on television. But," he added, "if somebody offered me a thing, I'd probably be stupid enough to do it."

Which explains why in 1985, Don Imus became a television "veejay" for the new VH-1 cable channel. Aimed at the twenty-five to fifty-four demographic, VH-1 was launched in January 1985 as an older sibling to the younger-oriented MTV. When looking to fill their veejay slots, the network's executives turned to an eclectic group of tried and true music personalities. In addition to Imus, VH-1 hired Scott Shannon, who also happened to be Imus's rival on New Jersey's WHTZ, Jon Bauman, better known as Bowzer of ShaNaNa, Frankie Crocker, and Rita Coolidge.

During the press conference announcing his being selected to be a VH-1 veejay, Imus was in top form, telling the throng of reporters that he'd been promised complete freedom in his material "if I could only get Linda McCartney to wash her hair."

L. Kevin Metheny, vice president of music production for MTV and VH-1, confirmed Don's leeway. "We placed the burden of entertainment more heavily on VH-1's veejays, so Don has as close to carte blanche as it can get."

And Don didn't disappoint. Although he kept his derision relatively low key while on the air, when talking about his new job he was typically blunt, such as when discussing some of the less slick videos. "I think the neatest trick these artists pull is to do these home movies and we play them as videos. I mean, Glen Campbell's got his grandmother out there picking grapefruit. I mean, we have a video of the Oak Ridge Boys where they have fifty of their fat relatives and their dirty kids with ice cream and watermelon smeared all over them. They took a Panasonic eight mm out there and they sent the video to us and we play it. I can barely tolerate the Oak Ridge Boys and their family. I mean, I hate their family. No one wants to see their fat family, you know."

Reviews for the new channel were mixed at first. *Newsweek* noted:

> VH-1's programming is a mishmash of soft rock, oldies, soft country, Sinatra, and soft rhythm and blues. Mostly, this diet of music is so bland that viewers might snooze through it if someone like Imus didn't occasionally jolt them into semi-consciousness by suggesting between videos that John Denver be sent up on the space shuttle and kept there.

It was vintage Imus, and although he got the lion's share of the press, others, such as Scott Shannon, felt it was their job to show more restraint. "Don comes closer to duplicating his radio personality, but you have to walk a line."

Although the VH-1 experience was more satisfactory than his previous television foray with *Imus Talks*, it merely reconfirmed to Don where his professional life really lay. "I'm mainly going to concentrate on radio. I'm probably one of the best ever on radio. I'm one of the few guys in America that can go to any market and make a bunch of money and get ratings. I'm not being smart. That's the truth. So, why not do that. Do what you do well, you know?

"I didn't plan a radio career. I just got in and I don't know how I wound up here. I really don't. I mean, I didn't realize I'd be this wonderful. I'm being serious. I didn't realize I'd be this good at it. And it's just the way it works. You know, you can make a lot of money and it's fun. I really enjoy doing it."

The tense alliance between Stern and Imus would come to an end in 1985, although Howard's departure from NBC would mark the beginning of a feud—whether real or perceived, genuine or put on, that would continue to present day. In 1984, Randall Bongarten had been promoted to president of NBC Radio Network, with John P. Hayes, Jr., named the new general manager on October 1, 1984. Unlike Bongarten, who had been instrumental in Stern's professional advancement, Hayes wasn't an advocate on Howard's behalf and therefore didn't make it a point to run interference for Stern, who seemed bent on pushing the obscenity envelope to the breaking point.

According to author Paul Colford, it was NBC chairman Grant Tinker who—over the objections of Bongarten—finally gave the order to fire Stern after Tinker learned complaints were being made about the content of Stern's show. In a rebellion all his own, Bongarten waited a full two months before making the firing official in September 1985.

In a press conference, Stern expressed his surprise. "I have a reputation for nobody knowing how I feel," he said. "I am genuinely upset over this, mostly because I didn't know it was coming. Had I known it was in the works, I could have sat down with management and worked things out."

Instead, he was now determined to get even for all the slights he felt he had suffered at the hands of both Imus and NBC, directly or otherwise.

Just a few weeks after leaving NBC, Stern was hired by WXRK-FM, known as K-Rock, and he openly declared war on Imus. "K-Rock asked me to switch to mornings so I could go head to head against Imus and destroy him," says Stern, who replaced Jay Thomas, who would go on to find success as an actor, appearing in the series *Mork & Mindy, Cheers,* and *Love and War.*

In earlier years when anyone challenged his belief he was the most popular disc jockey of the masses, Imus would heatedly join the fray. When a *Newsday* journalist suggested in 1981 that John Gambling was more popular than Don, he became testy. "John Gambling is not number one. I am number one. I don't give a shit what the ratings say. You walk out in the street and ask people who their favorite disc jockey is in New York and they'll tell you it's me."

But Imus responded to Stern's boasting with a retort more sardonic than ego-fueled. "If Howard Stern beats me, I'll eat a dead dog's penis."

In the end, it was Stern who would have the final bowwow. In 1984, WNBC had posted a four-million-dollar profit. In 1986, they showed a loss of $1.5 million. As he predicted, Stern eventually caught up with, then overtook Imus. "I said I would do it and I did. My ratings soared, and I dragged Shit Stain down to a one share."

But in some ways it wasn't a fair fight, because while Stern's entire focus was on vindicating himself and seeking retaliation against his former station and associates, which had included a feud with midday man Soupy Sales, Imus's was functioning at half capacity. Plus, he refused to fight Stern on the same obscenity-laced, sex-shop playing field.

As writer Howard Kurtz notes, "Stern is not politically inclined. His show, more often than not, is about sex. Imus may certainly touch on sex, baseball, and anything else that pops into his brain. But he's the kind of guy who watches Jim Lehrer, who watches C-SPAN."

"Imus never crossed the line," agrees Meredith Hollaus. "He always knew where the line was. He would just go so far, and you'd think he'd go over that, but he never did. That's what made him a true professional."

"What you see with Imus is what you get, on the air and off the air," Dan Rather adds.

Others were more passionate about their support of Imus. "Howard Stern is a vulgar, vulgar man," intones *60 Minutes* sage Mike Wallace. "He's not even sophomoric. I despise it. That's the difference. Imus is an infinitely more intelligent man, an infinitely more sensitive man."

Imus sums up their time as coworkers with a simple "We never hung out together. I don't think he likes me that much or that we got along that well. It's not what I do but that's irrelevant."

By 1987, Don was spending more and more time alone, in a forlorn attempt to hide his drinking from others. Although he had stopped for a while after he first started attending AA meetings in 1983, it wasn't long before he started again, "but secretly. What really was hideous in terms of my self-esteem was that I lied at AA meetings about drinking and I would speak at AA meetings about not drinking but I was still drinking. I was in a kind of O. J. Simpson denial," he says wryly.

Although AA is considered by many to be the premier organization for helping alcoholics get sober, Imus believes it doesn't work "for as many people as you would think. I went to AA meetings for years and I lied. I went to AA meetings and I still drank. I was horrible. I went to AA meetings and I would get up and give speeches about how great sobriety was. Then I go home and buy a bottle of vodka and get drunk. Then your self-esteem suffers. It was hideous.

"People would say to me, 'You look really great since you stopped drinking.' I was so disappointed in myself. I didn't know what to do. It didn't occur to me to stop."

By 1986, it was obvious to everyone that Don had fallen off the wagon. In an instant replay of the late '70s, Imus began missing work. This time his permanent fill-in host was Dan Taylor, who had begun his career in 1978 at WCBS-FM. He started at WNBC as a weekend deejay before taking over as Don's pinch hitter.

When he did show up, Don was often just barely functioning. Imus's producer, Lyndon Abell, remembers he was often "inconsolable. I was under strict orders from the station to pump Imus up."

Most alarming was Don's physical appearance. "His face resembled a death mask" is how Kinky Friedman describes his friend. "He looked like your garden-variety hatchet murderer."

Except the person he was killing was himself. In July 1987 Imus said, "It got to where the payback for alcohol got to be too much. I would go on these binges. My drinking escalated and it got worse and I was getting blackouts, where I would do things I didn't even know what I had done. There's a garage right next door to 30 Rockefeller and I used to sleep on a bench there, with thousands of dollars in my pocket. Crazy stuff. I got myself in such hideous shape that I had to go to rehab. I was on a book tour (for the paperback publication of *God's Other Son*) and I came back to New York and I went, 'Well, I'll have a couple of drinks' and . . . it was just horrible." Those few drinks turned into a nine-day drinking binge "on vodka, drinking warm vodka out of the bottle."

At the station there was genuine fear that something terrible had happened. Don had never disappeared for this long a time. "We tried calling him and we couldn't get a hold of him," Bongarten recalls. "We couldn't find him anywhere. So we finally had somebody go down to his apartment and get somebody to let them in. And we found Don on the floor and he was totally incoherent. Totally out of it."

When Don had tried to stop, he had gone into seizures, so as soon as he was found, Don was immediately hospitalized. Finally Don was ready to admit the problem was bigger than he could handle. NBC helped him make arrangements for rehab, and when he was released from the hospital, Imus went to the Hazelden Clinic in West Palm Beach, Florida, and spent six sobering weeks coming to terms with his disease.

He remembers believing "my life was destroyed." At Hazelden he shared a room with two doctors and a lawyer. "We were all junkies. I told myself, *I won't try to bullshit my way through this deal. I'm just gonna do whatever they say. I'll take their advice for thirty days and see if it works.* And once I made the decision, it wasn't tough. I've been taking their advice ever since."

After four weeks, Imus was made a group leader. "It was like being elected class president."

Although Imus, at least the public Imus, isn't given to much introspection, his time at Hazelden did impress on him some basic truths about alcoholism and drug addiction. "I don't think it's impossible to understand. It's not a big deal. It cuts across all segments of society. I've heard athletes and other people in the entertainment business talk about their depression and I think that's jive. There are as many guys on Wall Street doing coke as there are on the streets.

"I drank a little bit when I was in the Marine Corps and then

I didn't drink pretty much from the time I was twenty until I was thirty, when I came to New York. And I was successful almost immediately and I was very uncomfortable in any kind of social situation. I'm just a typical drunk," he says, then adds, "I don't think you ever lick it."

Unlike his lukewarm opinion about AA, Imus is almost reverential about the Hazelden program. "This is a great organization," he says simply with a trace of what sounds like humility.

Imus was also humbled by the reception he got at work, the fact he still had a job when he returned six weeks later. In looking back now, Don is amazed his drinking didn't literally kill him. "My life was a mess. I was really lucky. There's really not a day goes by that I'm not thankful that I'm sober. Not a day."

Don's recovery coincided with a career turning event. In 1988, WNBC sold its frequency to Emmis Broadcasting Corporation, which moved the underachieving all-sports WFAN from its old position on the AM dial to the newly acquired position at 660. Typically, Howard Stern took most of the credit and gloated that "NBC wound up selling the station for millions less than it was worth."

And the original Teflon Don once again found himself sought after—WFAN wanted him to stay on as their new morning man. Even Imus knew he hadn't earned such an opportunity, but he was grateful to have been offered it. Even so, he does worry that talking about his recovery "for somebody like me who was cut an enormous amount of slack by the people at NBC and other folks sends a mixed message [that some might mistakenly believe recovery is easy]. It isn't. People know I'm an alcoholic and drug addict, but had I been back working for the railroad or been back in the mines, I would have been fired."

The only reason Don believes he was spared by NBC was not because he was a celebrity or that they particularly cared about him, but simply because "I was making them money. You can't do what I did, conduct yourself the way I did, and still keep your job. I never had to function like a normal person. I didn't have to drive. I didn't have to write checks. So many people cut me so much slack that my recovery isn't a testament to anything other than luck."

But as he had showed so many times in the past, his continued success in radio was anything but luck. And Don Imus was presented with the chance to reinvent himself one more time.

Chapter Thirteen

CONFRONTING LIFE SOBER WAS A REFRESHING NEW EXPERIENCE FOR Don. Not because all his problems were suddenly solved once he was clearheaded but because he had eliminated an unnecessary set of obstacles that alcohol had added. "I'm amazed that I don't have any problems anymore other than the ordinary problems," he noted. "Because as I reflect on it, every single incident in my life that was a nightmare or unpleasant for either me or somebody else was an absolute, direct result of either drinking or doing cocaine."

But Don came to believe, with the guidance of the Hazelden counselors, that for all of the self-destructive behavior, he was still worthy of redemption.

"When I went to rehab, either the fourth or fifth step in AA, you have to sit down with some other person and you have to be honest and you have to tell them everything you've done in your life Everything. So I sat down with Sister Rose, a Catholic nun, and she looked at me and said, 'That's it?' Because I've never done anything I'm ashamed of that most people don't already know about."

After having had the dark side of his life laid bare, Imus seemed to be renewed. Instead of hiding in his house binge-drinking, he once again began exercising and would develop into a dedicated runner, keeping his lanky frame lean and his mind clear. Whether Imus suspected or not that he was about to enter into a new stage of career evolution, the symbolic significance of WNBC's dissolution on radio in general couldn't have been lost on Don.

The end came on October 7, 1988. The final hours' broadcast, hosted by Alan Colmes, were filled with call-ins from misty-voiced associates, melancholy-sounding former employees, and the public, all aware that an era was ending.

Colmes presided over the station's final moments with more pride than depression, intent on going out on the strength of WNBC's legacy rather than on its somewhat ignoble end.

"Let me say just a few final words then we're going to count down to the end of NBC, WNBC radio, that is. When I first broadcast on this station, it was the realization of a lifelong dream," he said, no doubt iterating the feelings of many of the former on-air personalities. "I never imagined during my first moments on NBC that the last seconds I would have on the station would be the last seconds anybody would have. It's a historic moment that belongs not just to me but also to every broadcaster who graced the microphones, every worker at WNBC who made this station great and each listener who supported us through the years.

"I'm Alan Colmes. Thank you, God bless you, and for the last time, this is 66 WNBC, New York. Let's do the countdown."

Then a chorus of voices counted down from ten and after sixty-six years on the air, WNBC was no more. The same day, at six-fifteen P.M. listeners heard the changeover announcement.

"Sports Radio 66, WFAN New York."

Immediately following the station ID, Larry Kenney's voice echoed over the radio:

And there came to pass a great change on the landscape and the numbers 1050 shone then faded into black. And there grew in their place the numbers 660. Emmis saw and said, "It is good." And then there also grew at 660 the letters WFAN. Emmis saw and said, "It is good." A courier appeared, Chet by name, and beckoned Imus to Emmis and Emmis saw and said, "We'll cross our fingers." And the courier brought forth a candle to illuminate the way and proffered it to Imus. Imus saw and said, "No, you idiot, I said a *Bud* light!"

And as Imus took to the air as the Reverend Dr. Billy Sol Hargis, WFAN was up and running. Although Imus's crew remained intact, it was quite a change in environment. Instead of being housed at Manhattan's 30 Rockefeller, WFAN was ensconced in Astoria, Queens, at the Kaufman-Astoria Studios, which had once been a thriving studio, producing over one hundred silent films during the 1920s before successfully making the transition to "talkies." The Astoria studios was also home to the legendary Paramount newsreels.

In 1942, however, the facility was bought by the army and turned into the Signal Corps's Army Pictorial Center, producing a myriad military films, ranging from how to survive in battle to personal hygiene. In 1976 the Kaufman-Astoria Studios were designated a national historic landmark and reopened a year later. In 1982, real estate developer George Kaufman, in partnership with Alan King and Johnny Carson, obtained the lease from the city of New York, which had been given the title to the studio earlier in the year. A $50-million expansion later, the Kaufman-Astoria Studios was one of the largest production centers west of Los Angeles.

While his sobriety may have humbled Don as a person, the competitive deejay in him still raged. "How does it feel to have your billings double in one hour, sucker?" Imus asked Joel Hollander, WFAN's general sales manager, referring to the immediate boost in sales revenue. But even though the change in dial position and the addition of Imus to their otherwise all-sports lineup had raised WFAN's profile literally overnight, it wasn't a cure-all. And for the first several months there was a persistent question of whether or not the radio station would survive.

Typically, Imus refused to worry about managerial concerns. Instead, he concentrated on his show, and as the weeks passed, Don was playing less and less music, replacing it with more and more talk and commentary. Michael Lynn saw the new station a fertile ground where Don's talents could be more showcased. "Before, when there was a broad music format, his show was more diffuse. The sports format gave an anchor to the creative thrust of the program."

Imus had been spinning tunes for so long, he did it out of habit. But as his show naturally evolved, it became clear that the music was now superfluous, so by the end of 1988, Don decided to stop playing records altogether. Through luck and serendipity, he had found a niche that allowed him equal parts silliness and thoughtful sensibility, a format that allowed him to use his comic talents to make commentary on the social and political landscape of the day while entertaining as well as provoking his audience. After almost twenty years in radio, Imus must have finally felt like a broadcast grown-up—no matter if some critics considered some of the humor on his show juvenile and sophomoric.

Even during his most self-indulgent drinking phases, Imus had always sought out collaboration. Charles McCord would remain Don's first and foremost writing partner because, despite possessing such disparate personalities, they shared the same comic sensibility and more important for Don, a time-tested friendship, and to this day they talk on the phone every night while watching *The NewsHour with Jim Lehrer*. "We joke about how fat former Deputy Secretary of State Larry Eagleburger is."

But McCord's importance to Imus goes far beyond the ability to share intellectual laughs together. "He's the single smartest guy I know. I couldn't do it without Charles," Imus says. "I don't even know if I'd want to do it," he says.

Curiously, many listeners view McCord as little more than a

toady, a perception of which McCord is well aware. "Many people see me as a suckup. I am! But I'm also smart enough to realize this whole thing could blow up tomorrow.

However, what most of the listeners didn't realize is that almost all of the material they were hearing was either written or cowritten by McCord, the born-again Christian from Missouri. Which is why Imus says, "He's a wonderful person . . . but, of course, there's a little Jeffrey Dahmer in him."

"He is a dear and valued friend. There are lots of facets to him," says McCord in return. "Those qualities are a deep caring and generosity. You see more the brashness and bravado, but he's a pretty good character. There are few requests for help that he wouldn't respond to—and probably negatively."

As his show developed and characters were now expanded to include more than just his own, others in addition to McCord became part of Imus's inner show circle, together forming a group who would become known as the I-Posse: sports guy Mike Breen, show producer Bernard McGuirk, and writers and all-around laugh guys Rob Bartlett and Larry Kenney.

As always, Fred was a significant if unofficial member of the I-Posse, a collaborator whose input Don sought out and often acted on. For example, it was Fred who suggested to Don that he ought to turn on everyone's mike in the studio to give them all an equally heard voice, giving the show the feel of a debauched town hall meeting.

However, Fred has no qualms about offering a complaint or two as well. "You know what? They don't pay me for being on the show," he told a reporter in 1991. "They won't even throw me a few bucks. And he'll deny this, but he gets pissed off if I don't come up with something funny every day. And I'm not a funny guy. I restore cars."

Although Imus still wrote some of the routines, his primary focus was becoming more directorial, preparing and conducting any interviews and running the show. So as Imus settled into a groove, he turned over a lot of the writing to McCord and the others. It was gonzo comedy writing, having to be funny on command. When Don would bark "Give me a Nixon," he expected the bit to be both written fast and written funny. Although he was a stern taskmaster, made no effort to hide when he didn't like a routine, and loved to demean his posse on air with sneering comments such as "I don't need any of them. They're all just insignificant little twirps," Imus in reality was also the first to acknowledge his team's importance to the show.

"If I were sitting in here by myself, it would be a completely different show, nowhere near as good as it is now."

Back in 1977, when Don was fired from NBC, he noted at the time, somewhat incredulously, that there was a rampant perception that he was difficult to work with. What seemed to bother Don was that the remark could be interpreted as a reflection of his on-air work. And the dichotomy that is Imus is that the very same people who freely acknowledged how horrible it was to be around him personally while he was a raging drunk were the same people who would work with him without hesitation. It must be seen as a measure of his person and his talent that the members of his inner team had all stuck with Don through the bleakest of times. Their history together helped weather whatever tensions might arise from the creative process of having to prepare a daily four-hour radio show and the mercurial nature of Don's personality. Hazelden had merely made him sober, not any easier. He still spoke his mind with painful bluntness, refusing to temper his opinions for the sake of anyone's feelings.

"I am not a nice person," Don has said. "This is the real me. You'll just have to believe that."

The show's producer, Bernard McGuirk, who had first worked with Don at WNBC in 1983, concurs with Don's self-assessment.

"What he does is no act," McGuirk says. "He's opinionated,

short-tempered, and funny. In short, he's like what he is on the air, cubed. It's survival of the fittest here. Darwinian radio."

McGuirk's on-air contributions to the show are a regular spot reading the daily lotto numbers in the voice of Cardinal O'Connor and interjecting the program's most potentially offensive ad-libbed comments. Although frequently chastised on air by a frequently chuckling Imus, Don alternately calls his producer "a bald-headed geek" and "a great kid. Very talented."

Fortunately, Imus already had a resident jock when WFAN took over, Mike Breen, whose playful sense of humor, such as doctoring sound bite tapes of athletes, fit right in with the Imus paradigm. After graduating from Fordham University, Breen's first job out of college was as a radio newscaster and sportscaster for WEOK/WPDH in Poughkeepsie, New York. He quickly branched out, doing commentary on television for the Colony Sports Network, and working as an analyst for Seton Hall basketball on radio.

In 1986, he was named producer and sometime host of WNBC's *SportsNight*, a weeknight talk show that was also simulcast on MSG Network, and also joined *Imus in the Morning* as the show's sportscaster. Breen is a seasoned radio play-by-play announcer, having covered football, basketball, baseball, and the Olympics. But for his professional accomplishments, which includes being named 1998 Broadcaster of the Year in New York State by the National Sportscasters and Sportswriters Association, Breen says his most notable achievement is "being fired by Imus sixty-one times."

While Fred, McCord, McGuirk, and Breen are all important elements to the show, the real point men are Rob Bartlett and Larry Kenney. Bartlett, who started his career as a stand-up comic, is a veritable endless well of material. "There are few people in comedy who write as well as he does," Imus says. "He's brilliant, I'm telling you, brilliant." Kenney is a natural mimic who Imus considers "the single most talented person

I've ever met." It is Kenney and Bartlett who supply the majority of material—and get the majority of Imus's wrath when it doesn't meet Don's comic standards. But regardless of whatever ill temper he subjects them to, both men seem to possess undying loyalty to Imus.

Larry Kenney began his radio career, such as it was, as a fill-in disc jockey in 1963 when he was fifteen years old, at WIRL, a tiny 5,000-watt station in Peoria, Illinois. It was love at first spin, and Kenney would eventually make his way to Chicago as the host of his own morning show. In 1973, Imus asked Larry to contribute comedy routines to *Imus in the Morning* via telephone. Later Kenney also wrote material for Don's comedy club act.

Thanks in large part to the exposure he received on Don's show, Larry moved to New York in 1974 and recorded a comedy album, *The Honest to God, We Really Mean It, Very Last Nixon Album* and was hired at WHN, where he would be named America's Best Country Music Disc Jockey by *Billboard* magazine in both 1976 and 1978.

Kenney and Imus subsequently recorded several country music songs, written by Fred, although the efforts were met with the same singular failure as Don's previous efforts to be a musical star. While Don went back to spinning records and spinning out of control, Kenney was hired to host the now-kitsch game show, *Bowling for Dollars.*

Although the program would do little for Kenney's TV career, it didn't matter because he was becoming Mr. Voice-over, aurally appearing in what now is literally hundreds of commercials, including the voices of Count Chocula and Sonny, the Coco Puffs bird. Larry has also worked extensively in cartoons, most notably on *Thundercats.*

But throughout all his other ventures, Kenney is still probably best known for his cast of characters on Imus, which has included Richard Nixon, Ted Kennedy, Ross Perot, Henry Kissinger, Walter Cronkite, Paul Harvey, Elvis Presley, Paul Lynde, David Brinkley, Howard Cosell, General George Patton, Jack Nicholson, and any number of others.

Kenney and Imus enjoy a bantering relationship, and Larry isn't afraid to ruffle Don's feathers. Once, in an interview, Kenney claimed that he and Bartlett were responsible for "ninety to ninety-five percent of the show's success." But while Imus tends to let his longtime friend Kenney get away with his trash talk, Don tends to keep Rob Bartlett, who in fact is probably responsible for at least half of the show's scripted sketches, on a shorter leash.

But Bartlett, whose regular cast of characters includes real personalities such as Rush Limbaugh, Mike Tyson, and Bill and Roger Clinton as well as the fictional, doesn't seem to mind being Imus's occasional whipping boy. "He calls me a fat bastard," Bartlett admits, "but he says it with love. Ninety-nine percent of the comics out there would kill to be in my position."

If Bartlett seems unusually tolerant, it's because Don Imus has been his idol since Imus first came on WNBC in 1971 when Rob was a teenager growing up in Massapequa Park, right in Jerry Seinfeld's figurative backyard. Bartlett had his bedroom clock radio set to 660 and was a faithful listener.

Bartlett's passion for performing surfaced at a young age, notably at a kindergarten talent show, where he performed a Pat Cooper routine about an Italian wedding word for word. A few years later he entertained his friend by doing an impression of a neighbor who had the charming habit of laughing, clearing his throat, and spitting.

At Farmingdale High, Bartlett was an occasional class clown and an exceptionally gifted academic student—and a bust in athletics. But Bartlett preferred theater to sports anyway, and appeared in school productions of *South Pacific* and *Mame*. He also immersed himself in television and pop culture, always honing his knack for mimicry.

Rob attended Alfred University on an academic scholarship but withdrew after he was stricken with Crohn's disease, a painful intestinal inflammation that can be physically debilitating. Because he was unable to attend school, he eventually lost his scholarship and once healthy found work as a building elevator operator in New York.

Like many stand-up comics before him, Bartlett first gave it a try just for fun and to see if he really could make people laugh. "There were eight people in the audience," Rob says. This included the friend who came with him. But the experience was enough of a rush that Bartlett went to another open mike bar, this time loading the audience with his friends. "I really killed the place that night," he says, and by evening's end, Rob decided to pursue stand-up as a career.

Among the struggling comics he befriended was Eddie Murphy, who often got rides to clubs with Rob because Murphy was still too young to drive, and a just-starting Jerry Seinfeld. For years Bartlett lived the on-the-road life of a stand-up and enjoyed it for a while. But after he married Sharon, a dancer and ballet teacher he met while performing at a club in Queens, Bartlett wanted work that would let him stay closer to home. He found a job as the resident stand-up at Club 1407 in Manhattan, which led to Rob being asked to do some characters on Don's show.

Although Bartlett was admittedly nervous in front of his former idol, he impressed Imus with an impression of Tom Carvel, a well-known East Coast ice cream mogul. After that Bartlett kept on impressing Imus by the sheer amount of material he could write.

"Most comics have six minutes worth of material; Rob kept coming up with the new stuff," Imus says. "Every time he'd come on, he had this prepared stuff that was simply hilarious."

Among his more popular re-creations is Scott Muni, a real-life deejay who had been a fixture at the legendary WNEW-FM.

Rob portrays Muni, who left WNEW only a few years ago, a bitter, aging hippie pining for the days he got stoned with 1960s icons such as Janis Joplin and Jimi Hendrix. On his show, Muni would interview rock stars in between spinning tunes, talking to them with a familiarity that suggested he was sitting in their living rooms.

Muni was once quoted as saying Bartlett's impression of him is so accurate that "people are always asking me, 'Does Imus pay you to come on?' It's the highest compliment I can pay him."

Over the years, Bartlett has delved more into political humor with his characterizations, most notably Bill Clinton and Rush Limbaugh. "I have no political agenda," Bartlett claims. "If a line I wrote really hurt somebody, I would probably feel horrible. Really. The stuff I like best is silly." Such as this ditty "Limbaugh" sings to the tune of Garth Brooks's homey "Friends in Low Places":

I like friends with white faces/
We're pretty big on the master races/
We wear slip-on sheets and pillowcases . . .

Or his homage to Robert Dole, written to Bob Seger's "Old Time Rock & Roll":

I like that old guy Robert Dole/
He's got no prostate but he's got a soul . . .

"It sometimes gets lost in the penis jokes," Imus says drolly, "but the stuff Rob does is the best political satire out there."

Because of his work on the show, other doors have been flung open for Bartlett in the last several years: he's headlined in Vegas and Atlantic City with his stand-up act, become a sought-after voice-over performer in both radio and TV commercials, and has been approached about possible writing and starring in his own television show.

But Rob has consistently said that even if that were to happen, he would want to continue his association with Imus. "To have this kind of steady work in show business is a miracle." Besides, he says, working with Imus is so much fun. "To be part of the whole atmosphere at the show, the insults, the banter, the energy, is great.

"I've got it all. Most of the time, I get to be here with my family, and I get to be in the position I'm in. I was in the right place at the right time. Being associated with the show and the way it's thought of in the broadcasting community is like a master class."

Perhaps the biggest reason Bartlett remains loyal to *Imus in the Morning* is that "there is nothing better than to make Imus laugh really hard. It's like praise from Caesar. It vindicates your existence."

Imus was well aware of the level of talent on his staff and has managed to keep his posse intact to the present by taking care of them. "You gotta remember," he told Larry King in a 1998 interview, "for just one local radio station, we're doing fifty million dollars a year. So we can pay 'em. They make huge amounts of money. I have guys who make twice as much money as the writers of *Saturday Night Live*."

Some of the most humorous segments of the show were fueled by civilians, as it were, who came from all walks of life. The only criterion was whether Don found them interesting and funny. The God Squad, Rabbi Marc Gellman, and Monsignor Thomas Hartman came to Imus's attention when he attended a fund-raiser on Long Island where the two clergymen were on hand to do a joint invocation. "I thought they were a riot and wanted to put them on the air."

So was born the Prayer of the Week segment. Hartman and Gellman, sponsored by Tri-State Jeep/Eagle, agreed to appear on the show gratis and try to inject a modicum of morality in between the penis jokes and toilet humor, with a little spiritual humor of their own. Once, Imus asked the clergymen, "Is it safe for me to believe in everything as a hedge against, you know, winding up burning forever, or do I have to pick one guy, like Jesus?"

"I basically believe that in life you've got to believe in goodness, truth, and humor," commented Hartman.

"Or," Rabbi Gellman added, "two out of three would be all right."

Another time, Imus mused that "you'd think there would be some tension there [between the two clergy] particularly during Easter."

"I just hide a lot," Gellman responded.

When talking publicly about his own religious beliefs over the years, Imus has been fairly consistent. "I believe in Jesus. I think it's okay, by the way, to believe in Moses too, or Buddha. I'm a Christian who believes that's not the only answer. Everybody has their own Jesus and I respect them all."

Although Imus says he doesn't believe in asking God for favors, "I do believe in thanking Him. He knows what you want. He also knows what you need. That's His decision. You can't ask God for things, but you should thank Him."

Also inhabiting the new incarnation of Imus's show were many of his longtime drop-in guests, either via phone or in person, such as Kinky Friedman. Don's old comedy club pal had gone on to become, among other things, a modestly successful mystery writer, leaving behind the world of music just in time or else "I'd probably be playing Disneyland now with the Pips," he cracks. "I'm only singing now in bookstores, whorehouses, and the occasional bar mitzvahs."

His series of novels feature a private investigator named, of all things, Kinky Friedman, who was assisted by his own posse of eccentric deputies. The plot of one book had the fictional

Friedman tracking down a missing documentary on Elvis impersonators.

In real life, Kinky, like Don, had undergone some changes since their wild days in the 1970s. Friedman had left New York in 1985, weary of all the drinking and drugging he saw around him that resulted in the death of several friends. He moved back to Texas, took stock of his life, and began writing. His philosophy that "life is too important to be taken seriously," reflecting an Imusesque wisdom that comes only from having survived where others didn't.

As the new decade dawned, Don Imus, against all sense and reason, was not only still standing, but was about to raise his personal bar to new, unexpected heights.

Chapter Fourteen

BY 1991, DON IMUS HAD COMFORTABLY SETTLED INTO THE EARLY scenes of his second act in public life. His record-playing days seemingly a lifetime behind him, Imus, who now preferred to refer to himself as the "I-Man," was leading the way in helping make AM radio not just financially viable once more, but intellectually vibrant. Plus, thanks to the strength of WFAN's 50,000-watt signal, *Imus in the Morning* was no longer simply a New York phenomenon. He was heard in at least seven states, as far south as Delaware, as far north as Massachusetts. In fact, he was so popular in Connecticut, he once quipped, to the extreme annoyance of Connecticut deejays, "You mean there are other radio stations in Connecticut?"

Although the bits and routines they did on the air were scripted, there were significant amounts of ad-libbing too, off-the-cuff and top-of-the-head comments that might just as easily be brilliantly witty as vulgar and offensive. Don preferred his show to have no discernible pattern, leaving the audience always wondering what would happen next. The topics covered were the topics that interested Imus, who still pored over newspapers religiously on the day of his broadcast. And as was evident even in his earliest days as a rock 'n' roll deejay, politics usually topped his list of interests, followed closely by all levels of potty humor.

Tony Kornheiser, who currently hosts his own talk program on Washington, D.C.'s WTEM, once asked after his station picked up *Imus in the Morning,* "How can he do five minutes on the size of his penis, and then interview Bill Bradley?" To which Don replied, "I have varied interests. They range from NAFTA to my penis."

Journalist Jeff Greenfield doesn't understand the indignation. "He's out there talking the way most of us talk when we're not in public. Most people go through life not being able to say some things. There's the id and superego. He knows what most of us know but find harder to admit: it is possible to become deeply involved in an intelligent discussion of health care at nine in the morning and then make risqué jokes five minutes later."

It was this combination of intellectual discourse and high school locker room banter that appealed to his listeners, particularly the guys who outwardly held down important jobs in business, finance, and government but inwardly wished they would crack wise and tell it like it was the way Imus did. Since they'd get fired for telling the boss just how they felt and charbroiling the status quo, they lived vicariously through Imus, who in contrast was now making $1.5 million to insult whoever he wanted, including the hand that fed him.

> This concludes the entertainment portion of the WFAN broadcasting day. WFAN now presents the rest of its programming schedule, 8,612 hours of imbecilic prattle between contemptibly limited provincial program hosts talking on the telephone to a band of thirteen equally insignificant housebound agoraphobes with sports obsessions.

"I have the luxury of being able to say anything I want," Don pointed out with accurate self-importance. "Who else does? Tom Brokaw? Somebody who works for the *Times*?"

In the beginning of his career, Imus took liberties not granted to him and had willingly risked, and ultimately survived, the many fallouts that resulted. But by the early 1990s, he had earned his creative freedom, not just in years served behind the mike and number of career comebacks, but in the way radio stations care about the most—in cold, hard cash.

By the summer of 1991, according to Arbitron, *Imus in the Morning*, which aired from five-thirty A.M. to ten, was ranked number three, behind WINS's all-news station and Howard Stern in the top spot on WXRK (K-ROCK) among the male twenty-five to fifty-four demographic.

But Imus was number one with advertisers because he had more male listeners making over $100,000 than any other morning talk show—the golden calf demographic of advertisers.

"The number of listeners Imus has is mind-boggling," noted Bernadette Castro, who was one of the show's sponsors back then. "I go to board meetings in the city with really important bankers and executives and they'll pull me aside and say, 'What is Imus really like?' "

With such a high level of interest among such a sought-after group of consumers, it was obvious why advertisers were crawling over each other, throwing money at WFAN. In May 1991, thanks largely to Imus, WFAN earned the most revenue a radio station ever had in a single month up to that time. One industry analysis projected WFAN would earn $20 million for the year, with Imus accounting for a full half of that.

What is ironic, though, is that once they made it on the air with Imus, sponsors were never sure how their product would be treated by the I-Man. "We're gonna lose *that* account," McGuirk intoned on air after hearing Don say:

> You know, Miller beer is celebrating the sale of its three-
> billionth case of beer . . . and it's two-millionth car wreck!

After Don made fun of an outfit called Try-A-Bed, the company pulled its advertising in a fit of pique, only to have a change of heart a short time later. But when they tried to buy more ad time, Imus made a Try-A-Bed representative bark like a dog live on air during a broadcast before he would agree to do any more commercials. "I really feel horrible about that," Don told a reporter later, who noted he didn't seem to feel horrible at all about it.

Despite never knowing what Imus might say about their product, many advertisers were more than happy to pay the $1,500 a minute (circa 1991) it cost to have *Imus in the Morning* listeners pitched their product; it was $300 extra if the I-Man read the copy himself. Many times, advertisers felt as if they were playing radio Russian roulette.

"I have to be on the phones constantly to hold clients' hands," Joel Hollander admitted. "We lose a sponsor a couple times a year, maybe three." Mostly for comments such as . . .

The roach problem has been cleared up.

. . . when reading an ad for a local restaurant. But Hollander, who Imus calls "a thieving little fucking rug merchant who I happen to like," would never lack for advertisers because despite roach jokes, a spot on Imus's show could make a significant difference in sales, especially if Don himself gave it his personal seal of approval, as he once did with Stonyfield Farm Yogurt. According to the company's president, Gary Hirschberg, within a week of Imus casually commenting on how much he liked the yogurt, Stonyfield Farm sales were up between ten and twenty percent.

Whatever love/hate relationship Imus had with his advertisers, it seldom got personal because usually the I-Man's insults were done for comic effect. As it had so frequently been noted by friends and coworkers alike, for as snarky as Don could be on air, he was by and large thoughtful and toned down in person. In both television and print interviews he would still be unflinchingly honest in his opinions and not shirk from describing public figures in unflattering portraits, although his insults seemed spoken with more amusement than meanness.

"Are there elements of his personality that come out on the radio?" asks *Daily News* writer Mike Lupica. "Yeah. But is he *Imus in the Morning* twenty-four hours a day? No, he's not. He's not any more than Carson is, or any of those."

But Don's notoriety and infamy preceded him into Southport, Connecticut, the socially tony and financially exclusive enclave located within Fairfield and home to the Pequot Yacht Club. In January 1991, Imus had bought a million-dollar weekend retreat that sat on Long Island Sound, just down the road a ways from Paul Newman. But his seven-figure pied à terre wasn't the bastion of tranquility he had hoped for, at least, not once he set foot outside his front door. The fact that he decorated his house with a southwestern flavor, in colors reminiscent of sunset in the Painted Desert, served as a reminder that Imus was an outsider. Even if he could match the locals bank account by bank account, his background left some of the longtime residents cold. In their eyes, while he might be nouveau riche, he was still a social interloper.

That fact was emphasized in the most nongenteel manner possible when the *Bridgeport Post* ran an interview that had been conducted by the paper with his new neighbors. The comments made it clear Don should not expect a welcome wagon at his door anytime soon. Comments ranging from "He'll never be one of us" to "Move out" screamed off the blue-bloodied page.

The irony was almost Kafkaesque. As a youth, Don endured ostracism by many of his high school peers and Prescott neighbors because he was different, didn't fit in, and had a chip on his shoulder about it. On top of that, he was poor. Fast-forward several decades, and now Don is a wealthy, successful radio personality with a loyal legion of prominent, important fans, and he finds himself once again an outcast among a group of alleged peers. It must be somewhat stultifying to realize that we're never really all that removed from the insecure adolescents we were in high school and that the baggage we assume in our youth tends to remain part of our wardrobe no matter how we try to distance ourselves from it.

Don reacted to his neighbors' ridicule in the same fashion he had his taunting high school classmates—with disdainful dismissal.

"They are insignificant specs on the I-Man's windshield."

One former resident of the area remembers that "it was just such a scandal when he moved there because they're such snobs. There was this big movement to keep him from joining the yacht club."

Not that Don would ever let on it mattered to him, even if it did. "I would rather tongue-kiss Al Sharpton than go to the Pequot Yacht Club," he snarled. "These people really have spent their lives being snotty and horrible to people. They live their own insulated, pretentious lives, and nobody's ever had any recourse with them. Well, fuck them. I don't care what they think. And if they ever fuck with me, I'll make their lives a fucking nightmare."

As the legitimacy of that threat sank in, the residents of Southport who had been offended by Imus's presence thought better of making a public issue of their distress. Indiscreetly put, nobody wanted to get into a pissing contest with Don Imus. In a war of words, Don was the Robert E. Lee of verbal assaults. Plus, he held the high ground—he had control of the microphone.

Later, Don would downplay his Hatfield-McCoy feud, claiming most of his on-air commentary was, again, just comic fodder, although he has admitted, "I have thin skin and a tender little ego." Which is why others weren't so sure the opinions expressed by the *Bridgeport Post*'s article hadn't stung Don more than he was willing to admit. "There's always a certain amount of truth in every shot he takes," commented NBC president Robert Wright. "You kind of have to sort it out for yourself."

Although Imus still got plenty of notoriety for the caustic commentary and pubescent humor that pervaded his show, he was also being recognized as a wily social and political satirist. In *GQ* magazine, Peter Richmond once called Imus "the closest thing we have to a modern H. L. Mencken. Imus is no shock jock. He's no Howard Stern. Stern has all the intellectual acuity of a farm boy who drinks an entire keg by himself and thinks he's profound and hilarious when, in fact, most people want him to shut the hell up.

"Imus, on the other hand, spends as much air time delving into the political as he does the libidinal—and he does his homework."

Imus at his best was when he brought both facets together, such as in a bit Charles McCord wrote for Larry Kenney to perform as Jeane Kirkpatrick—while speaking in a profoundly male voice. McCord had written the piece in response to the *New York Times*'s decision to name the alleged victim in the Kennedy rape case.

> And what is one of the salacious tidbits that the *Times* profile reported? That the alleged victim has a bad driving record. Hello, wake-up call! A newspaper doing a story involving Ted Kennedy commenting on someone else's performance behind the wheel? Earth to Chappaquiddick . . .

It was summa cum laude *Saturday Night Live* and it was about to get national exposure thanks to two turns of events, the first being Infinity Broadcasting buying WFAN. In a show of karma Imus must have appreciated, he and Howard Stern were once again working for the same company. Although they would remain separate but equal, Stern and Imus together would help make Infinity an even greater radio powerhouse than it already was. Infinity was owned by radio mogul Mel Karmazin, who had grown up in a Long Island housing project with his parents, who had emigrated from Eastern Europe. To support the family, his dad drove a cab and his mom worked in a curtainrod factory. Still, Karmazin says, "My family had zero money. We never had a vacation and we never had a car."

After high school Mel worked his way through college, attending only part-time until he earned a degree in business administration. His first job was selling radio ads for WCBS for a base salary of $17,500 plus commissions. He wasn't just good at his job, he was *too* good. He sold so many ads that management cut his commission rate. After he went on to earn $70,000 anyway, he was informed salesmen shouldn't make that much money. "It was the dumbest thing I'd ever heard in my life, so I quit."

Karmazin spent the next eleven years working for Metromedia, then in 1981 he took over control of Infinity, which at that time owned just three radio stations. Over the next several years, Karmazin increased Infinity's holdings, buying stations such as WFAN and the L.A.–based oldies station KRTH-FM. He also added sports broadcasts wherever possible because "we want programming that can't be replicated."

That nose for the unique is what led Karmazin to hire Howard Stern after he was let go by NBC. And why, after Infinity bought WFAN, Karmazin went out of his way to be solicitous to Imus. The first time they met, Imus let Karmazin know he would like a digital workstation in the studio because it would make producing some of the routines easier. Imus had made this request before, but the previous owners either couldn't or wouldn't comply. Not only did Imus get his new toy, Karmazin signed him to a five-year contract reported to be worth $12 million. (When that contract was up, Imus signed again with Karmazin, saying, "I know everybody from Sumner Redstone to Ted Turner, but I wouldn't have considered working for any-body else.")

But not even Karmazin could have predicted how much the unexpected opportunity afforded Imus by the United States going to war in the Persian Gulf earlier that year would ultimately benefit his investment. It was during that conflict, America's first techno-war, that Imus more boldly ventured into not just commentary but actual journalism. It was a time when Americans from all walks of life were glued to CNN's play-by-play, albeit at-a-distance, coverage, starved for information, because for the first time in modern history journalists were prohibited from being near the battle lines during an American conflict. This was the Bush administration's effort to sanitize the carnage United States fighter pilots and ground troops were wreaking on the Iraqi forces.

Imus jumped into the fray and began calling politicians and media pundits to appear on his show, based on whether or not Don thought they were compelling enough. "At first," he admits, "they were reluctant to come on the show because I had a Howard Stern reputation. But a few did agree, and among the early guests were then *New York Times* columnist Anna Quindlen and *Nightline's* Jeff Greenfield—both of whom became Imus favorites and still appear regularly on his program. It wasn't long before politicians, smelling a sound-bite op, also lined up to chat with the I-Man.

Just as Imus had come of radio age during a time when the country was undergoing a paradigm shift of mores, enabling him to stretch broadcast boundaries that would have previously been rigid, he adopted a more journalistic approach to his show as the explosion of cable and increased number of television networks was serving to homogenize news coverage. In a chorus of interchangeable media voices, Imus spoke out with singular distinction. Whether listeners "got" him or not, whether he was seen as being a refreshing dose of honesty or an obnoxious dilettante, was another issue.

For the most part, the politicians who braved a session with Imus believed the former. According to Eric Hauser, press secretary for Bill Bradley, Imus speaks "in common, practical terms." Plus, there was the not-so-insignificant matter of his audience. While Howard Stern might have a bigger listenership in terms of sheer number, Imus had the listeners politicians cared about. Not because of income or profession but because Don's listeners were much more apt to vote than Stern's. As comic Drew Carey once noted, "I don't think marijuana smokers get to the voting booth as often as they'd like to."

Journalists also knew an appearance on Imus could give them a hip panache they might otherwise lack. "When I speak to a group, nobody asks anymore about Clinton or *Nightline*," Greenfield commented early in his association with Imus. "They all want to know about Imus."

Quindlen explained she and Imus got along because "I think he's a feminist, which might surprise some people."

What the Gulf War afforded Imus, beyond a personal platform, was the opportunity to change the perception by nonlisteners that he was a Stern also-ran in style and content. Imus readily admits that prior to the Gulf War, *Imus in the Morning* "wasn't held in the esteem it is now by journalists and politicians."

The same man Cleveland newspaper columnists were trying to run out of town were now being greeted on the phone by the likes of Senator John Kerry, saying, "Hi, I-Man, how're you doing?" Broadcasting from New York, it would have been easy enough for politicians to come to the studio and appear on the show in person, but Imus preferred the distance of telephony. "I try not to have any actual personal contact with the politicians and mostly keep them on the phone."

Imus enjoyed talking to pols from all political persuasions, and once made the seemingly disingenuous claim that the only criterion to get on the show was that his guests "have to be smarter than I am. Sometimes we have to go pretty deep to find them."

But the complete fruition of *Imus in the Morning*'s Gulf War breakthrough wouldn't occur until the 1992 primaries and subsequent presidential election. As the New York primary neared, Imus spent much of his shows skewering the field of Democratic candidates, with particular attention paid to ridiculing Clinton's campaign. But there would be a sea change for both Imus and Clinton after then-Governor Clinton agreed to be on Don's show as a telephone guest. Clinton's political adviser, Paul Begala, later admitted that "it was a high-risk move," considering the loose-cannon nature of Imus's show.

James Carville, another of Clinton's strategists, says the decision was made to accept the *Imus in the Morning* challenge, as it were, "to show that Clinton was a hip guy and that although he was from Arkansas, he was someone who could come to the toughest thing in New York and, if you will, sort of play in that league."

It was apparent from the first moments that Clinton was going to be able to hold his own with Don.

"Good morning, Governor Clinton."
"Good morning, Don."
"How're you?"
"I'm all right. . . . I'm disappointed you didn't call me Bubba. It's an honorable term where I come from. It's just southern for mensch."

Clinton's quick wit and self-deprecation obviously appealed to Imus, who you could hear laughing over the mike.

"I read someplace where you do an Elvis impression. Is there any truth to that?"

"Well, when I've got my voice I do. I can barely talk today, but I used to know all the Elvis songs and all the Jordanaires' backgrounds. As age has taken my voice, though, I'm better on the Jordanaires than I am on Elvis."

Whether anyone likes to acknowledge it or not, one of the enduring prejudices in our country among most non-Southerners is that when we hear a distinct southern accent, there's a built-in assumption that the person speaking is somehow of lesser intelligence. Television, films, and stand-up comedians such as Jeff Foxworthy with his *You must be a redneck if . . .* routines have all sent the subliminal message that the South is more white trash than White House material. To New Yorkers listening to Clinton exchanging repartee with Imus, it was clear that Clinton was no rube. The appearance on Imus managed to humanize Clinton not only for New Yorkers in general but for Don personally. "I thought he was a bright guy and he was funny and spontaneous and he had no idea what we were going to talk about."

Imus himself was surprised to find out that when he was speaking to Clinton over the phone, "there was a *Nightline* crew in my studio and I didn't know this. And Ted Koppel was with Clinton in his hotel room when he called me. That was a big risk—he didn't know who I was. I could have said anything to him and I did, I talked about him sleeping with Roseanne. I said, 'Let me make this observation, Governor, and it's a sexist observation, but at least you're not being accused of sleeping with ugly women like Roseanne.'

"His response was good, he talked about what a great palimony suit he would have. But when you saw it on *Nightline*, you see ten or twelve guys sitting around the table there in the suite, and he's in his baseball hat and T-shirt, sitting there, talking on the phone, and they're all just kind of reading the paper and stuff, but when he said *palimony*, their heads all jerked around, not knowing what context he's talking in."

Not only did Clinton's appearance open doors for the future president, it was the springboard for Don to get his first national exposure. There was so much buzz in New York about the Clinton-Imus tête-à-tête that the *Today* morning show came knocking on Imus's door. Suddenly, there was Don chatting with Katie Couric and Bryant Gumbel for the whole country to see.

"I personally hope Clinton wins, because it means a lot to me personally, having endorsed him," Imus cracked to Couric.

"I'm sure that endorsement means a lot to New Yorkers as well."

"Unfortunately, it probably won't mean anything and it'll just mean further humiliation for me. It's been great fun for us because when these folks come to New York we get to beat them up for a week or two and we all have a sense of humor here, which is why a lot of us have bought the thirteen percent flat tax and been able to listen to some of Bill Clinton's explanations for some of the hideous things he's done in his life."

Then, in a moment of stunning prescience, Imus added, "I'm sure there's a couple of bags of laundry in his closet we could have looked at. I'm sure there's a number of things they could have found out about him but haven't gotten in to. If this primary were like next week, we could ruin these people's lives."

That was primary day, April 7, 1992. The next morning, with Clinton having been declared the winner and new front-runner, Imus was back on *Today*.

"I don't think he owes it to my endorsement. I do think the pivotal point of the campaign was when he appeared on this program last Thursday. At seven-nineteen last Thursday he was a dead man. A dead man. At seven-twenty-one he got into his Elvis impression. He then became a viable candidate and I think will go on to get the Democratic nomination." Then showing that not even the I-Man is right all the time, he added, "But he's not gonna be president."

Couric, who seemed as enamored with Imus as Clinton was, asked Don what advice he'd give the governor.

"I'd advise him to continue singing Elvis songs and imitating Elvis, but I would also advise him to stop eating like Elvis. Because this guy is one gravy sandwich away from being *with* Elvis."

While it's true Clinton shot up in the polls after he was on *Imus in the Morning*, whether or not Imus really had anything to do with his eventual win is debatable. Still, many credited the appearance with resuscitating Clinton's primary campaign, and Imus was more than happy to take credit. "I think he was going to win the New York primary anyway, but I do think it helped him a lot because he'd been beaten to death and nobody knew whether he had a sense of humor or not."

And as is true with everything, particularly politics, it's the perception that matters and with the lemming mind-set that all elected officials seem to possess, other politicians were soon following suit and just like that, Imus was a political player. Not everyone, however, understood the appeal, such as Leonard Shapiro of the *Washington Post*. "I admit that I don't get it. Why would somebody like Bill Clinton, a decent human being, go on a show where there are constant references to genitals and Jews and derogatory comments about blacks?"

The politicians who appeared on the program pragmatically pushed aside those concerns because *Imus in the Morning* was now a recognized hip place to be heard. And when the Democratic convention rolled into New York in July 1992, *Today* once again came a-calling. For those viewers who weren't familiar with Imus, it must have been confusing to hear him express his support of Clinton while simultaneously making fun of him.

"It's been painful for me to watch him, for example, jog,"

Don told an ever-attentive Katie Couric. "Man, you know, it's a mile and a half around the reservoir in the middle of Central Park and it should take a normal person about fifteen minutes to jog around it. It took the governor almost half an hour. It's been a gruesome sight. I actually ran around it once in twelve minutes. That's pretty good for an old guy, huh?

"You know, the best thing to come out of this Democratic convention is George Bush and Ted Williams walking out in the All-Star game and getting booed. I mean, if you're the president, and you've got Ted Williams and you're in the baseball game and you get booed, I think you got big problems."

But, as always, Imus's jabs were based on keen observations, some of which, heard in retrospect, border on the prophetic. "I do think he has a chance. You know, he doesn't bring to the table the same kind of integrity and moral authority that, for example, Governor Cuomo did last night, but I think he has a chance tonight.

"He has some baggage. We have this image of him being onstage with these two steamer trunks full of stuff and putting them down, but I really do think he has the chance to reintroduce himself to the American public. And you know, he's not a bad guy and a lot of people have made mistakes and this country is in horrible trouble and I don't know that he's necessarily the answer, but I do think he has a chance."

In November 1992, for the first time since Jimmy Carter's fall from grace, America elected a Democratic president. Clinton was also the youngest president since John F. Kennedy and was the first baby boomer. His election in part would forever, correctly or not, be tied in with Don Imus, who had grabbed the golden political ring as a result. "You know," he said, "I'm a very powerful and influential person."

It was a position he'd been waiting his entire life to be in. At fifty-two, he finally knew what he was going to be when he grew up.

Chapter Fifteen

IF IMUS'S PROFILE HAD RISEN THANKS TO CLINTON'S APPEARANCES ON his show while a Democratic candidate, it was gilded when now-President Clinton took the time for another live on-air chat in April 1993. This time his appearance would be simulcast on *Today*, once again exposing Imus to the national masses.

"If you haven't seen Imus, this may seem very out of place," Bryant Gumbel told his television audience.

"And even if you have, it still may seem very out of place," interjected Katie Couric.

"But it's his stock-in-trade and he does very well with it," Gumbel continued. "He's obviously very bright, very witty, and very irreverent, and the President enjoys that. And he's obviously come to the conclusion that it would serve him well" to appear on *Imus in the Morning* as commander in chief.

Clinton's adviser, Paul Begala, explained why. "Imus has incredible reach and that's why his show is important. It's not some tribal ritual of Washington that only insiders watch, or the media elite, like *Crossfire*. You go on Imus and reach everybody. In Washington, I'm known as Bill Clinton's adviser. In New Jersey, where the entire state listens to his show, I'm the guy who goes on *Imus*."

While waiting for the call to the Astoria studios to be put through, President Clinton explained the appeal Imus had for him. "I've enjoyed talking with him in the past and, as you pointed out earlier, he did endorse me in the New York primary. He's got an enormous listening audience of people who talk about politics in the course of other things in life. He's also on an all-sports radio station, so there are people who listen to him who may not follow every in and out of development here in Washington, so I think it gives me a chance to reach a different sort of audience. And I also think he's an interesting man. I just enjoy him."

While Clinton was talking, the phone call to Imus had been established and a somewhat nervous-sounding Couric mentioned that they were cutting in on Don's time. With no pleasantries directed at the *Today* hosts, Don addressed Clinton.

"Good morning, Mr. President."

"Good morning, how are you?"

"I'm fine. How are you?"

"I'm all right."

"Let me ask you something. What the hell is going on down there in that White House? What do you mean you've 'lost your focus'?"

"I haven't lost my focus, you've just been seeing me through the foggy lens of television instead of the direct way of radio. There's a big headline in the *Washington Post* today, *Clinton Wins Third Major Victory in Congress*. I think we're doing fine. But you know, we lost one bill and a lot of people think it's like the last days of Pompeii. If you fight for change, you gotta be prepared to lose a few as well as win some. But I think we're well on track. . . .

"There's always going to be people who want to be in control, and some days I'd like to give it to them. If I did that, at least I'd have a telephone conversation with you before I'd give it up so you can call me President Bubba. I've been waiting for that all this time."

"Mr. President, I don't know what you've heard about what's been going on with this program, but it's always been very respectful, and anything you've heard to the contrary would just be further evidence of the collapse of the intelligence community."

For the next twenty minutes or so, Imus engaged Clinton in a wide-ranging discussion, covering topics from the economy and defense to foreign relations and the grim situation in Bosnia, which was undergoing "ethnic cleansing" while the world watched.

Clinton also let himself be led into a discussion of sex, with Imus fixated on the story of the Astro Turf in the bed of Clinton's old pickup. When the President played it coy, Imus prodded him. "Frankly, Mr. President, that's a little like saying you didn't inhale."

"Let's just say," Clinton lobbed back, "I didn't inhale in the back of the pickup."

Although that last bit of repartee would come back to haunt Clinton, once again both he and Imus afforded themselves well. Although the President would still endure some rough political days ahead, the appearance gave him a platform to discuss issues in detail and a forum where he could solidify his position—and not just to Imus's listening audience but Today's national audience.

For Imus, now making $3 million a year, it was another feather of validation in his cap. He believed his success mostly "had a lot to do with the people who we have on. It's the mixture of the people I interview, the nature of the interviews." And as far as his clout as a political player, Imus didn't hedge. "In some cases it can make the difference between getting elected and not getting elected."

If there had been any lingering doubt as to the difference between Howard Stern and Don Imus at this point in their careers, the April 1993 presidential interview resolved it once and for all. Imus's resurrection and transformation was complete, and now he was more comfortable drawing the distinctions between himself and his broadcast rival.

About the only similarity Imus saw was that "we work for the same company now, Infinity Broadcasting, and we used to work together back at NBC in New York. Lots of times they sell the advertising as a combo. I don't listen to him because I'm on the air at the same time. Plus, I have an education. No, I don't listen to the radio, but I have listened to him. He's entertaining and he has at least twice as many listeners as I do. I think he's funny sometimes. It would be hard for me to disparage him if he makes me laugh sometimes. I mean, though, I'm not going to go on an awards show as Fartman. There are just some of those things I won't do, but that's subjective. That doesn't make it not funny."

All that said, Don would reiterate and hone in on the overall intelligence-quotient disparity between their listening audience. "I don't know what the difference is, but I think if you wanted to draw a distinction between me and Howard Stern, you would at least have to have a GED to listen to me. I'm Howard Stern with a vocabulary. I'm the man he wishes he could be. I have a greater interest in talking to Anna Quindlen or Nina Totenberg or Bob Dole than I do Jessica Hahn or Joey Buttafuoco.

"That's not to suggest one is necessarily any more valid in terms of either their interest value or entertainment value, it's just *my* interests. My interests change. And I'm comfortable getting older. I don't try to pretend I'm thirty. I'm fifty-two. That's what I am. My show's just more sophisticated. I don't do this show based on what I think people want to hear. I do it based on what I'm interested in. I've always done it that way.

"They do these qualitative surveys of all the radio programs in New York and we skew higher with people who make more money, who've had more education, have more managerial kinds of jobs, more professional people and those kinds of things. But that's not to suggest he doesn't have some of those people, because he does. His audience isn't exclusively low-rent morons. I know some people who listen to both of us. I know some fairly bright people who listen to him."

But when asked point-blank by Bob Costas during a television interview if it bothered him that a show like Stern's had more listeners than Don's estimated one million plus, Imus didn't dodge the question. "Yeah," he acknowledged, then added, "I hate *everybody* who's on in the morning."

But there was little Don had to worry about from his other competitors. Not only had Don become recognized as an influential talk radio host because of his guest list, he was also being hailed for something suspiciously close to wisdom, such as when George Vecsey, the *New York Times* sports columnist, called him "the poet laureate of morning drive."

Washington Post media critic Howard Kurtz thought it was more primal than poetical. "He just comes on and gives you pure ego. Or pure id. And there's something weirdly compelling about that."

Others simply marveled at his personal maturation.

"It's been very interesting to watch his evolution," says his former boss Randy Bongarten. "He's developed from a guy who basically said very outrageous things on the radio to a personality who's almost a contemporary philosopher."

Make that a philosopher with a healthy public ego. "I've become a king maker," he said, tongue tickling cheek. "I only endorse people when I'm positive they're going to win, so that I can take full credit for the victory."

He was also quoted as saying "Here's the evolution of radio: Marconi invented it and I decided to talk on it."

But as always with Don, behind the facetious comments and megalomaniacal bravado lay a certain element of self-awareness. Don *was* an influential figure to many of his listeners and through his show he *did* have the power to help make or break a fragile candidacy. But he also knew not to mistake pandering for respect, so he never stopped doling out his pointed jabs and barbed comments out of concern that he might offend. Even though his success had made him an apparent insider among many circles, his cowboy mentality ensured he would not let success make him go soft. If anything, he felt even freer to say what he thought because he knew the people who came on his show needed to be there more than he needed them there.

"It's pathetic, isn't it?" Imus asks happily.

So for all the external success, daily life on *Imus in the Morning* went on, business as usual.

Donald Trump: "A hideous, transparent goon, an unctuous, gauzy, pumping twit."

Rush Limbaugh: "He'll be long gone, and I'll still be here."

Howard Stern: "I'm no big fan of that boner-nosed meathead, disgraceful idiot."

Newt Gingrich: "Doesn't he look like a guy who'd barbecue road kill? It's like he would run over something and then eat it. I mean, I'm sure he's a nice guy but . . ."

Kenny Rogers: "He's horrid."

"You sometimes get the impression that because Imus has been through so much—drugs, alcohol, being fired from jobs—that he's beyond any sense of danger," notes Howard Kurtz. "That he can say whatever he wants and feel he can get away with it."

Which, according to Jeff Greenfield, was precisely the point. "With Imus there's no restraining impulse, so he appeals to a lot of people who wish they could let the beast run free."

Not only was Don peddling free-wheeling political influence on his show, he was also using his radio pulpit to make his brother Fred a comfortably wealthy man by hawking a line of

Auto-Body Express mail order merchandise over the air, an enterprise Fred says "just happened by accident."

In late 1992, Fred had one hundred T-shirts printed to try to help promote his El Paso auto-body paint business. After Don gave away fifty shirts on the radio one day, listeners jammed the phone lines wanting to know where they could buy their very own T-shirt, and an entrepreneur was born. Within months Fred was selling hundreds of items a day, which would be expanded to include mugs, caps, and even salsa.

The younger Imus was savvy enough to know that it was his familial association with Don that made his merchandise so sought after. "Being the brother of somebody rich and famous, hey, I was the brother of somebody poor, and I like this a whole lot better. I want Don to work until he's eighty, otherwise our salsa business will go to hell."

Even though Fred is tucked away in El Paso, people regularly make pilgrimages to his shop. "We're right by I-10, so a lot of people from back east actually come by the shop to get shirts and mugs. And a lot of people won't buy anything unless I talk to them personally."

But when talking to potential customers, Fred was strictly low key and soft sell. The most aggressive sales pitch might be to observe that "the cap makes a great Easter basket if you turn it upside down."

For Don, promoting the Auto-Body Express line was the chance to do a good turn for the person he loved most in the world. It also gave him new material. One of his favorite taunts was to insinuate that many of Fred's customers were Texas-border drug dealers. "A lot of my brother's business is in cash."

But Fred was always able to more than hold his own with big brother. "I saw you on the Brinkley show yesterday," he said during one of his phone-in appearances. "Did you slouch down so they couldn't see the logo on your shirt? You're turning into a wimp. You're not tough like you used to be. You've lost that hard edge. Sam Donaldson loves you."

Although Fred was unarguably more laid back than Don and admittedly far less ambitious, he was just as quick-witted and would frequently turn the tables on Don and make him the straight man.

"All your stuff is made in the U.S.A., not in some sweatshop in Asia," Don once noted while plugging the clothes.

"That's right," Fred concurred. "It's made in a sweatshop in El Paso."

By the time the business was less than two years old, Auto-Body Express would sell over 100,000 items, none priced under $19.57—almost two million dollars in gross sales. And as *Imus in the Morning* expanded its reach beyond the coterie of states reached by WFAN's signal, Fred would soon be selling his salsa as fast as he could make it.

In July 1993, Unistar Radio Networks started syndicating the show nationwide, shortly after the network was bought by Westwood One, Inc., which is managed by Infinity Broadcasting. According to Kirk Stirland, then senior vice president, affiliate relations, Infinity-owned Westwood One Radio Networks, the decision to syndicate Imus was based on the ratings history he had racked up covering three decades of broadcasting.

"Imus had all the right stuff for national syndication: a consistent billings and ratings success story in a big market, good recognizability to radio people and listeners, and a show with a brilliant ability to make you laugh as well as think. We figured you couldn't miss that—and we didn't."

Sam Michaelson, a senior vice president at Zenith Media, added that Imus was "a better personality, he's not as controversial and he's better produced."

Although Imus was still considered controversial, he was not considered obscene. The same, at least from the government's point of view, could not be said about Stern. While it was precisely Stern's crudeness that appealed to his listeners, his raunchy escapades on air had resulted in the Federal Communications Commission levying record fines in excess of a million dollars against his employer, Infinity, for what they considered "indecency." It also threatened to revoke Infinity's broadcasting license. Most problematic to Mel Karmazin, the FCC would put on hold Infinity's acquisition of three FM stations for $170 million because of its objections to Stern.

Broadcasting is the only segment of the American press that is licensed and regulated by the federal government. Historically, the FCC has been judicious in flexing its muscle regarding broadcasters, usually trying to keep radio kid-friendly during hours when children might be listening. Stern was targeted because of comments such as:

> AIDS baby, come here. You know, the big know-nothing Barbara Bush. Can't even speak up to her husband about abortion. Anyway, so I'm reading *People* magazine, then I get upset by that, so I lay down, and I figure, well, I gotta masturbate.

The last time the FCC got so riled was back in 1959, when an announcer at a Denver station joked:

> Say, did you hear about the guy who goosed the ghost and got a handful of sheet?

In that case, when the FCC threatened to revoke the station's license, the announcer was immediately fired. But Infinity refused to muzzle Stern and refused to pay the fine, so the FCC felt it had no choice but to make an example of Stern and it wasn't long before some politicians got involved in the fray. Representative Jim Moran (D-Va.) accused FCC chairman Reed

Hundt for not levying Infinity with even bigger fines. "If you're going to hit 'em, hit 'em hard."

Stern responded by rabble-rousing his audience. "Moran is our enemy. Let's get this guy out of office!"

But after trying to fight the fines in court, Karmazin eventually paid up in the guise of a $1.75 million "voluntary contribution" to the government in exchange for Infinity getting a clean slate. Karmazin's decision to settle the case was strictly pragmatic. "I had a business to run."

Karmazin had no such legal worries, and no such financial expenditures, with Don. *Imus in the Morning* was his cash cow. To start, *Imus in the Morning* was syndicated on thirty stations in twenty-three markets, including Boston and, of course, Washington, D.C. In Boston, Imus aired on WEEI, another sports-talk radio format. Phil Sirkin, the programming director in 1993, said after Imus was picked up, the station went from twenty-first to eighth in the morning drive time. And among men twenty-five to fifty-four, WEEI rose to third.

"Imus was certainly the missing ingredient. At most sports stations you have a problem finding a morning show that fits with the format. But the Imus show carries its own weight and amplifies the rest of the format."

It was a scenario that would be repeated over and over, and it quickly laid to rest some concern that had been voiced over whether or not Imus would "play" outside New York. "People don't turn off Letterman because he does his show from New York and makes a lot of references to New York," Sirkin pointed out. "New York doesn't have to mean boring to people outside New York when a show is handled by a professional like Imus."

Now that Imus was a verified, rehabilitated-comeback-kid success story, his publisher, Simon & Schuster, decided the time was right to reissue Don's book, *God's Other Son*. In 1987, Pocket Books, the publisher's mass market imprint, had released a paperback edition, and it was after being on tour for that release that Don had come back to New York and gone on his nine-day binge that led to Hazelden.

Even though Imus had effectively retired Billy Sol from his repertoire, Simon & Schuster felt the time was right, based on Don's increased profile, to release a $22 hardback edition.

His first experience with the world of publishing had left Don cold because he never believed the book had been promoted properly. "I thought they should have done a better job, and now they are. . . ." Of course, there was also the matter that back then, Don wasn't the most reliable of souls, it being at the apex of his drinking and drug use. But this time around, between the publisher's marketing commitment and his millions of loyal listeners, *God's Other Son* became a solid best seller.

Even though he didn't have to, Don appeared at book signings, explaining, "Well, you know I do like it. You get to see who listens to you. And if you agree to do one of these things, you gotta be enthusiastic about it," he told a reporter, then added in an Imus aside, "I mean, I'm honest about it. I'd just as soon run over 'em in the limo."

When asked to comment on Howard Stern's number-one best-selling autobiography, *Private Parts*, Imus critiqued it as "vile." Imus said at the time that he, too, was writing another book, tentatively titled *Imus Unabridged*, that had a 1995 publishing date. The book was to be a collection of essays written with "exquisite literary quality," and filled with plenty of laughs.

As Imus gradually insinuated himself more into the national consciousness, others in the media began to try to dissect Don and fit him into easily classified, orderly categories. But as a 1993 *Newsday* profile noted:

> The trick is not to search for consistency. The I-Man doesn't like consistency. Consistency is for the hideous, small-minded

dorks and stooges who think life is a set piece. Imus voted for Clinton but digs Bob Dole. Cuomo is swell, and so is D'Amato. Handguns should be outlawed, he says, but notes that he owns a .357 Magnum and packs a .32 snub-nosed revolver at all times.

Q. Why do you carry the .32?
A. In case I have to shoot somebody.
Q. But you go to and from the studio in a limousine.
A. I may want to knock over a [expletive deleted] minimart.
Q. Can you show me the gun?
A. I'm going to shoot you with it if you don't move on.

Imus's pique aside, the article's point was well taken. Even though most thoughtful and honest individuals are acutely aware of their own incongruities of personality and beliefs, it's a human paradox that we insist on trying to define others with broad strokes and superficial labels. Imus refused to be pinned down, and in so doing managed to protect and retain his essence. When told that Imus claimed to have voted twice for Reagan and for Bush in 1988, Anna Quindlen responded with a surprised "Well, he must be a liberal Republican, then."

The point was, it didn't really matter what Don Imus believed in. As long as he got others thinking about what they believed in and entertained them in the process, he was doing his job.

Between the show, the television appearances, and his literary commitments, Imus was running on all cylinders. Despite his jammed schedule, since his stay at Hazelden, Don's absenteeism on the show had fallen to zero. So it was ironic that just two months into being syndicated, Imus would miss work. But this time he had a legitimate excuse. While relaxing at his house in Southport, Imus's lung collapsed on August 2, 1993. After being treated at New York Hospital–Cornell Medical Center,

Imus was cleared to go home. But two weeks later, on August 15, his lung collapsed again and he was admitted to St. Vincent's Medical Center in Bridgeport.

"I feel fine, except that the thing went down again," Imus told *Newsday* from his hospital bed. "The lung is back up now, but I guess I'll be in the hospital a few more days."

A St. Vincent's spokesman sought to assuage the concerns of Imus fans by issuing the following statement: "His condition is satisfactory, all vital signs are stable, and the prognosis is favorable."

Despite the obvious discomfort he must have been in, Imus still had his wits about him, calling into his show via the phone in his hospital room and having on-air chats with McCord. In addition to noting which politicians had sent him get well wishes and expressing annoyance over the way gift baskets were wrapped, he also noted, "I've learned that not a lot of models gave up careers to be nurses."

Not so amusing was the diagnosis, made after Imus was transferred back to New York Hospital, that surgery was necessary to prevent a recurrence. On September 3, doctors cut an incision that went from Imus's chest to his back. Although he was in good physical shape, the surgery took its toll, and nearly two months later he was still feeling weak and sore, complaining, "I'm in more pain than I should be," and taking pain medication to alleviate his aching body.

In addition to the pain, he had trouble bending over and was easily chilled, but even so, Imus missed only a handful of days at work. He compensated for his ailments by furnishing his office with a portable electric heater and by being marginally crankier than usual, not in small measure due to his craving a cigarette that no amount of nicotine gum seemed to quell. But even when he was the picture of health, Imus was still subject to fits of unreasonable anger; although he was stone cold sober, it didn't necessarily mean his temperament had improved.

"The hell with Koch," he snapped one day when someone suggested the former mayor as a guest. "Koch blew us off. He's done."

It was such days that prompted Bernard McGuirk to sigh that sometimes coming to work was "like wandering into Hitler's bunker," adding that when Don was on edge, "it's like having a gun pressed to your head all day long. He can say he never shot you, but the gun is still there."

Martha Sherrill, who suffered at the hands of Don while researching a profile on Imus for *Esquire,* believes "he's angry in the way that a lot of former drunks are angry. He has the kind of anger as though he were wishing he were still drinking, maybe. Wishing the world were a different place."

It was small consolation to his staff that Imus doled out his ill temper equally to guests when the mood struck. One day Regis Philbin was scheduled to do the show so he could promote a benefit he was hosting for his high-school alma mater, Cardinal Hayes, in the Bronx. As arranged, Philbin called Imus at eight-thirty but was told by an assistant that the show was running commercials and asked Philbin to call back in four minutes.

Instead, Philbin waited six minutes, and in so doing, enraged Imus, because while two minutes seems insignificant to most people, it's a lot of air time in radio to fill. So because he didn't follow his instructions exactly, Imus never put him on the air and informed his audience that Philbin was just "an old queen with a TV show" while suggesting that Regis was also a cross-dresser. Rather than get into a game of one-upsmanship, Philbin chose to joke about the incident later on *Regis & Kathie Lee.*

But Koch's or Philbin's loss was another's gain. From then-Governor Mario Cuomo to singer/songwriter Paul Simon to former George Bush campaign official Mary Matalin to authors and newsmen, Imus ordered his staff to find guests that fit the *Imus in the Morning* bill, which meant just about anyone other than actors. Imus admits that his staff complains that he features "too many politicians, that the show is too abstruse." But Imus has little regard for thespians. "The Alec Baldwins of the world, it's frightening how stupid they are."

Elitist or not, few chose to disagree.

"He knows what's up," commented Jeff Greenfield.

"He sparks new sunbursts of thought in my mind," Dan Rather said in that peculiar Dan Rather way.

Not that Don was always on the mark, mind you, but he still sounded more intelligent than most when making a faulty prediction, such as when he endorsed David Dinkins for mayor of New York over Rudolph Giuliani, even though he did add the disclaimer that Giuliani "wouldn't be horrible either." Nor did Imus's prediction that James Florio would be the next New Jersey governor instead of Christine Whitman pan out. Worried that Imus was on a bad roll, Bob Dole rubbed salt in the I-Man's political wounds by calling and asking Don to please not support him should he decide to run for president in 1996.

That call merely further endeared Dole to Imus, who had revealed to Katie Couric that he would vote for the then-senator "in a heartbeat" if he ran for president. "I have enormous respect for Senator Dole. I just think, having had—and I wouldn't describe it as anything other than an honor to meet him and spend some time with him when we were in Washington. He's an extraordinary human being and a marvelous person personally. You know, they talk about Bob Dole's dark side, but he's a marvelously witty, smart guy. He's got a great sense of humor.

"Obviously there's some of his politics that folks may not agree with, that I may not agree with, and the same goes with Bill Clinton, but he's personally and extraordinarily ethical, a moral person, one of the most extraordinary people I've ever met. I don't think anybody's going to accuse Senator Dole of taking his pants off in a hotel room.

"I'm not one of those people," Imus added, "who thinks it's his turn to be president."

In fact, when Bill Clinton's approval ratings were at their lowest in the autumn of 1994 and the Republicans took over Congress in the Democratic bloodbath known as the midterm elections, Imus refused to join in the feeding frenzy against the President, even if his opinion wasn't the most popular at the time.

"I am a fan of his," he said on *The Today show*, "and I think even folks like us who revel not only in his agony but everyone else's acknowledge he hasn't gotten the credit for a lot of the things he's done. It's been a rocky two years, this was a humiliating defeat for Democrats and probably for him personally, I think a lot of people would agree. But not to be just a Bill Clinton suckup, but most folks, even those who don't like him don't think he's gotten a fair shake and gotten the credit for a number of good things he has done."

Imus has said his philosophy of interviewing was simply to get people "to reveal a part of themselves. I like to get people in a position where their defenses are down. You tend to get real answers then," such as when Senator John Kerry from Massachusetts commented that "Steve Forbes is Ross Perot without thirty-five voices going on in his head. Think about it." However, Kerry notes that Imus doesn't like his guests *too* polished. "You may want to think up a good line, but he'll clip you if you're too pre-prepped."

NBC's Andrea Mitchell says Imus is able to "get us to say what we really think."

Cokie Roberts equates it to "the conversation you have with your sources before the mike goes on, before it gets all solemn and kabuki-like."

Whittling down someone's defenses can also lull them into making the occasional embarrassing faux pas. Imus was delighted the day Alfonse D'Amato called then-Defense Secretary Les Aspin a "jackass" over the situation in Somalia. "I thought he was fucking fabulous!" In an alarming display of not learning his lesson, D'Amato would later incur the wrath of Japanese Americans everywhere for his Charlie Chan-esque imitation of "little Judge (Lance) Ito," who presided over the O. J. Simpson murder trial. That display of thoughtless humor resulted in the senator making a public apology the next day on the floor of the Senate.

By 1994, *Imus in the Morning* was reaching an estimated nine million listeners. And in almost every market where the show was broadcast, the station enjoyed an increase in either overall ratings or demographic share. More than just being glory to WFAN and money to Infinity and Westwood One, Imus was shoring up AM radio in general.

"He's just been really good for radio," believes Terry Nelson, Don's longtime friend who had left New York for a job in San Francisco. "He saved a lot of AM radio stations from going completely belly-up with his talent, it brought recognition to AM radio that literally saved radio stations, saved AM radio. He's one of the two or three people we credit with saving AM radio or else all of AM radio would be nothing more than sports and talk. It's high praise and the honest truth."

But for as good as Imus had been for radio, for as fulfilled as he was with his work, there had been a noticeable void in Don's life. Then, when he least expected it, Don found the woman who would make the Imus heart melt.

Chapter Sixteen

FOR YEARS, LISTENERS HAD HEARD DON IMUS FORSWEAR THE DESIRE to ever get married again. He had dated a number of women, but joked how he was waiting to marry a cross between "Anna Quindlen, Martha Stewart, and the woman from Voyeur Vision." That, of course, was until he met a woman who was actually a cross between Jim Ryan, Oscar de la Hoya, and Cindy Crawford. Deirdre Coleman was a twenty-seven-year-old aspiring model and actress who first met Don "while literally just walking down the street."

"Yeah," Imus likes to say, "she was being accosted by six thugs and I leaped out of the limo and came to her rescue," to which Coleman just laughs.

Deirdre had attended Villanova on a track scholarship and once out of school supported herself by alternately working as a model-actress and personal trainer. "Then, about six months later"—in November 1992, Coleman recalls—"I was on his show, in a modeling contest, some cheesy thing."

"What do you mean, some cheesy thing we were doing?" Don interrupts, feigning shock.

"It was for models who were also into sports, like boxing; if you were hip enough and up-to-date on what was going on in boxing. And I was." In fact, a year later Deirdre would be featured in a newspaper article about the growing popularity of boxing as a workout sport for everyday folk from housewives to Wall Street executives. The piece followed Coleman doing a workout at the legendary Gleason's Gym in Brooklyn, which the reporter notes:

> . . . is packed with sweat-soaked boxers sparring, shadow-boxing, pummeling speed bags, and jumping rope. Off in the corner, the one they call "the Animal" is taking out the frustrations of the day on a 100-pound heavy bag. Right hook, boom! Left hook, boom! Uppercut, boom! At 5 foot 8 and 122 pounds, Deirdre Coleman is barely winded. That may explain the nickname.

"There is nothing as physically or mentally challenging as boxing," enthused Coleman, who had taken up the sport three years earlier. "It's like playing chess."

A chess-playing model who can whip someone's butt with a mean left jab . . . no wonder Imus was smitten. Actually, Coleman now says that it was pretty much love at first sight. When Don tends to downplay his initial attraction, Coleman needles him. "You're always in denial about all this stuff."

Partly because in the beginning Don did his best to try to talk himself out of his feelings. Deirdre was literally young enough to be his daughter, and in fact she *was* younger than his two adopted children. So for a long time Don settled for being just friends with Coleman.

"We knew each other for at least a year before we ever went out because, to be serious, I thought, *She's too much younger.* I thought it was ridiculous. It doesn't bother me anymore, but it did bother me."

Plus, Deirdre says, Don "also thought I was younger than I really was."

Even so, there was not only a twenty-five-year age difference between them, but their life experiences had been vastly disparate. She was a health-conscious athlete looking to establish herself in a career, and he was a recovering drug addict and alcoholic who had enjoyed not one but two opportunities, as a music deejay and as a radio talk show host, to be recognized by many as the best in his particular field. Many times a May–December romance, such as the headline-grabbing relationship between Jerry Seinfeld and Shoshanna Lonstein, becomes victim not so much of age as expectations. When one life, chock full of experiences, is ready to wind down and the other life, just gearing up, is craving to experience what the other already has, often the gears strip; what they individually need and want out of life just simply doesn't mutually mesh. So, being the thoughtful man he was, it makes sense Imus would think long and hard before entering into a relationship with a woman who had been a three-year-old when he got his first radio job in Palmdale, California, as a married father of four.

"I wasn't running around looking for a younger woman, but I fell in love with her. She's interesting, funny, and smart. She's one of the best people that I've ever known. I mean, aside from being in love with her, she's just a great person. You can say anything to her. What was I supposed to do?" he asks, then adds, "What can I do? She's in love with me."

For Coleman, the years between them was simply not an issue. "He is the sweetest, most charming, adorable, compassionate, warm, extremely affectionate. I love him a lot. I love him more than anything. I don't think the age difference is a factor. I don't see the age difference. I forget."

Imus jokes that sometimes he wishes she *would* see the age difference. "I have to remind her, 'You know, honey, I'm twenty-five years older than you and I'm tired.' "

Once Don set aside his worries over their ages, he fell fast and he fell hard and soon proposed to Coleman by, according to one report, having a talking doll made that when the string was pulled asked, "Would you marry me?"

As usual, one man's gain is another's loss, and in this case the other man was Coleman's ex-boyfriend, Alan Nathan. Imus has admitted to hiring a security guard to make sure Nathan left Coleman alone, implying that he was in some way harassing her—an implication with which Nathan takes issue, saying he "didn't appreciate reading," what Imus had said about him.

Although he is reluctant to give many details of what he says was their six-year relationship, Nathan does say he believes he and Don "overlapped," although it took him a while to realize it because "I am a relatively trusting person and actresses do go out with various people, go out with friends to promote their career. I have no problem with that. I have no problem with Don Imus. I'm sure he was led to believe something by Deirdre."

According to Nathan, after he realized she was seeing someone else, "I asked her to leave but I put her up at a friend's place as parting couples do." Nathan says he went to talk to Coleman but says, "I don't think there was a great deal of honesty going on. When I talked to her, everything was more or less fine." Then he says the next thing he knew, "a bodyguard showed up in the lobby and I was accused of molesting her."

Nathan suspects he might have just been caught in the cross fire. "I think what actually transpired was that Imus was calling all evening and was very annoyed with her." But Alan says he'll never know for sure because Don "wouldn't confront me." As far as he's concerned, the whole incident was blown out of proportion and he says he was never a threat to Coleman and wishes her and Don well.

But aside from Nathan's concern over his reputation, the Imus-Coleman union seem to elicit only good cheer and unending ribbing. As soon as their engagement became known, Imus endured a lot of teasing from the I-Posse, who would do things like play a snippet from the commercial where the little girl asks, *Can I marry you, Grandpa?* After a lifetime of giving it out, Imus showed he could take it as well and laughed with obvious delight. Others, like Tim Russert, would call Deirdre "a living saint." But Fred perhaps got to an important essence of their relationship when he noted, "She can laugh at Don, who's not always easy to live with."

Coleman agrees. "I make fun of him all the time. Half the time that's what we do. I make fun of him, he makes fun of me, and we make fun of everybody."

And never one to miss a comic opportunity, Don made fun at his own expense. "There was a question of whether I should adopt her or marry her," he has said. "She's already practicing wiping the oatmeal off my chin."

Apparently, however, not everyone thought Deirdre had filled the void in Don's life. Whether a reflection of her attitude toward his then fiancée, a genuine concern over her father's well-being, or a sign that his relationship with his children was still occasionally turbulent, Don told *Esquire* that his daughter Ashleigh called to tell him "how self-destructive I am. How obviously unhappy I am."

But to all appearances, Don was anything but unhappy. Especially when he and Deirdre were married December 17, 1994, in a small ceremony held on a Navajo Indian reservation near Four Corners in the heart of the land that Don felt was his soul's true home. The symbolism was fitting, because in Coleman, he had apparently found his heart.

Although Don would say things like "There's nothing like a good-looking woman loving you back," which smacked of superficiality, his feelings about his marriage were anything but that. "I mean, I don't want to sound like a sap about my marriage, but it's somebody to talk to about everything. Somebody you learn stuff from."

The age issue now is brought up mostly for laughs, such as when Imus is making jokes in *People* magazine about playing ride the horsie with her. Also in that interview, Deirdre was quoted as saying, "I do like it when he reads to me. He tells me these *really* bizarre bedtime stories like 'Little Red Riding Hood' or 'The Three Bears,' in a very modern version." It's an amusing thought to imagine Don pulling out old Crazy Bob routines from years past to entertain his bride.

But there were aspects of Don's life that Coleman did influence, at least partly. She tried to get Don to eat only "pure foods." She has also said that she and Don "don't eat anything that's been killed or trapped or hunted," although he's been known to taunt her by eating a hot dog on air.

If Don fancied himself a runner before, boasting to Katie Couric of his time around the Central Park reservoir, he'd met his match in Coleman, for whom running was a passion. And thanks to her newfound higher profile, she was able to combine her love of running with causes close to her heart, such as her participation in the Race for the Cure, held in Central Park, which hoped to raise awareness and money for breast cancer research, with many of the participants survivors of the disease, including men.

"It was overwhelming," Coleman said at the 1994 event, prior to her marriage to Don. "My grandmother is a breast cancer survivor for thirty-five years. So this is a very emotional thing for me."

At the time, Coleman was in training for her first New York City Marathon and Imus was on hand to cheer her on and act as ad hoc publicity guy. When a *Newsday* reporter asked Deirdre her time for the 5K course, Don answered, "Fifteen-oh-two!" which would have made Coleman a world-class runner. Her actual time of under twenty minutes was still very respectable.

And as she would prove on the next two New York City Marathons, she was a serious runner and competitor. "The first year she ran it," Imus says, "she ran it in four-twenty, and the next year she ran it in three-thirty." Don went on to say that he and Fred figured, if she kept improving her time proportionally, "she could win it because the women who win it run it in two-twenty, two-twenty-five." Coleman just laughed.

If listeners, or Infinity management, worried that love would mellow Don Imus, they didn't understand the I-Man very much. Although incredibly tender when speaking of his wife and partner, and despite his admission that "I'm not nearly as angry as I used to be," Don's critical eye and sharp tongue had lost none of their edge. His bite could still be just as bad as his bark. None of which bothered Coleman. When asked once if she thought her husband and his show went over the top, she laughed. "Oh, no, I like it. I get it."

Nor had wedded bliss made Don any less moody or less apt to come in with a short fuse threatening to fire everyone in sight, whether they worked for Don or not. "He's not mellow," Coleman says. "He hasn't changed, really. He's very much like he is on the air. He can be grouchy if something's bothering him. But I'm probably worse than he is."

What his newfound personal happiness provided Don was the security that comes from being loved. Rather than temper him, it made Imus more jovially prickly. "The purpose of this show," he proclaimed, "is to goad people into saying hideous things about other people that end up on the newscast, to perpetuate a feud or to create one." Especially those politicos who were running for office.

But Imus emphasized that the show's foundation was still cemented in entertainment when he stressed that politicians "are on only if they bring something to the program in terms of just being willing to play ball and if they have some information and are willing to say something hideous about other people. The candidates think that by getting on the program and humanizing themselves it's gonna help. Well, maybe it does. But I don't put them on to help their political careers," says Imus.

Maybe not, but in many cases that was indeed the result, because Imus had the knack for getting people to drop their carefully composed public faces. "He gets to talk to people as if they're just sitting in a bar somewhere as opposed to the kind of formal, careful, guarded interviews you see on so many television talk shows," opined Howard Kurtz, who in 1996 would write a book, *Hot Air: All Talk, All the Time*, about the often dysfunctional relationship between the media and politics.

Esquire's Martha Sherrill agreed. "He makes them look like human beings. He makes them look like funny, cool, wonderful people who you might even allow in your house."

CNN's senior analyst, Jeff Greenfield, believes "for a lot of people, going on Imus is a way for them to be a different person."

However, the risk anyone ran appearing on Imus's show was that if they didn't measure up to Imus's double standard of having to be both smart and witty, they could find themselves on the receiving end of an Imus thumbs-down, such as then-Governor William Weld did. "What a dud," Imus announced. "He wouldn't play."

Exactly why a politician was willing to be an Imus-certified dud again was a function of both wanting to reach his upscale audience, which included a whole lot of people who are statistically more apt to vote, and, according to Imus, because "people appear on my program because they just don't want me to make fun of them. . . . It's fear." And, he added, "It has some value to them."

In April 1994, *Imus in the Morning* lost one of the show's most comedically mined politicians when Richard Nixon passed away, a man who had survived as many professional deaths and resurrections as Imus had. For several days, the I-Posse discussed whether or not Larry Kenney's Nixon should be buried with the once-disgraced ex-president. "A decision hasn't been made yet," Imus announced, "but I think this is it." But in the end he just couldn't bear to bury Nixon and the now-dead president remains in the program's repertoire. Ironically, though, there were certain living politicians Imus wouldn't even consider, most notably, members of the House of Representatives, which is why Imus gloated, "Joe Kennedy is dying to come on the show, but I say no."

Lest nonlisteners think that Imus is crudely rude directly to his guests, the real test of how Imus felt about the guest comes after the call is over. That's when he will let loose with a stream of consciousness verbal assault, which was not necessarily indicative of whether the guest would be asked back or not.

"Anything I've ever said about anybody who's been a guest at least twice, I couldn't have meant, because I would have never had them on a second time. I only have people on who I like and who I think are smart."

Although Don must exert some restraint while interviewing his guests, some of the I-Man's sharpest barbs were usually reserved for those public servants he viewed from afar.

> America hates you and we hate you. He's a fat loser, which is why Newt Gingrich has the approval ratings rivaling those that Nixon had right before we impeached him. He's just so personally offensive and abrasive and a fat know-it-all. If he'd just shut up and stay off *The Tonight Show* with squealing pigs snarling at him, he'd do himself and the Republicans a lot better than he's doing now.

Imus has also felt no discretion was called for when giving thumbnail sketches of others in the political limelight of the moment, with comments such as "Lamar Alexander is a solid-gold-plated phony" and "Tom Daschle is one of the scummier weasels in Congress, by the way."

"But you know what?" observes Mary Matalin. "That's how people hear and think about politics. People have an intuition and judgment about politicians and policy and that's how he approaches it."

Often, Imus's commentary is in conjunction with the daily news reports, where he will interject his personal take on the happenings of the day. That, to Jeff Greenfield, may be one of the I-Man's strongest bonds with his audience. "The way news is traditionally delivered is laden with emotional dishonesty. The style is Olympian, formal, pompous, and detached. Then along comes Imus with a whole other kind of dialogue: rich, colorful, always irreverent."

"I think people are onto the politico-journalistic dance. They know when they watch a press conference or an interview show they are getting predigested stuff; people are saying the same things they always say. With Imus, people feel he's going to ask them blunt things and not take bullshit for an answer."

Imus seems to be well aware of his news deconstruction when he calls the network anchors "dinosaurs, haunted by the ghost of Edward R. Murrow. The evening news show—it's over."

The key to understanding how Imus can on the one hand say he's "the last media person who will still admit liking the President," then on the other play a parody of "The Lady Is a Tramp" called "The First Lady Is a Tramp,"

> She goes to state dinners with her lesbian friends/
> Makes big investments with high dividends/
> Forgets to pay taxes but then makes amends/
> That's why the First Lady Is a Tramp . . .

is to understand that nearly nothing he says on the show is personal. If something is funny or he fixates on an absurdity such as millionaire Steve Forbes promoting the flat tax, it has no bearing on whether he likes or respects someone as an individual. They are two separate issues. "This is a comedy show," Imus finds himself repeating constantly.

Those guests he gets along with the best understand this, such as former Clinton adviser James Carville. "I don't think of it as a political show. He just uses politicians to entertain people."

Of course, the issue to most people is how they come across to Imus's millions of listeners, which is why the "First Lady Is a Tramp" ditty raised the hackles of the White House, with Hillary Clinton's press secretary huffing that it showed "a complete lack of respect for Mrs. Clinton, for all women."

However, it was those millions of listeners who also kept people willing to come back and brave Imus again and again. "Radio is a great medium to reach people," rationalized Neel Lattimore, Hillary Clinton's press secretary. "I wouldn't discourage anyone from going on any show where their message could be heard."

The irony of the whole fracas was that what seemed to get missed is that the song was "sung" by Rob Bartlett's Rush Limbaugh.

But politicians' paranoia aside, among many of Imus's critics, and even some fans, the question was being raised over what exactly *was* the I-Man's message? What political agenda was he *really* promoting?

Even though Imus stressed that the foundation of the show was still cemented in entertainment, "I mean, you can't endorse Ted Kennedy and Oliver North and have a political agenda," as he drolly pointed out, there were many observers who weren't convinced. It was the overall unsparing nature of the humor on *Imus in the Morning,* particularly the ethnic and racial routines, all overseen and approved by the man himself, that was of concern to those who were more politically correct, especially when considering the ever-growing size of Imus's audience.

What some saw as jokes, others interpreted as base slurs, and although they began as whispers, the shouts of racism would soon be ringing in Don's ears, and once again Imus would be forced to defend his on-air behavior, only this time in the politically and socially charged arena of race relations in America.

Chapter Seventeen

"I'M GOING TO BE VERY HONEST WITH YOU," DON IMUS HAS SAID. "I may be the most self-absorbed person on the planet." While there may be an essence of truth to Don's hyperbolic assertion, it's impossible to believe that anyone so thoughtful, well read, and keen minded could be oblivious of the fact that some of the dialogue on his show could easily be argued as racist. Therefore, either Imus is indeed a racist hiding in satirist's clothing, or he's a calculated, equal-opportunity offender whose point is to show the absurdity of bigotry and bias while getting a laugh at the same time.

Imus calls the charges of racism, "a cheap shot. Nitpicky and stupid and simple-minded. "We satirize everybody. I mean, are black people or Hispanics or any of these other people, have they been inoculated and are they immune now to satire? I don't think so. Everybody thinks it's funny until it's about them. I'm not a racist. There's not anybody on the program who's a racist. Is it racial sometimes? Probably."

Looking at his show, from the more-Irish-than-Irish brogue of Bernard McGarik's recreation of Cardinal O'Connor to Rob Bartlett's lisping "fag" routines, it does seem that nobody is spared, not even Imus, who's heard himself described as a "pencil-necked, wrinkled geezer." Perhaps, then, the reaction to Imus actually says more about the individual listener than it does about the man they are listening to. Plus, as Charles Grodin once said on his CNBC talk show, the Imus show is funny until you're the one in the cross hairs, meaning, it's always easier to laugh at others than it is to laugh at ourselves and our own foibles.

There doesn't seem to be a group that hasn't at some point taken issue with Imus. One of the most heated editorials came from Rick Hill, chairman of the National Indian Gaming Association, over some antigaming comments made on *Imus in the Morning*.

> It's hard to make a really good joke about poverty. Disease is a real tough subject to laugh about. So is early death. Unless, of course, you are Andy Rooney, Bill Maher, or Don Imus. Of course, Andy, Bill, and Don don't have to worry about such things.
>
> Apparently, Indian gaming is now funny. Which, when you think about it, is an improvement. The thieving ancestors, the murderous policies, and the lying government officials (including more than a few "honorable" American presidents) were our dirty little American secret. Maybe, with Andy, Bill, and Don helping out, America can finally talk about Indians and laugh at their efforts to dig themselves out of the hole (grave?) in which they were place [sic].

It's a particularly ironic accusation, considering Don's family history and the fact that his ancestors lived peacefully and cooperatively with the indigenous tribes of Arizona and, in fact, married among them.

The unnerving fact for many is that unlike so many celebrities who cater to the whims of their audience, Imus doesn't care if he ruffles feathers or if people don't like his brand of humor. They don't have to listen. As always, he remains the supreme individualist willing to incur the wrath and condemnation of others in order to forge his own path. In high school it was about individual style and thumbing his nose at peer-group pressures. As an adult it could be argued that it's about finding the true path to wisdom and tolerance. After all, the first step to curing prejudice is to admit it even exists, and Imus seems to be promoting the belief that the first step in acknowledging the problem is to laugh at the stupidity of it all.

When asked just how much of the show is show and how much a reflection of Imus himself, Don says, "It's part me, part all the guys who work on the program, part Charles McCord, it's part Rob Bartlett, part Larry Kinney, McGuirk." Although most of the bits are meticulously worked out in advance, there are plenty of spontaneous moments, such as when Imus loses his famous temper on air. That, he assures, is no joke. But just about everything else is.

"I don't pick on anybody who doesn't deserve it and who hasn't already asked for it," Imus explains. "I'm not arbitrarily attacking people. There's always a reason. We don't have a political agenda but we're interested in current events. We sit around the office every day at ten and say, who do we want to have on tomorrow? What's going on and what's interesting and what are we interested in."

To those listeners who fret over whether someone's feelings might have been hurt, Don is dismissive. To him, those are "idiotic" concerns. "Of course it's infantile and obnoxious for me to make fun of people's physical appearance." If he knows that, then why do it? "I sometimes think it's amusing, but it's not serious and I don't want to hurt anybody's feelings, but nobody gets made more fun of than me. The fact that I have wrinkles, that I'm old, that I have a young wife, yadda-yadda. I get brutalized on my own program. I'm not immune—everybody makes fun of me."

It seems that what's most infuriating to people about Don is the fact they can't quite nail him down; it's that old defining-by-labels bugaboo that Imus so deftly avoids. He's both pro-choice and pro–death penalty; he decries the rise of AIDS but ducks the opportunity to set an example of safe sex by boasting he refuses to wear condoms. His routines might seem consistently demeaning to blacks and yet on Martin Luther King Day he always plays the I Have a Dream speech in its entirety.

But the fact remains, while the political satire is generally considered acceptable because politicians are public figures as well as time-honored fair game, a substantial amount of *Imus in the Morning*'s material does have a racial, homophobic, myso-gynistic, nonwhite ethnic slant that plays on often hurtful stereotypes. Worse, at times there are comments that are directly humiliating and offensive. In a bit of ideological irony, Rush Limbaugh has even taken it upon himself to call Imus to charge that the inherent racism contained within some of his material is simply a reflection of Imus's actual feelings. But parody, counters Imus, is exactly the point.

"We all get bogged down in this absurd area of political correctness, worrying about somebody being offended in the spirit of enlightenment and fairness. If you consider all that, you can't be funny."

Perhaps critics might accept the I-Man's claims if the humor seemed more evenly distributed and his I-Posse occasionally zeroed in on someone who might better fit the mold of his Wall Street banker listeners than someone of color. In a 1996 article for *Newsday*, Murray Kempton wrote:

> "Racism" happens to be one of a good many words that are peculiarly unfitted for loose usage. All the same, since O. J. Simpson is a more-than-suspect double murderer and Alex Kelly a more-than-suspect double rapist, minimal justice would appear to mandate, say, that for every fifty darts sharpened for hurling at O. J. Simpson, at least one should be honed and thrown at Alex Kelly. A proportion of fifty to zero, day after day, may not be an indubitable proof of racism, but it can quite try the patience.

Ironically, it's not so much remarks made by Imus himself that have drawn the most fire. In particular, Rob Bartlett and Bernard McGuirk have most often been held up as prima facie evidence that the humor is really a clever weapon for promoting racial stereotypes and ethnic degradation. Bartlett, of course, takes issue with the characterization of his characters, such as Shecky Bhuda, the wacky Paki.

"Stereotypes? I prefer the word caricature," he says. "I make fun of everyone and everything, but it's not meant to be mean-spirited." To prove his point, Bartlett describes his own cultural and ethnic ancestry as coming from "trailer park" Anglo-Saxons. Plus, he says there are lines he won't cross. "I don't think tragedy makes for good comedy."

The same cannot always be said of his boss, who has no qualms about tossing in a joke or two on the death penalty, because "you're talking about mass murderers! They *should* be fucking fried!"

Because Imus is the unchallenged and undisputed ringleader of the I-Posse, everything that gets said on the air leads directly back to him. If he wanted to, he could rein in Bartlett and McGuirk. Obviously, he doesn't want to.

"Some stuff gets said that you think whoa, but seldom does something happen that I really regret," Imus has said. "Bernard says some things I'd prefer he wouldn't say. But, I really hate to admit it, we do it because I find it amusing."

Imus singles out his producer because even more so than Bartlett, McGuirk has become a thorn in the side to those most enraged by what they see as insidious racism on *Imus in the Morning*, with comments such as "heaven is like a country club. No blacks and no Jews."

Les Payne of *Newsday* is one of those who remain unmoved and not swayed by Don's assertions that it's all just poking fun at our unfounded prejudices, not encouraging bigotry. "He chastises, 'Oh, you shouldn't say that.' Right," Payne says sarcastically. "He stage-manages the whole thing, of course."

In an editorial, Payne elaborated on his dissection of the show and his position that McGuirk is a "badger in the studio" and that Imus denies "responsibility when this beast slurs people."

> Though Imus has curbed Bernard McGuirk, this sidekick still carries the night soil for this televised radio show.
>
> Much of the program flows in jocularity if not in particularly good taste. Talented mimics and satirists make neat work of the individual foibles of politicians and celebrities. Although Imus and McGuirk pull no punches with each other, the sidekick specializes in slurring a subject's race, religion, or ethnicity.
>
> It is fair game to satirize, say, O. J. Simpson in a voice approximating his grainy baritone as a self-possessed golfer, a schmoozer, a bad actor, a dummy, a murderer even. It is quite another matter to satirize Simpson as a generic black man with an "Amos 'n' Andy" voice. Imus's otherwise intelligent listeners laugh along as his troupe demeans African Americans a hundred times, only to arouse themselves when McGuirk's claws rend the flesh of someone they care about.

What Payne is referring to is a hubbub that ensued after Imus insulted *Washington Post* writer Howard Kurtz by calling him a "beanie-wearing little Jew boy," only to have McGuirk go one step further and call him a "hook-nosed dirt bag." What annoyed Payne was that others rushed to defend Imus, such as New York *Daily News* columnist Lars-Erik Nelson, who pronounced, "Imus is no anti-Semite." Nelson goes on to quote Rabbi Gellman, half of the God Squad, as saying, "I wouldn't be on the show if I thought he was an anti-Semite. It's obvious that Imus has re-created himself into something new and more respectable, and he has a whole slew of guests who would bail on him if he went back to racist and sexist jokes."

Even Kurtz, the victim of the slur, notes that Imus "certainly can turn on you in a minute. He spent two weeks saying nice things about my book, for which I was very grateful, but then I did something that annoyed him and for four hours the next day he just kicked the stuffing out of me. I don't think he was trying to injure anybody, but sometimes he crosses the line. He just comes on and gives you pure ego. Or pure id. And," he admits, "there's something weirdly compelling about that."

Although Imus has often said he seldom apologizes for what he says on the air, his actions seem to belie that claim. The fact is, Imus has been known to call people, primarily non-public figures, presumably to apologize if upon reflection he feels some comment went too far, saying, "I don't want them to feel bad."

When confronted about the Kurtz castigation, Don sounded almost contrite. "I was obviously kidding. I would never say it in a disparaging way. We think we're kidding around on the air, and we don't realize how it sounds." It was precisely this mea culpa over Kurtz that in Payne's mind was the exception that proved the racial rule, because Imus has apparently never gone to such lengths to apologize for any comments made toward a black figure. Even his reaction to Payne, who says all he wants is for "African Americans to pass through the dialogue satirized as individuals, not slurred as blacks," carries a decidedly different tone; Imus tends to dismiss him as "some punk from *Newsday*." Payne must be aware of the irony—in his case, Imus is indeed insulting him specifically as an individual and not generically as a member of a particular race.

But Payne is not alone in his assessment of Don and *Imus in the Morning*. Morton Kondracke revealed that he "got a call from WTEM asking if I'd do some commentary every morning. So I listened to Imus and realized there was no way I'd be on that show or even have my remarks intercut with that show. It's at least eighty percent as bad as Howard Stern."

Even among Don's own inner circle there is some concern. His agent, Esther Newberg, has mused, "I've always wondered about the show playing in the heartland or the South, where people belong to the KKK and won't know Imus is kidding."

And it's not just pundits paid to quibble who have contemplated the issue. In a letter to the editor, one *Newsday* reader from Long Beach, California, noted:

> It was ironic to discover, one page after Les Payne's fine column regarding Don Imus and Bernard McGuirk, that the first two letters to the editor dealt with preventing hate crimes. . . . If millions tune in daily to listen to this hateful swill and find it not only acceptable but funny (my husband among them), why should we be surprised when we read about homosexuals being beaten, swastikas painted on homes and synagogues, blacks treated as subhuman, and women the objects of sexual violence?

Therein lies the quandary that Murray Kempton noted when he wrote:

> The songs that mock the bigot can either wake the angels or stir the demons in the Imus votary.

In the end, it's up to each individual listener to decide whose side Imus is really on and ultimately, again, the final interpretation probably says more about the listener than about Imus himself, who can remain above the fray by saying those who see racism are really reacting to their own projections. He's simply the verbal mirror. Because of that, in some ways Don does indeed seem to fit Jeff Greenfield's conception of being the "court jester to the powerful. The court jester could say things nobody else could."

But the court jester was also beholden to the crown and Imus seems incapable of bowing before anyone, as was proven by his ongoing feud with Manhattan Supreme Court judge Harold Rothwax that turned into a lawsuit when the judge sued Imus for $50,000, charging he had been libeled and "embarrassed, ridiculed, and disgraced."

The contretemps began when Deirdre was called for jury duty in September 1996 and was selected to be an alternate juror in a murder trial over which Judge Rothwax, who was best known for having presided over the trial of Joel Steinberg, who was convicted of killing his daughter Lisa.

Once she found out what trial she had been selected as an alternate, Coleman asked the judge to excuse her, because, according to court documents,

> . . . her husband, Don Imus, had arranged for a reporter to cover the Gibson case for . . . radio. Ms. Coleman expressed her belief that the presence of the reporter was affecting her judgment.

While it's true Imus had assigned a reporter to cover the case, freelancer Michael McGovern, it might not have been out of journalistic curiosity as much as a ploy to make sure Coleman had a good reason to ask to be excused. From the beginning, it was obvious Don wasn't thrilled with the possibility of Deirdre sitting on a murder trial, as evidenced by his hiring a bodyguard, Jimmy Wagner, who worked for *Imus in the Morning* regular, ex-police detective Bo Deitl to accompany Coleman to the courts. Imus said the personal protection was necessary because there were "so many creeps hanging out" at the courts.

Imus also told his listeners, "If I wanted to, I could have gotten her off." And after McGovern was assigned to the case,

Deirdre did indeed ask to be relieved of jury duty. But unwilling to let Deirdre out so easily, Rothwax . . .

> . . . asked Ms. Coleman whether it was possible for her to tell her husband that he should not cover the trial on his . . . radio broadcasts. Ms. Coleman said that although she could ask that he stop covering the trial, she felt that Defendant Imus would continue to do what he wanted to do in spite of her indication to him that his coverage of the trial might affect her ability to be an impartial juror.

Judge Rothwax then instructed Deirdre to go home and talk to Don, then return to court in a couple of days. When she came back and told him her husband was in fact not willing to not cover the case,

> Rothwax then excused Ms. Coleman from the jury. At this time, Steven Gibson, his counsel, the assistant district attorney, Judge Rothwax and the court reporter were present.

And therein lay the rub. Imus believed the judge had been disrespectful to his wife, a charge Rothwax vehemently denied; not that it mattered. Imus's red-haired temper had already been riled.

> Shortly after Judge Rothwax excused Ms. Coleman from the jury panel with consent of all parties, Defendant Imus sent a letter to plaintiff's chambers in which Defendant Imus stated that plaintiff's supposed disgraceful behavior regarding [Ms. Coleman] "will be the subject of my nationally syndicated radio program for as long as I live."
> Defendant Imus also declared that plaintiff's "attempts to humiliate her—by insisting that she stand and face the courtroom when you were fully aware she had the right to speak

with you privately—was the action of an embittered old fool
enjoying the fruits of a failed and not all too distinguished
judicial career." Finally Imus wrote, "By the way, your book
sucked."

It actually might have been that last barb that was particularly insulting to Rothwax, who had become a bit notorious
himself for his 1996 book, *Guilty: The Collapse of Criminal Justice,*
which he called an attack on irrationality. Others called it an
attack on basic civil rights. Among his suggestions was to admit
some evidence even if it was illegally obtained by police; dis-
mantling the Fifth Amendment by allowing a jury to infer that a
defendant may be guilty if he doesn't say anything to defend
himself; and doing away with the Miranda warning against
self-incrimination. Norman Siegel, executive director of the
ACLU, said the judge was destined to become the "poster person" of conservatives everywhere. "It seems the judge is moving away from the presumption of innocence." And in fact
Rothwax seemed to confirm that observation by his assertion
that "the fact is, most defendants who come to trial are probably guilty."

So even before he tangled with Imus, Judge Rothwax had
known his share of criticism and should have developed a thick
skin in his then twenty-five years on the bench. Not so. He took
umbrage when Imus, despite Coleman having already been dismissed, told his listeners:

> The judge is a creep. He's a wise ass . . . I think it's dis-
> graceful jerking her around like this. And the judge being a
> jerk, he's not a jerk, but the judge I think, is being unreason-
> able. His response is: "Well, see if you can get your husband
> to stop covering this." That's not a response. That's just being
> a hard-ass. It's an inappropriate response to say to her, "Tell
> your husband to stop covering it." I mean, that's idiotic.

Imus also went on to colorfully describe the judge as, among other things, "Judge Scuzwax," "Rothworm," "senile old dirtbag," "a misogynist," "a creep," and "a drunk."

During Don's original tirade, he had said:

> I'm not willing to apologize to Judge Rothwax at all. I think he's a jerk. And I'd go down there and punch him in the mouth if he wasn't seventy years old.

But Don did eventually apologize to Rothwax in May of the following year. Rothwax, however, was not appeased and a few months later filed his lawsuit, noting

> Defendant Imus is widely described as a "shock jock" for his efforts to foment controversy and for his practice of insulting and humiliating certain public figures on the program he calls *Imus in the Morning*.

Imus was incredulous. "I think it's ridiculous. I already apologized to the judge, anyway, which I don't expect to do again. The judge is a public figure and I believe what I said about him at the time." Although Imus was ready to rumble: "Let's get it on; let's go to court." In a moment of reflection, though, he added, "He seems like a nice old guy. I don't know what the problem is."

As it happened, the lawsuit was settled by intervention of the divine kind. Just two months after filing his suit, Judge Harold Rothwax died of complications from a stroke he suffered September 6, so what would have no doubt been a sound-bite-intensive court drama was averted, to the chagrin, no doubt, of many Imus devotees. But the entire soap opera did little to diminish Imus's legend and in all probability added to it. It seemed everything Don did—and didn't do, such as go out in public much—only added to his aura.

"Because people don't get to see him very often, there's a real rock-star mystique about him," commented Mike Lupica. "I've been out in public with him enough to know that I can't imagine that anybody provokes the kind of reaction he does."

Not that Imus cultivated such attention. In fact, at one promotional event Imus let it be known to the crowd of fans that "I don't want you people to touch me. I don't want you people who are actually willing to come down here to touch me." As often happens, though, reticence made people want to flock to him even more.

But it wasn't just anonymous fans whom Imus kept at arm's length. Although it would seem that Don must have close relationships with at least some of his regular guests, the reality is, he hardly ever meets, much less socializes with his frequent callers.

"I tend to discourage people from coming in live," he admitted in a 1996 *People* interview. "I think people on the phone are more candid, more conversational. Like Al D'Amato, who says hideous things, then spends the next week trying to explain what he meant."

But Imus was also cautious about maintaining distance. Perhaps it's his mordant individualism that makes it difficult for others to get close to Don. Jeff Greenfield admits he and his wife "had a really long talk . . . about whether we wanted to actually be friends with Imus or not," only to discover their desire for friendship wasn't the issue. It was Imus's protective emotional vest to keep his core group small and the fuel of his creative fire to maintain an us-few-against-the-world mentality. The more who became part of "us," the more dilute "the world" he raged against became.

Anna Quindlen, who is one of Imus's absolute favorites, admits she has met him just once and rationalizes it by concluding; "Like so many on-air personalities, contact isn't easy in person."

And as Imus would prove with biting clarity, contact with the I-Man often meant facing the verbal equivalent of a sawed-off shotgun blast, an experience of which President Clinton and the First Lady would soon be on the receiving end.

Chapter Eighteen

WHEN IMUS ATTENDED THE ANNUAL WHITE HOUSE CORRESPON-dents' dinner in 1994 as a guest of *The New York Times*, he and Deirdre sat at a table along with the *Times*'s Maureen Dowd, Frank Rich, Michael Kelly, and Andrew Rosenthal, and according to published firsthand accounts of the evening, Don looked uncomfortable and strangely out of his element the entire night. Perhaps Don's unease stemmed from being simply one in the crowd and not the one controlling the action. For so many years, for better or worse, in drug-induced sickness and rehabbed health, Imus was used to running the show and not being an audience for others. Inciting and provoking people was second nature to him; socializing and schmoozing were not, so it's hardly surprising that Don felt, as ever, the outsider even while sitting in a roomful of media peers.

Two years later, in March 1996, Imus was asked to be the guest speaker at that year's radio and television correspondents' dinner, and the I-Man who showed up that evening was completely in his element as the eyes of the Beltway media and political establishment focused on him. Although in retrospect many would ask why Don, of all people, would have been invited to address such an august crowd, considering his *unpredictable* nature, looked at objectively, Imus was a perfect choice.

For one, the dinner was supposed to be on the loose side, the format reminiscent of a Friar's roast, where politicos and journalists poke fun at one another, share some laughs, and mend wounds and affronts suffered over the previous year. Plus, it was no secret that President Clinton was a fan. Even Mrs. Clinton had stopped by the Kaufman-Astoria Studios to say hello to Imus during one visit to New York. Dan Rather recalls the time he was at the White House and became engaged with Clinton in a discussion about Imus and according to Rather, the President "brightened right up."

Somewhat surprisingly, though, Imus says he didn't immediately jump at the chance to address the gathering. "I just didn't think it was a good idea," he admits, explaining that Rob Bartlett was instrumental in changing his mind by convincing him it was a great opportunity. Once he had committed to speaking, the next step was to write the speech. The guidelines given Imus were brief. "They didn't want any penis jokes. They didn't want any swear words, which was fine."

As always, his writers helped Imus put together a twenty-five-minute rumination on all things Washingtonian, skewering both sides of the Senate aisle equally. The material contained in the speech was the same kind of material Imus and his I-Posse had been creating for years on the radio—raunchy but witty, unsparing but not inaccurate. However, insulting people on the radio from the safety and dispassion of distance was one thing; presenting the same material in person and to their face was a perceptually different risk altogether. Not only did the people who were the target of Imus's barbs have to endure them in the company of others, the rest of the audience would be put in the equally uncomfortable position of laughing publicly at someone else's expense. But that seemed to be Imus's intent. If you can laugh in the privacy of your car or home, then don't be a hypocrite and not laugh now.

Even though Imus could claim that the material was no more shocking or insulting than his daily porridge of humor, he knew he was about to cause a stir and turn the Washington elite upside down. The dinner was held Thursday, March 21, 1996.

At the pre-gala cocktail party, Imus had a chance to talk with President Clinton, who asked Don "How's your speech?" I told him, "Well, it's a little tough," Imus said. "Oh, it'll be fine," Clinton responded, to which Imus then noted, "The only people who will probably talk to me afterward are you and my wife." As it turned out, Imus would be only half right in that conjecture.

Prior to Imus, addressing the audience, President Clinton took to the podium to say a few words about the evening's primary speaker.

"I'm really glad Don Imus came to Washington. You know, all politicians pander to Don Imus, because real people listen to him. He actually takes credit for getting me elected in 1992, and he might have done it," Clinton noted with a chuckle. "But what I want to know is, what has he done for me lately?" The President was about to find out.

Imus opened the speech with a bit of shtick, pretending to find a mystery dossier on the lectern, saying, "Where did this come from? Well, nobody just leaves stuff like this just layin' around," making sly reference to Whitewater documents the White House claimed to have misplaced. "Let me see if I can see what it says: *S. McDougal called again . . . says bank needs check and statement; told her both were in mail, ha-ha-ha. Jesus, she looks stupid in those tank tops.*"

Nobody laughed harder than Hillary Clinton. But, of course, Susan McDougal wasn't there, she was busy trying to fend off prosecutors looking into her Whitewater dealings and would soon be in jail for refusing to testify before a grand jury on whether or not the President had been truthful concerning his role in Whitewater. But Imus had seemingly gotten the crowd on his side—until he launched into the main body of his presentation.

"Good evening Mr. President, Mrs. Clinton, honored guests, ladies and gentlemen, radio and TV scum."

While the politicians smiled at his characterization of the media, which of course included himself, the jaws of some of the journalists in the crowd clenched a bit. Soon they would be hanging open, because Imus went straight for the second touchiest topic he could find—Hillary's involvement with the Whitewater scandal. It was one thing to make fun of Susan McDougal, the Clintons' old friend and business partner, but nobody thought Imus would be quite so pointed about the First Lady when she was seated less than twenty feet away.

"You know, I think it would be fair to say, back when the Clintons first took office, if we had placed them all in a lineup—well, not a lineup—if we were to have speculated about which member of the First Family would be the first to be indicted . . . I don't mean indicted—I meant to receive a subpoena—everybody would have picked Roger. I mean, been there done that.

"Well, in the past three years, Socks the cat has been in more jams than Roger. Roger has been a saint. The cat has peed on national treasures. Roger hasn't. Socks has thrown up hairballs. Roger hasn't. Socks got his girlfriend pregnant and hasn't . . . oh, no, that *was* Roger."

By this time President Clinton was watching Imus warily.

"And as you know, nearly every incident in the lives of the First Family has been made worse by each and every person in this room of radio and television correspondents—even innocuous incidents. For example, when Cal Ripkin broke Lou Gehrig's consecutive game record, the President was at Camden Yards doin' play-by-play on the radio with John Miller. Bobby Bonilla hit a double, we all heard the President in his obvious excitement holler 'Go, baby!' I remember commenting at the time, 'I bet that's not the first time he's said that.' "

At that point Imus turned to face President Clinton. "Remember the Astro Turf in the pickup?" Imus asked as the audience gasped in surprise at the insinuation of Clinton's womanizing ways—which at that point was still mostly speculation. "My point is, there is an innocent event, made sinister by some creep in the media."

Later, Don would explain that the *Go, baby* line wasn't new. According to Imus, the morning after the President had done play-by-play at a baseball game with John Miller at Camden Yards, "Mike Breen played it on the radio. I said, 'I bet that's not the first time he ever said that.' I just repeated that line.

"But I repeated that line at this dreadful speech to illustrate how innocent remarks by the President get twisted. So that was my point, but, of course, I was unable to make that point. Then I turned around"—and even months later—"I can still see that guy just glaring at me, the fat bastard. He had the option of laughing or not laughing. He chose not to laugh and glared at me as if to say, *I'd like to shoot you, you son of a bitch.* And I thought, *You want to play hardball? Fine. Here we go. Fasten your seat belt.*"

In watching Imus speak that night, it's interesting to note that never once did he display any hesitancy or nervousness over the reaction he was getting. If anything, he seemed to gain more than just confidence as he spoke, but a sense of purpose. *You want to play hardball?*

"In some cases, the Clintons have not exactly helped themselves. Imagine if back in 1978 Mrs. Clinton had *not* said to Mr. Clinton, 'Honey, Jim and Susan are here and they've got some riverfront land for these great vacation homes, maybe we can make some serious money.' And he said 'God, I love this Reaganomics!'

"Or later, she'd said, 'Bill, I talked to Web and he said "put down six hundred hours," ' and he'd said, 'Well, that's a lot,' and she'd said, 'Yes, I think sixty makes more sense.' And recently somebody said, 'I don't know, I left them on the table in the book room.' "

And with that, Imus was essentially done toasting the Clintons, leaving them to sit and stew in the comic morass of their own shortcomings. For as stone-faced as the First Lady was, the President positively glowered. "I've seen that look before," CNN White House correspondent Wolf Blitzer said. "If you could kill, that's the look you would give."

Although the speech is mostly remembered for his few jokes at the Clintons' expense, Imus had much more to say.

"And then there's Senator D'Amato—It Takes a Village Idiot. The senator suggests the Clintons hung around with unsavory characters. What the hell was he talkin' about? All of *his* friends have bodies in the trunks of their cars.

"When I was asked to speak here tonight and was told who would be in attendance, my initial thought was *Well, I've already said almost every awful thing you could say about almost everyone in the room.* And then I thought, *Well,* almost *everyone.* And I recognize I'm not going to be invited to Renaissance Weekend, or that Bohemian deal where Newt, Rush, and Dick all sit in a tepee naked, beatin' on tomtoms. I won't be having lunch with Peter Jennings and some Hollywood nitwit, so this could actually be fun."

Imus announced he was going to start at the bottom rung, the journalists and work his way to the low middle, the politicians. He started with Dan Rather.

"Dan has these utterly incomprehensible bucolic expressions he punctuates the conversation with. Several times after talking with him, he would say to me, 'Tamp 'em up solid.' Having something to do, I later learned, with fortifying underground tunnels his father dug, for reasons that remain unclear. Now, I'm hearing-impaired a little bit from wearing headphones for a long time. I thought he was saying, *tampons up solid* and . . . I'm wondering, *I know he's nuts, but what does that mean?* Anyway, I'd laugh and I'd say uh-huh, and I would hang up. And he's a great reporter, but he does not have all of his bait in the water. And he's a little tense. Watchin' Dan Rather do the news, he looks like he's making a hostage tape. They should have guys in ski masks and AK-47s just standing off to the side. . . ."

The audience seemed to be split into two camps—those who were completely put off by the Clinton remarks and refused to react to any of the other humor, such as White House Press Secretary Mike McCurry and journalist Cokie Roberts, and those who were just going with the flow, such as former Bush strategist turned MSNBC talk show host Mary Matalin, who appreciated the way Imus combined current events with his roasting.

"By the way, nobody wants us out of Bosnia more than Tom Brokaw does. Just so he doesn't have to pronounce Slobodan Milosevic. Or report on fighting on the outskirts of Vilikakladusa. We know Brian Williams is standing in front of the White House thinking, *I'm two Serb war criminal names away from Tom Brokaw's job.*

"And then there's Peter Jennings, who we are told more Americans get their news from than anyone else—and a man who freely admits that he cannot resist women. So I'm thinking, here's Peter Jennings sitting there each evening, elegant, erudite, refined. And I'm thinking, *What's under his desk?* I mean, besides an intern. The first place the telecommunications bill should have mandated that a v-chip be placed is in Mr. Jennings shorts."

Imus recalled "Bill Clinton's worst media day, when Kaplan left as executive producer of *World News Tonight* because he'd humped the Clinton administration harder than O.J. has his video. The only thing he didn't do was run a crawl of the Clinton defense fund's 800 number with a shot of Sally Struthers sobbing into the camera.

"By the way, I like Sally Struthers. And I think she's a sweet, harmless soul doing God's work. But if you're going to go on television and beg for food for starving children, shouldn't you maybe like eat a little less of it yourself? I mean, I don't think the plight of suffering children is amusing. I've personally raised millions of dollars for children with cancer, and millions of dollars for parents who've lost children through sudden infant death syndrome. But what are these people thinking about when they send her to a village in Ethiopia full of starving people? They might as well send the fat guy from Wendy's."

Imus was on a roll, which led to the one joke he might have taken back given the chance.

"By the way, and this is really awful, if you're Peter Jennings and you're telling more Americans than anyone else what's going on in the world, shouldn't you at least have had a clue that your wife was over at Richard Cohen's house?" Although many in the audience laughed at the reference to the Jenningses' marital woes, a few people booed.

Upon reflection, Imus would admit, "I regret what I said about Peter Jennings. I apologized to him and he accepted it."

But that was the only remark Imus would atone for, although plenty of other network and cable journalists were singled out.

"Bernard Shaw and Judy Woodruff round out our network news anchors and deserve mention only to recognize that Bernie has greater nut potential than even Dan Rather. If not for CNN, Bernard Shaw is at the post office marching somebody around at the end of a wire coat hanger and a shotgun. . . .

"I love Mr. Brinkley. He's adorable. He also looks like ET. One of these mornings I expect him to say, *Cokie, phone home.* And he's not the only extraterrestrial on the program. There's also Sam Donaldson, the New Mexico sheep rancher. You would think that anybody who's taken as much money from the government in wool subsidies as he has could come up with something better to put on his head—I mean what is that? . . .

"And then there's George Will—and they call Steve Forbes a geek—anyone that buttoned up, I guarantee you, is spending part of his weekend wearing clothes that make him feel pretty. . . .

"*Meet the Press* with the utterly charming and gregarious Tim Russert has brought a new sense of adventure and enthusiasm to Sunday morning television. Mr. Russert's unique and probing interrogation of guests is widely seen as bold and refreshing. . . . By the way, Russert, as many of you know, came to television from the world of politics, having once worked in New York for Senator Moynihan and Governor Cuomo. He was a fine aide whose duties included hiding the bottles for Pat and the bodies for Mario.

"Some of you may have noticed Mike Wallace wandering around here tonight. For some insane reason I agreed to be interviewed by Mr. Wallace. It's a good thing actually, because frankly, time is up over there at *60 Minutes*. I mean, they've gone from biographical essays of Martin Luther King, Mother Teresa, and Stephen Hawking to profiles of loudmouthed morons on the radio. I mean, have they no standards?"

Although the remark never got much play, its inclusion was crucial to understanding Imus's belief that nobody, especially himself, was above being satirizing and made the butt of a joke. That said, some of his comments definitely carried a sharper edge than others.

"Speaking of people whose place on the planet is a waste of space—the White House press corps. I mean, no wonder the President doesn't want to hold any news conferences. Who needs to be assaulted by a pack of rodents whose idea of a question is to confront the President with an insulting observation designed to impress their equally rude and arrogant colleagues. *Mr. President, Rita Braver, CBS News. We all know you're a pot-smokin' weasel, that you once ate an apple fritter the size of a baby's head, that you actually run a twelve-minute mile. Can you, therefore, tell the American people why that thing on your lip looks like a Milk Dud, and if it is a Milk Dud, and I'd like a follow-up . . .*

"Rush [Limbaugh] may not, as Al Franken suggested, be a Big Fat Idiot, but I'm sick of him. The radio show, television show, the stupid books, and now men's ties—bold, vibrant, colorful, and all designed to look great with a brown shirt. Remember the old joke, what's got a hundred feet and four teeth? You know, the front row at a Willie Nelson concert. Well, of course, now it's a Rush room. How appropriate that these ditto dorks all get together and eat and listen to lard-butt . . ."

But some of his most creative jabs were directed at Newt Gingrich, including a little ditty inspired by the Johnny Cash song, "A Boy Named Sue" that included the lyrics:

> He's a guy who spends a lot of time in the fridge
> And it's no wonder he wants to bring back the orphanage
> You would too, if your parents named you Newt
> Now all you atheists had better beware
> 'Cause schoolchildren's heads'll be bowed in prayer
> Beseechin' the Lord to get rid of the poor and the
> queer . . .

"And it was Newt, remember, who wanted to give every kid mired in the poverty of urban America a laptop computer. Not nearly as popular as Phil Gramm's plan to give every white male in the country a lap dancer. I was in Las Vegas when the news broke that Senator Gramm had financed a porno movie. It was better than having Ed McMahon hand me a check for ten million dollars. . . .

"Senator Gramm was fond of saying he was too ugly to be president. Well, that was not his problem. I know he has a Ph.D. in economics. But you can't sound like you just walked out of the woods in *Deliverance* and not scare people. . . ."

Imus seemed to be onstage forever, moving from Pat Buchanan and his family to Jimmy Carter and his. After concentrating on the Republicans, he then switched his laser to the Democrats.

"While President Clinton's cabinet is not technically a family, they are the single oddest-looking group of people ever assembled. Like the bar scene out of *Star Wars* . . .

"I miss the Democrats that were in charge. Especially Joe Biden. And Joe Biden's head. Tracking the progress of his plug job was like watching time-lapse photography of a Chia Pet.

"I also now recognize that it was irresponsible to suggest that [Senator Kerry of Massachusetts] was a suspect in his own wife's unfortunate mugging. If the authorities thought it made sense that a senator from Massachusetts would be in Puerto Rico on a fund-raising mission during the time of family crisis, it should have made sense to me as well. However, when I initially thought about it, it seemed only slightly more plausible than chipping golf balls at ten o'clock at night," Imus said, referring to one of O. J. Simpson's alibis the night of his wife's murder.

Twenty-five minutes after he started, Imus was ready to step down. But his closing comments weren't a few more zingers. In a decidedly unexpected shift, Don spoke thoughtfully of who a politician really was.

"One of the things that it seems to me that the media ought to think about in the coming months, particularly in this election year, consumed by the chaos of the campaign, is the sensibilities of the people you are covering. The way you cover them, and your treatment of them as individuals. For if nothing else, they are all good and decent people who, for whatever reason, have chosen to devote the bulk of their adult lives to public service. People who possess a passion for ideas and ideals to which they have committed extraordinary energy."

Then, in a reference that clearly included himself, he noted, "It is almost always irrelevant and shortsighted to seize *only* on the unfortunate human imperfections of people who frankly have demonstrated an often puzzling willingness to endure great sacrifice, both personally and professionally, for what they see as a noble summons to serve the greater good. More often than not, however, that is exactly the case. You folks focus on each misstep, every misspoken word, each testy outburst. Do they not deserve some degree of our respect? To be treated with the dignity that at least acknowledges the mission of altruism they believe they're conducting. Shouldn't we be willing to give them some benefit of the doubt?"

However, those last remarks were quickly forgotten in the ensuing furor over his barbed handling of the First Couple. Ironically, as the Clinton administration had a knack for doing, it was an impulsive act by Press Secretary Mike McCurry that brought even more attention to Imus's speech than would have otherwise happened. In a moment of spin-doctor panic, Mc-Curry contacted C-SPAN, which had aired the dinner live, and asked them not to rebroadcast the dinner as it had originally planned. C-SPAN refused to pull the taped broadcast and suddenly McCurry—and, by extension, the White House—were having to answer questions about censorship.

At the first press conference following the dinner, McCurry was asked about the Clintons' reaction to Imus's speech and his attempt to have the taped broadcast pulled off of C-SPAN.

"I haven't had an opportunity to talk to the President and the First Lady about last night's entertainment because they fled the scene as quickly as they could. I cannot attest whether that was due to the lack of quality of the entertainment programming, or whether it was more likely due to the basketball game that was televised last evening involving the President's alma mater. I think he was probably a lot happier doing that than he was sitting there," the press secretary told the assembled press corps. McCurry then explained his rationale for contacting C-SPAN.

"I think that there was about 99.9 percent agreement of most of those in attendance that it wasn't a compelling event that reflected well on any of the participants. I personally believe a large part of that entertainment—that's what we call it—offered last night was fairly tasteless, and I didn't know whether young children ought to be subjected to it, courtesy of C-SPAN.

"I raised that issue; it's clearly within their province to decide. I just flagged the issue for them and said, before you automatically replay this, think about the issues. I don't know what they've thought about it. I called Susan Swain down at C-SPAN and said, 'Look, before you guys re-air this, just think about whether you think that's something that ought to be on the air.' I have no idea what their reaction to that was."

But he denied it was an attempt at censoring Imus.

"I have no ability to do so, nor would I intend to do so, but I think it's appropriate for me to raise the issue of whether or not they themselves consider that appropriate programming. I didn't cite anything specifically, I just said look and see if that's something you think you want to have on the air.

"I'm not going to define community standards for indecency. How many of you were here? Show your hands—how many were there last night? Okay. Just talk to your colleagues and find out how they regarded that. I had plenty of people there last night come up to me and not only apologize and ask me to express to the President their sense of regret at the nature of that performance, but I had a lot of people sort of indicate to me that they didn't think the President should have to sit through that kind of thing again."

But even those who might have been offended with Imus's brand of humor or agreed that many of the jokes were in poor taste still could not condone what appeared a blatant attempt at censorship. And looked at in retrospect, knowing what everyone knows now about the President's extramarital affairs, it smacks even more so of a desperate, incredibly misguided attempt to prevent Imus's taunts of womanizing from reaching the ears of Americans.

But it didn't take McCurry long to realize that the knee-jerk reaction, whether truly his alone or done so at the direction of the President, had served only to stoke the fire. "Look, this is very simple. I called them and said, just think about whether you want to put it in the air or not. If that was inappropriate, I'm sorry. But I just thought it was so bad that they ought to just think about it before they automatically re-aired it. If they do it, they do it. I mean, there is not much we can do about it."

McCurry then went on to intimate that in any event, while sticks and stones may break the President's bones, being called names by Imus couldn't hurt him, because he didn't really even like him. That brought another barrage of questions pointing out that the President had been publicly effusive about Imus. All McCurry could do was respond by saying Clinton hadn't been on *Imus in the Morning* "in quite a while."

Unwilling to let him wriggle out of yet another gaffe, reporters kept after McCurry, citing example after example of the President's obvious enjoyment of Imus, right up until he became the after-dinner mint the evening before. Exasperated, McCurry said, "I don't know. I was not here when he—he apparently was a long time ago on it, but I wasn't here then."

In the immediate aftermath of the speech, nobody involved with *Imus in the Morning* knew for sure what kind of fallout to expect. Rob Bartlett, for one, who had contributed about a fourth of the material in the speech although not the lines that had drawn the most criticism, admits he was nervous for both Imus and himself. The person least concerned was the I-Man, even when the first wave of commentary was mostly negative. These reporters were shocked, shocked they would tell you, that Imus would dare be so disrespectful. Lloyd Grove of the *Washington Post*, for example, commented, "My own reaction, hearing this untoward remark and actually feeling my stomach tighten." And ABC correspondent National Public Radio political reporter Cokie Roberts, who up to that time had been a frequent guest, accused Imus of going ''way, way, way over the line.''

But the concern wasn't really what other journalists had to say; if they lost the Washington political crowd as guests, the show would surely suffer. But it was, in the end, much ado about nothing. Although there might have been a very brief cooling from some Beltway politicos, it was soon back to business as usual. With the exception of Roberts, who probably not so coincidentally is the daughter of one-time House Majority Leader Hale Boggs and retired congresswoman Lindy Boggs.

"A lot of people thought that nobody would come on again," Imus acknowledges. "Cokie thought she was going to lead the lemmings over the cliff, but none of them followed." As punishment for taking her stand, Imus announced he had banned Roberts from the show for life.

For every indignant journalist or politician, there seemed to be ten who felt the criticism was not only unjustified but hypocritical. First and foremost, Imus was hardly an unknown commodity. "Let's say I buy a pet alligator, put it in my swimming pool, invite you over for a swim, and it bites off your leg," analogized Sam Donaldson. "The alligator is doing what alligators do. Don Imus did what Don Imus does."

Bruce Bradley, whose show followed *Imus in the Morning* on WIBV in St. Louis, commented, "Imus went for the jugular. He wasn't hypocritical. He said it to their faces. Imus doesn't look like a fool, but the rest of them do."

"What did they think he was going to do?" asked Mary Matalin. "It's a thin line between calling him Bubba and everything else he did to his face when he was on the air and what he did there. It was the vernacular President Clinton, unfortunately, invites."

Even staunch Clinton supporters, such as Matalin's husband,

James Carville, found no fault with Imus. "They didn't invite him to stand up there and sing the National Anthem. The press brought him down to make these kinds of jokes and then they professed horror when he did."

Howard Kurtz, who had endured many slings from Imus himself, added, "What he said to the Clintons was really much milder than what he says every day on his radio show. But there was something about sitting there in that black-tie audience with all these prominent journalists, the President, and First Lady sitting right there that gave it a lot more sting."

Even Don's radio nemesis, Rush Limbaugh, gave a swipe of backhanded support. Even though he considered the speech "tasteless," he also used the occasion to comment on the broadcast journalists who had no problem being on Imus's show and laughing at others, but were upset when they became the target. "If one thing proves how self-absorbed these people are, it's this incident," Limbaugh said. "They can't take it."

But, as it turned out, most could, especially the politicians. Among the first guests to appear after the dinner were some of the very people Imus had stung: Senator Alfonse D'Amato, Senator John Kerry, and Senator Christopher Dodd. Bob Dole phoned Imus after his announcement that he was retiring from the Senate to run for president.

Senator Joseph Lieberman, who first urged then-Governor Clinton to appear on Imus's show during the New York primary in 1992, admitted some of the jokes made him wince "a little bit," but had no qualms about going back on the show. "It's a lot of fun, and he's a very serious student of current events."

He also still had the knack for being able to read the mood of the public. Had Imus taken Ronald Reagan to task for being senile while Reagan was in office, the fallout probably would have been more substantial, because Reagan was revered. The contradiction with Clinton is that while most Americans strongly approved of his job performance, few thought he was particularly honest or trustworthy. As a result, Imus was simply voicing what many Americans already thought about their commander in chief. Just because he might be a shyster and womanizer didn't mean he couldn't be a good president too. All it meant was that Bill Clinton wasn't someone you'd necessarily want as a business partner or husband. It was a dichotomy Imus had understood from the moment Clinton reached the national spotlight. The biggest difference is that now we know Imus was simply hitting too close to home, closer than even he realized. As Imus would later note, "Little did I know that ten days later he resumed his affair with Monica Lewinsky."

The controversy that really wasn't not only gave the show's guest list a boost, it also was directly responsible for *Imus in the Morning* picking up twenty new radio stations, and raising ad rates twenty-five percent. It also brought new advertisers such as Digital Equipment Corporation, American Express, and Merck, the pharmaceutical giant. Other than Cokie Roberts, about the only true casualty of the evening was the relationship between Clinton and Imus.

Although Imus has commented it might have been "hideous judgment" to make insinuations about the President's lack of marital fidelity, he claims he is completely untroubled at being the object of Clinton's displeasure. Indeed, in light of the President's troubles, which culminated in an impeachment, it seems somewhat beside the point for him to hold a grudge against Imus, who, it should be noted, had long commented on Clinton's wandering eye. In a 1994 appearance on David Letterman's show, Imus was asked what he thought Bill Clinton wanted. Imus answered, "I think he wants babes." And with

Clinton's admission of adultery with Monica Lewinsky, the chances of Imus ever apologizing evaporated, not that he ever would have anyway.

"I don't think so! I let them off the hook! What the President needs to do is get a sense of humor, and so does she. It was pretty funny material. But it was in such idiotic taste."

Perhaps this is why Imus makes a point of not becoming socially engaged with the guests on his show, so that he won't let personal feelings interfere with his political judgment and cause what in his eye would be misplaced regret. "I wasn't hanging out with him. I have not talked with him since then. I didn't care. The way it turned out, I'm glad."

When asked if he's ever considered having Clinton back on his show, Imus quipped, "We might. Maybe when he's indicted—or when she is."

The White House went out of its way to make clear that Imus and his show were officially persona non grata. Even after the furor had quelled, a spokesman for the President told reporters somewhat huffily that "we have a mile-long list of press requests for interviews with the President, and Mr. Imus is not on it." And even if Imus were to be on it, "he would be low on that mile-long list."

Perhaps the biggest irony is that time and Monica Lewinsky would make Imus look like a sage and put a completely different understanding—or in Washington terms, spin—on the President's pique that night. Time would also prove Imus right when he said, "It's the best thing that ever happened. It really has helped us. In fact, it has even enabled us to get guests who we couldn't get before."

What that showed was that either our elected officials understood that political humor helps us all keep perspective, or, as talk radio analyst Bill Adams opined, "Politicians are shameless."

Perhaps journalists are too. Despite swearing she'd never

grace the phone lines of *Imus in the Morning* again, Cokie Roberts, too, eventually returned to the fold in late 1997, presumably because by that time the President had disgraced himself far more effectively than Don ever could and, just maybe, because she was promoting her book, *We Are Our Mothers' Daughters*. Imus explained his rationale for reversing his lifetime ban by saying, "We always liked Cokie Roberts. She's a great guest."

For Imus it ended up being yet another feather in his cap of controversies and added yet another chapter to his legend. "It doesn't get any better than this," he said with satisfaction shortly after his speech had put him squarely in the public consciousness.

But Don was wrong about one thing. It *would* get better than this.

Chapter Nineteen

IF HOWARD STERN HAS CROWNED HIMSELF THE KING OF ALL MEDIA, then the argument could be made that Don Imus is the Crown Prince. While it is true that Stern's radio program has more listeners, and his book, *Private Parts*, sold more copies than *God's Other Son*, and the film based on *Private Parts* was a box office success, Imus's media reach somehow seems deeper and more substantial because it has developed organically as opposed to being the result of raw ambition.

Because Stern was so determined to push into television, Imus was often asked whether he, too, wanted to pursue a television career of some sort. Don always brushed aside the suggestion. "No. I'm not a television performer. I don't want to be. I like doing the radio."

So, MSNBC came up with an idea to satisfy both the network's desire to have Don as one of their broadcast personalities and Imus's wish to stay firmly rooted in radio when it was announced that *Imus in the Morning* would be aired live for three hours, from six to nine A.M. EST, on the upstart twenty-four-hour cable network, which was jointly owned by NBC and Microsoft. Being on MSNBC would give the program access to as many as twenty-four million TV households, in addition to its already estimated twelve to fifteen million daily listeners.

"He's exactly what MSNBC needs in the morning," said Andrew Lack, president of NBC News. "He's smart and he's got his own take on things."

The concern many of his radio listeners had was that once the show started being broadcast, it would mean Don would have to tone the content down—a worry Imus laid quickly to rest. "From my standpoint, I'm simply going to do my radio program," he said. "We'll have the same old people we always have—lying, thieving politicians or liberal weenie pundits. I'll still be talking with people like . . . that goofy Deborah Norville. And I have to hold up all the books I'm required to plug from all the publishers who bribe me." And no, he added, he wasn't suddenly going to go glam for the benefit of the cameras. "Anyone who knows me knows I don't care about my appearance."

What made the deal particularly unusual from a business standpoint was that CBS, via its parent company, Westinghouse, was about to take over Infinity Broadcasting, which distributes Imus's show, meaning, in essence, NBC would be promoting a competitor's product.

Unsure just how well his show would work as a television program, Imus adopted a wait-and-see attitude. "The deal initially is for three or four months, but then we're both going to sit down and decide whether it's working or not."

Imus in the Morning made its broadcast debut on September 3, 1996, and what viewers saw was the equivalent of a statically staged one-set play, which for some reason was still oddly compelling, perhaps because of the voyeuristic sense of watching through the eye of the camera.

For the most part, Imus paid no mind to the camera while bantering with his posse or conversing with guests, but he did have to make some technical allowances. "The commercial breaks they take on this hideous little cable channel are apparently computer generated, so I've got Mike Wallace in the studio and Jeff Greenfield on the phone and we're talking, when all of a sudden we're into a commercial," Imus mildly griped. "But they can adjust these things. It'll all work out."

And apparently it has, because *Imus in the Morning* has become a fixture on MSNBC and is the network's highest-rated show. Although Imus won't deign to admit he enjoys the simulcast per se, his competitive side will allow, "I'm happy that we kill CNN."

Moreover, the televised broadcast has introduced Imus to a new legion of listeners who discovered Imus only because he was on TV. In William P. Warford's column for the *Antelope Valley Press*, retired postal worker Fred Lienhard admitted he was a new convert. "I knew who he was and I knew that he used to work here, but I didn't know much about him until I started watching. I like him because he's honest. He's funny. He tells it like it is. He's probably somewhere between a moderate and conservative, but he can be persuaded. He'll listen to people. Now, you take that Limbaugh. With him it's *My way or no way* and I don't like that. Imus is never predictable."

It was converts like Lienhard who were important to the continued success of *Imus in the Morning*. While the conventional wisdom held that Imus "played" in the large, more cynical metropolitan areas such as New York, L.A., Chicago, and Boston, there had always been concern whether or not he would play in America's heartland. For many station owners it was an expensive gamble but one they were willing to take despite the licensing fee that ran well into the six figures, such as Detroit's WYST-FM, which picked up Imus in June 1996.

"We needed someone who could break through the clutter of morning radio," said WYST general manager Rich Homberg. When promoting his show to the Motor City, Imus described his show to the *Detroit News* as "a cross between Beavis & Butthead and the Jim Lehrer report. It's a talk show, but I talk.

"I don't expect young people who are into Smashing Pumpkins to listen. I don't expect older people who are into whatever they're into to listen. And I don't expect the same people who listen to Howard Stern to listen to me, because it's a different show. You have to have a fairly good knowledge of what's going on, particularly in politics and the world and literature and the arts to understand what the fuck we're talking about."

KPHN in Kansas City, Missouri also jumped on the Imus bandwagon. "It's a big step for us," said owner William Johnson in December 1997. "Not only because of the money, but because of the change of focus. We've been known as a qualitative station not concerned with ratings, but this is going to give us a significant boost."

At least one competitor, Bob Zuroweste, had his doubts. "Don has some attraction in certain markets, but I didn't feel his style of marketing and programming was one that was going to win a big audience in Kansas City. Midwesterners have a different attitude." But Imus had already proven he could attract an audience in cities like Milwaukee and Wichita, and expected to do just as well in Detroit and K.C.

Unlike being on a television network where affiliates have no choice but to air the prime time shows given them by the network, when a show is syndicated, each affiliate becomes of equal importance because they can choose to cut a program loose independently. One of the best ways to establish a relationship with radio listeners is to go out and meet them in person. Just as Imus had done personal appearances and remotes when he was starting out in Palmdale and Sacramento, he decided to take *Imus in the Morning* out of the studio and into the field.

Even before *Imus in the Morning* was syndicated, though, Imus had learned the value of taking his show literally on the road. In 1992 he traded places with then-Governor Lowell Weicker of Connecticut for four hours. Although Imus taunted those who were appalled at the idea by saying he couldn't wait to order a condemned prisoner to death, his brief moonlighting stint passed uneventfully. But it was an example of how to make his New York–based show more inclusive of other communities.

"We like going on the road," Imus says. "They're fun. They have live audiences and it's a big deal for them."

Two cities Imus seemed to particularly enjoy were Memphis and Atlanta. The visit to Georgia happened in part because WQXI-AM picked up the program and after Governor Zell Miller sent Imus a note and a signed copy of his book, *Corps Values: Everything You Need to Know I Learned in the Marines.* Imus was clearly enamored with Miller, who was quick with a quip and had the I-Man laughing. When he presented Don with a proclamation, he warned, "I don't know if you want me to read it or not. It'll wet your leg."

Later, Miller let Imus know that despite his wholesome image, "You're not the only one who could start out the night with good intentions and get sideways and end up in places you don't belong."

And he seemed to permanently endear himself to Imus when he responded to a question about whether he had discussed the Monica Lewinsky question with President Clinton by saying he had "skirted the issue." Later Imus would call Miller "one of the most extraordinary politicians in this country because he is not a crook, he doesn't cheat on his wife, and he loves the baby Jesus. God, what a wonderful guy."

In return, many in the audience found themselves drawn to Imus. "I like his cynicism and his brutally honest talk on politicians," said one of the audience members to the *Augusta Chronicle.* Even though he was in the South, Imus carried on as usual, such as noting Strom Thurmond was a "turnip with a suit on."

But it was in Memphis that Imus seemed to take on the mien of fan himself when he toured Elvis's gauche palace, Graceland. It was also prime Imus comic fodder. When informed that the house was 17,000 square feet, he joked, "That's pretty big—big enough to make a peanut butter sandwich," because "fifteen thousand square feet is the kitchen."

While in Memphis, *Imus in the Morning* broadcast from B. B. King's club on Beale Street, the musical Mecca for blues performers.

"You know, in honor of Elvis's birthday, I'm having a jelly doughnut," Imus told the assembled audience. "He's not going to eat one, I'll tell you that. He's deader than Dean Martin." Then he recounted his trip to Elvis's mansion. "A lot of people in Memphis claim they've never been to Graceland; it's like people in New York never been to the Statue of Liberty. But we were there and they had this, actually, it was a larger place than I thought it was, and they had this display of Elvis's jump suits. And the guy says, 'You'll notice they get progressively . . .' and before he could say anything else, I said, 'Larger?' And he just glared at me."

While most of Imus's syndicated outlets did well with his show, there were some notable failures. In St. Louis, *Imus in the Morning* debuted in June 1995 on WIBV-AM, but unlike other stations which promoted the coming of Don, WIBV management apparently hoped to attract an audience by sheer word of mouth. It didn't happen. So less than a year later, in April 1996, the show was pulled in favor of a local duo named Wendy Wiese and Bill Wilkerson.

However, his failure to bring in listeners seemed more a function of misguided promotional strategy than a rejection of Imus by St. Louians. One of his biggest fans was Bruce Bradley, whose talk show came on after Imus. "He's been my favorite in broadcasting for as long as I can remember," Bradley said. "He's the best broadcaster I've ever heard."

In 1995, Imus yanked his show in, of all places, El Paso, his brother's former home. (Fred had since moved his Auto-Body Express business to Santa Fe, New Mexico.) But this was a case of Imus making the decision, not the station, after his affiliate there, KROD, moved *Imus in the Morning* to the afternoon and put Howard Stern in the morning slot. The switch came about after the station's owner, New Wave Communications, bought KAMZ, Stern's former El Paso broadcast home. When New Wave changed KAMZ format from classic rock to adult contemporary, it dumped Stern's show and decided to move it to KROD. Contractually, though, *Imus in the Morning* is required to be aired between five A.M. and nine A.M. KROD, however, claimed *its* contract said five A.M. to nine *p.m.* And with that Imus pulled the plug.

There were also unexpected guilt-by-association experiences unique to syndication. In May 1996, a woman named Kellie Jacobs filed a complaint with the state Department of Human Rights in Minnesota after a school-bus driver refused to turn off Imus's show, subjecting her son, Zachary, to it. According to Jacobs, Zachary had kidney problems and physical disabilities and was upset over hearing Imus and company engaged in a graphic discussion. "You can talk about penises, but not cutting them off and putting them in jars," she said. "He's had a lot of medical problems. That's not a fun thing."

When he heard about the incident, Imus sides with the boy. "The bus driver's a jerk, and once the kid complained he should have changed the station."

The irony is that once again the impression left to the uninitiated was that *Imus in the Morning* was Howard Stern for the AARP set. And while the locker room banter would always be a central part of the show, Imus was branching out from politics into the literary arts by mid-1996 in a big way.

Although Imus tended to avoid most movies and rarely if ever rented videos, from the time he was a young boy spending the long and quiet nights at the ranch reading, Imus had been instilled with a passion for literature and love of books that had remained strong throughout his adult life. And since *Imus in the Morning* was more or less a treatise on the ruminations of Imus, he would frequently talk about the books he had read, both good and bad.

And as his audience grew in national scope and he became a presence on television, he began to indirectly have influence on the publishing world; not only were his listeners more apt to vote, they were also a book-buying group. So when Don endorsed *One True Thing* by *Imus in the Morning* regular Anna Quindlen, which told the story of a daughter coming to terms with her dying mother, sales immediately jumped. (The book eventually became a film starring Meryl Streep and Renee Zellweger.)

But the true impact of his ability to affect and influence the reading public became clear only with his serendipitous discovery of *I Was Amelia Earhart* by Jane Mendelsohn. Actually it was Deirdre who came across the novel while browsing at a bookstore near their home in Connecticut on a weekend. She read the book, a 146-page fictional memoir of the world's most famous female aviator who disappeared, with navigator Fred Noonan, during her 1937 attempt to fly around the world. In Mendelsohn's story, Earhart is living on a tropical island, stranded after her plane has gone down in the Pacific. The next day Coleman insisted her husband read the book.

"She was intrigued by the title and brought it home," Imus said. "She said, 'You've got to read this.' And I thought, *Well, all right.* And I'm telling you, I was absolutely just waylaid by this book. I was blown away by it. It's an extraordinary book. So I just talked about it the next day."

Imus was so taken with the novel that he actually spent the next several days on his show raving about it, and by the end of the week, *I Was Amelia Earhart* had leaped from obscurity to the best seller list. First time author Mendelsohn, who admits she wasn't a big fan of radio, suddenly became "a big Imus fan."

In that short period of time, Mendelsohn went from struggling writer to literary darling, all because a foul-mouthed, grumpy radio guy waxed poetic about her work. As often happens, the story behind the book was as dramatic as the novel itself, because *Earhart* almost never got published. Mendelsohn, a native New Yorker, graduated from Yale and spent a year in Yale Law School before she "decided I wanted to be a writer and left. I started reading a lot on my own, kind of giving myself a private, intense course in writing."

She says the book, inspired by an article she read in *The New York Times* in 1992 about Earhart's flight, had originally been conceived as a historical novel. But over the two and a half years it took to write, *Earhart* transformed into a lyrical first person narrative—not the sort of thing that makes editors take notice. "They said different things, but they didn't want it," Mendelsohn says. "A lot of people said, 'I like it but it isn't commercial' or 'It's inaccessible' or 'It's too short.' "

Eventually she found an editor at Knopf willing to take a chance on her. The book's first printing was thirty thousand copies, which is fairly typical for a first novel. At first it seemed the naysayers would be proven right, as sales were limp. Odds are even the marketing people at Knopf had shrugged and moved on. But after being tub-thumped by Imus for a week, bookstores couldn't keep the novel in stock and Knopf had standing orders for sixty thousand books.

"Imus is a guy who can make a book happen in this country," said a thrilled Paul Bogaards, director of promotion for Knopf. "What Imus accomplished in the space of five days is extraordinary. It almost happened in a vacuum. There was nothing else going on. It was his endorsement that propelled it onto the best seller list. In the span of one month, April to May 1996, we went from thirty thousand copies in print to two hundred twenty-five thousand. For a lot of people in the industry, that was a clear compass point."

Nobody seemed more surprised than Mendelsohn. "I'm

really happy. I'm surprised but really happy. It's really sort of head-spinning."

Mendelsohn's husband, filmmaker Nick Davis, acknowledged Imus literally turned their life around. "It's nice to know where the rent is coming from. Jane worked so hard for so long. It's great for people who love her to see her happy."

Many believe Don later did for Pete Hamill what he did for Mendelsohn. After strongly plugging Hamill's *A Drinking Life*, which Imus decreed "deserves the Pulitzer," listeners flocked to buy the book. In it Hamill, a longtime reporter who eventually became the editor of the *New York Post*, tells of growing up in Brooklyn during the days the Dodgers were still playing at Ebbets Field, and how drinking shaped his life. Imus firmly believes, "we absolutely put it on the best seller list."

For all his literary tastes, though, Don wasn't above doing a bit of shameless hawking for himself and family. It was largely through his relentless promotion of *God's Other Son* on his program that the oft-published book finally became a best seller nine years after its original publication. He also urged listeners to check out the photography book he had done with his brother, *Two Guys, Four Corners*, which made the *New York Times* best seller list.

Although radio remained his primary source of income, the change offered to Imus by publishers was substantial. "I did take a bunch of money from Doubleday. I took a million dollars to do a nonfiction book."

Perhaps the worst example of nepotism was Don promoting *The Fred Book*, written by Mike Lupica. According to the publisher, "Collected here for all the ages is the wit and wisdom of Fred Imus, brother of Don and king of Frontier Salsa and 1957 Chevys, who is never shy with his outrageous opinions on his brother's wildly popular *Imus in the Morning* radio program, where he regularly appears. Whether waxing nostalgic about country music, ranting about American politics, needling Don, or hawking his western goods sold through his million-dollar catalogue company, Fred is always outrageous, often outlandish, perverse, and a hilarious alter ego to his big brother Don, the I-Man. Think Garrison Keillor from hell."

While some readers found the tome humorous, others didn't," said Paul Ferguson on amazon.com. "When I finished, I wished I could sue the author to get back the twenty minutes of my life I wasted on it. Since I can't, I'll have to be satisfied with warning off other unsuspecting souls.

"In the introduction, brother Don also tries to warn you off, calling the book 'a piece of shit.' But at the time you may think he is speaking with tongue in cheek. He is not."

Others were kinder. "I found the book to be amusing, but for those unacquainted with Fred and his brother Don, it might fall flat."

But the point was really Don's influence more so than his taste. "All you need do is hear him wax poetic about your book and you say, *Hell, I'd buy that book,*" commented Anna Quindlen.

Simon & Schuster publisher Jack Romanos credits Imus with increasing the sales of Howard Kurtz's *Spin Cycle* from twenty-five thousand copies to two hundred thousand. "Imus is the second most powerful person in the country in terms of selling books," he said, putting Imus behind Oprah Winfrey, whose monthly Book Club feature on her syndicated talk show had generated sales in the millions. Imus, however, didn't like taking a backseat to anyone.

"Oprah couldn't have put *Spin Cycle* on the best seller list if she'd bought all the copies herself. If you said, Have you read *Spin Cycle*? she would have thought it was a washing machine manual," he said after being apprised of Romanos's perceived slight.

"So here's the new policy. We are never, ever, in the history of the program, ever, going to have an author on this show who has a book at Simon & Schuster. Why would you want to go on the number two show?"

However, he then told *New Yorker* writer Ken Auletta that the ban only "lasts until the photography book my brother and I are doing for them comes out."

Imus has also had other issues with Winfrey, though, and has gone on record calling her a racist. "I think you can promote Toni Morrison, who I think is brilliant, without disparaging Anna Quindlen."

But their personal disputes aside, and whether Imus and Oprah actually had a hand in it or not, 1996 was the biggest year ever in book sales. Oprah's first book pick, *The Deep End of the Ocean* by Jacquelyn Mitchard, sold over five hundred thousand copies and her second selection, Toni Morrison's 1977 *Song of Solomon* also landed on the best seller list.

Whether to set himself apart from Winfrey or out of genuine pique at the book industry, in 1998 Imus would establish the Imus American Book Awards. With chain giant Barnes and Noble providing financial backing, three awards of $50,000 and one for $100,000 would be awarded.

Don says he got the idea to establish his own awards after a book he liked didn't win a National Book Award, the organization behind which he characterizes as filled with "elite weenies." Finalists would be selected by Imus and a panel of editors. Among the fiction selected for his first awards were Richard Price's novel *Freedomland*, based on the Susan Smith murder case in Union, S.C., *My Year of Meats* by Ruth L. Ozeki, *The Archivist* by Martha Cooley, *The Farming of Bones* by Edwidge Danticat, *The Mourner's Bench* by Susan M. Dodd, and *Cities of the Plain* by Cormac McCarthy.

The nonfiction finalists included Taylor Branch's *Pillar of Fire: America in the King Years, 1963–65, Life Every Voice* by Lani Guinier, *King of the World: Muhammad Ali and the Rise of an American Hero* by David Remnick, *Titan: The Life of John D.*

Rockefeller, Sr. by Ron Chernow, *Confederates in the Attic* by Tony Horwitz, and *Pack of Two: The Intricate Bond Between People and Dogs* by Caroline Knapp.

It was this ability, if not to actually change people's minds, then at least expose them to new ideas or possibilities or ways of looking at events, not just in politics but in the world of literature and the arts as well, that prompted *Time* magazine to include Don Imus in a list of the twenty-five most influential Americans. Those surprised at the selection included more than just his former high school classmates who had so tacitly but so effectively designated Don a loser. Martin Nolan of the *Boston Globe* wrote:

> *Time* has apparently decided that influencing the influential is a tradition. If Al Gore, with a target audience of one Arkansas politician, made it last year, Imus was an easy choice.
>
> Like all media magnificos, *Time* editors approach Don Imus cautiously, apologizing that "the grizzled, cello-voiced host of *Imus in the Morning* has fewer listeners than Howard Stern," his rival for morning radio dominance. *Time* apparently regards Imus as a guilty pleasure.
>
> It may also feel guilty about a cover story pairing Stern as the liberal alternative to Rush Limbaugh. If "people whose styles are imitated, whose ideas are adopted" are influential, where are Rush and Howard?

However, as Nolan himself pointed out, *Time*'s originally stated mandate cited "being influential as the reward of successful salesmanship, the validation of personal passion, the visible sign of individual merit. It is power without coercion, celebrity with substance." So regardless of whether you appreciated or abhorred what lay beneath the surface, it would be hard to argue that Imus lacked passion, merit, or, especially, *substance*. To compare the intellectual breadth of the topics discoursed in *Imus in the Morning* to Howard Stern's daily raunch romp seems akin to comparing *Beavis & Butt-head* to *Seinfeld*. While Imus frequently stooped to sophomoric levels, rarely if ever did Stern or Limbaugh display the wit or comic and intellectual sophistication that clearly set Imus apart and justified his inclusion on the list, for better or worse.

When asked his feelings about being labeled influential, Imus was typically both self-deprecating and mocking. He also said precisely what the majority of people would feel but not have the nerve to say. "The best part is the people I know who didn't make the list who wanted to make the list. That makes me a small, petty person."

And that was indeed the image Imus had always seemed most comfortable projecting. But the on-air I-Man seldom advertised the other, lesser known side of Don; a paternal side that first found expression helping the children of others, then would ultimately find full flower with a child of his own.

Chapter Twenty

F OR MANY ALCOHOLICS, BECOMING SOBER LEAVES AN UNSETTLING void in their life that was once filled by their desire to drink but now needs to be constructively redirected. Some who simply need an activity to replace the hours previously spent drinking become AA meeting devotees, which effectively serves the dual purpose of filling time as well as surrounding oneself in a support group that encourages continued sobriety. Then there are those who devote themselves to helping others, which gives both personal focus and, in a sense, expiation for having wasted however many years in an alcoholic haze.

For Don, Alcoholics Anonymous was not the best way to go, so he depended less on support-group pressure for continued sobriety and more on personal will and effort and by never forgetting what it was like when he used to drink. "I stopped doing drugs thirteen or fourteen years ago," he said in a 1996 interview. "I stopped drinking coming up on nine years, and I noticed my life got almost instantly better when I stopped drinking."

And, as always, humor helped too. "I'll tell you how you can tell a real drug addict, which I was or am, a recovering drug addict," he told his radio audience. "You can swallow pills with no water."

"You talk about memories," Larry Kenney intoned in an old voice. "I wish I had some."

But Don had made other changes in his life, some noticeable, some not. The exuberant social life he enjoyed in the early 1970s had been buried in the past. He seldom went out at night and tended to shy away from cocktail parties. He was only half joking when he said, "You want me back in rehab again, crawling around on the floor looking for a vodka?" It's also been reported that Imus has the liquor removed from his hotel room before he checks in "just in case I sleep-walk over to the cabinet."

Jokes aside, Imus altered his life out of simple self-knowledge. "I realize there are things in my life I can change and things that I can't change." He can't change the fact that if he has one drink, he'll drink until he is back crawling on the floor, so his everyday life is, in some measure, a constant struggle to keep that first drink at bay. So like every other recovering alcoholic, Imus finds distraction in family, friends, work, and other outside interests.

It's no surprise that Imus didn't get involved in charity work until after he stopped drinking—until he was sober he couldn't help himself much less have the wherewithal to help others in any significant way. But when Don did finally become involved, he would do so in a meaningful way. Unlike some celebrities whose idea of charity is to simply write a check, Imus would put his heart, time, and money into changing the lives of children.

Freudians could have a field day speculating why Imus, an admittedly absent father to his four daughters during their formative years, would be drawn to charities for children. But whether his subconscious motives are rooted in a search for paternal atonement or simply the result of a friend's tragedy is moot. What does matter is that Imus has become one of the most effective money raisers in radio. Between 1990 and early 1999 he has helped raise close to $50 million for the C.J. Foundation for Sudden Infant Death Syndrome, and Tomorrow's Children's Fund, which helps children afflicted with cancer and other serious diseases. His involvement with SIDS came about after Joel Hollander, Imus's general manager, lost a daughter to the mysterious syndrome. As for his association with Tomorrow's Children's Fund, Imus says, "When you see a seventeen-year-old girl lying in the middle of her bed, all her things around her, and she knows she's going to die in a month, it's got to get to you."

Every year since 1990, WFAN has held a twenty-eight-hour radiothon to benefit Tomorrow's Children's Fund, during which Imus works an eight-hour shift. The 1999 radiothon, held February 25 and 26 and broadcast live from the World Financial Center's Winter Garden Atrium, raised $2.5 million for the two charities. The co-president of Tomorrow's Children, David Jurist, has called Imus "a hero to the kids. I don't think he understands the depth of what he's done. He hasn't just raised money, he has given the children a purpose. When he talks about them, he makes them feel important. He's their hero, their leader, their mentor.

"I honestly believe there is nobody, not one person, who can do for our charity what Don Imus has done over the last nine years. It's not only the money raised that is so important to our children, but the awareness that is raised about the charity."

In their mission statement, Imus says, "I have been deeply moved by the commitment of parents in their loving efforts to alleviate the burdens borne by their children and to allay their fears . . . a commitment that continues even among parents whose children were lost in this courageous struggle. Their fight, our fight, goes on. Stand with us. It is a conflict that must be won."

The money raised through the radiothons helped build the Don Imus-WFAN Pediatric Center for Tomorrow's Children at Hackensack University Medical Center, a seven-story facility. In recognition of his efforts, Don was made the group's honorary chairman.

Although Imus does promote the charities on the air, he tends to downplay his own significance. Back in August 1991, Imus made two public appearances for the Connecticut Special Olympics and at the time Mark Mason, WFAN's program director, told *Connecticut* magazine: "Imus has a very big heart, but it's bad for his image."

Then there are those, Howard Stern for one, who accuse Imus of simply being interested in self-promotion. "Imus trumps up phony charities to make himself look like a good guy." To which Imus replied that Stern was a "boner-nosed, Linda Tripp–looking dirt bag who has never raised a penny in charity and has never done anything to help anybody except himself."

However, those who might have doubted Don's commitment would be hard pressed to explain the Imus Ranch, to which Don has not only devoted time and energy, but a million dollars of his own money. The idea for the ranch was planted during a trip in 1997 back to his childhood. "Fred and I and Deirdre went out to the old ranch where we grew up, the Willows ranch outside Kingman, Arizona. Then we came back to New York and Fred, Deirdre and I talked about buying a ranch somewhere in New Mexico, which a lot of people do. [Tom] Brokaw has a ranch up in Montana, Ted Turner owns everything in New Mexico we don't own."

After he got back from Arizona, one of Imus's first guests was Paul Newman, who talked about his line of food products which all benefit charity.

"Then I went home and Deirdre was downstairs on the treadmill and it just came to me. I thought, *Wouldn't it be great if we could take these kids with cancer—and by the way, they want to just be treated like regular children—wouldn't it be great if they could have the same sort of experience we had growing up on that ranch?* We're going to buy a ranch anyway, let's buy and build a little working cattle ranch, like a *City Slickers* deal. Take these kids from Tomorrow's Children who are in various stages of cancer

treatment—some get better, some are not going to get better—
and make it a camp, not a dude ranch but an authentic working
cattle ranch.

"So the original idea was to create this cattle ranch, to run
Texas longhorns on it, with horses and sheep, get some buffalo
and take these children out there for ten days, two weeks, but
actually put them to work." These kids would be teens, he explained. "They will come to the ranch, live in the big ranch
house. They're not going to live in little cabins or bunks.
They're going to live in the big ranch house with me and Deirdre and Fred and we'll spend every summer out there. There's
no charge. We've made arrangements through a friend of mine
to fly them all out there. And they come to the ranch and we
turn them into little cowboys."

In addition to Tomorrow's Children, Imus also opened the
ranch to children who had lost brothers and sisters to sudden
infant death syndrome. Together the children would learn the
ways of ranch living.

Although it would be a huge commitment, Don had all the
necessary business and political contacts to make bring his idea
to fruition. One of the first people to help was Hamilton Jordan.
"He and his wife run a great camp down in Atlanta, the Sun-
shine Camp. He heard me talking about it and he called me. It's
a mammoth undertaking and I didn't have all the money in the
world."

What Imus ultimately worked out to help fund the ranch was
to actually sell acres to investors. "I put up a million dollars of
my own money, in cash, to buy the original 810 acres, so it was
free and clear. And I bought privately another 640 acres adjacent to that. We subsequently bought another couple of thousand acres, so the entire ranch now is around three thousand
acres.

"What I originally wanted to do was take a mortgage on it. I
didn't see anything wrong with that, but the people who handle

my money said you can't take a mortgage on a property you're buying for a foundation. It's got to be free and clear. What I learned was after you establish a foundation and put up money, you can't take your money back. It's the foundation's money, and if you don't build the ranch, you give the money to other charities.

"Dick Grasso, chairman of the N.Y. Stock Exchange, said, 'Why don't you symbolically sell these acres?' I figured I needed about ten million dollars to build the ranch—six to seven million to build it, three to four million to run it. So I just came up with this idea that people could become founding members and official Imus ranch foremen and actually own an acre. And I would cut their name in a piece of stone—and I got the idea from seeing my grandfather's name cut in the old Willow ranch out in Kingman."

So in April 1998, Imus told his radio audience he needed 810 people to "buy" one acre each for $5,000 in exchange for becoming an honorary ranch hand. Before his show was over, all the allotted parcels were gone. In fact, there were people, many of whom were former or regular guests, who were clamoring to donate money even though the parcels were all gone. When it was suggested to Imus the response may have in part stemmed from a desire by some politicos and pundits to get on his good side, he chose not to believe it. "I'd be surprised if they did it for cynical reasons. Maybe I'm naive. I don't think so."

Nor was Don willing to pat himself on the back. "I'm not some great guy. I'm not putting myself out by doing this. I already said I was going to buy a cattle ranch. I already said I was going to go spend my time out there in the summers. I'm not going to go to the Hamptons. I'm not going to go to St. Barts and drink beer with Mike Glynn. It's not a big deal."

The four million dollars raised by selling the 810 acres was still not enough to cover all the construction costs. So after the individual sponsorships ran out, he appealed for corporate sponsorship to pay for three barns at $500,000 each, the bunkhouse for $250,000, a dining room and an executive kitchen, ranch office, infirmary, and general store, all sponsored at $500,000 each. Among the companies to heed the call was American Express, the N.Y. Stock Exchange, and Mentadent toothpaste, each donating $250,000 to the Imus Ranch cause.

And Don made sure the money was put to good use. In keeping with his desire to give the kids a true western experience, Imus hired Santa Fe designer James Smith to fashion the ranch, located in Ribera, New Mexico, approximately fifty miles northeast of Santa Fe, after a nineteenth-century desert town. "We're building an infirmary to look like an old Tombstone saloon, so when the kids go to get their chemotherapy, it's like going into the saloon," Imus explained.

While the ranch, which was scheduled to open in mid-1999, brought Imus personal satisfaction, it also brought its share of unexpected headaches. In July 1998, Imus made the headlines after it was announced the New Mexico attorney general's office was investigating whether he had unlawfully torn down some "historic structures" on the ranch. The state's involvement came about because part of the 3,000 Imus Ranch acres included 878 acres of land leased from the state. Under New Mexico law, people who lease state land have to get permission from the state to make any changes. According to the attorney general's office, Commissioner of Public Lands Ray Powell had requested the inquiry.

The main focus of the investigation was whether or not Public Safety Secretary Darren White and Transportation Secretary Pete Rahn broke the law by bulldozing ranch properties as a favor for Imus when they ordered a Transportation Department crew to tear down the structures on July 1. In addition to the failure to have mandatory studies done to determine the historical and cultural value of the barns and corrals, it was also against the law to use public money for private benefit. (Archaeologists who later examined the site estimated the buildings dated back to the 1880s and may have been used in the 1920s as a rest stop for travelers.)

In July 1998, the New Mexico attorney general's office was investigating whether state officials had broken any laws. "I wouldn't use the word *investigation* yet," said Kay Roybal, spokeswoman for Attorney General Tom Udall. "It's an inquiry."

What the inquiry discovered was that Fred had called Darren White and asked to have the buildings torn down because they seemed to be a safety hazard to the children at the ranch. The transportation secretary said there had been miscommunication, because he believed the Land Office had given permission for the demolition. "The motivation for all this was the idea we were trying to help kids with cancer," explained Pete Rahn. "If I would have thought I was being asked to do something that was not right, I would have said no."

Imus immediately agreed to reimburse New Mexico $6,696 for the cost of tearing down the buildings, and to pay for a survey of remaining historical and cultural sites on the land.

"It's an appropriate solution to an unfortunate situation," said Ed Moreno, Ray Powell's assistant commissioner for public affairs.

"It was never our intention to get something from the state we weren't supposed to get," said John Silver, an attorney representing Imus. Don's opinion, however, was less diplomatic. "We weren't trying to do some sleazy deal. We weren't trying to build a casino."

Three weeks after launching its inquiry, the attorney general's office announced, "We have found no evidence of criminal intent, so we closed the criminal inquiry," said Kay Roybal. "We have also spoken to all the parties involved, and they all declared themselves to be satisfied with the deal that was worked out." That deal included the Land Office agreeing to let the Imuses temporarily take over the existing agricultural lease while another type of lease, more suitable for a camp, was negotiated.

When word of the ranch first became public, among the first words of encouragement had come from New Mexico. The *Santa Fe New Mexican* noted: "A source who works on his radio program says Imus increasingly has been contemplating a retreat for youngsters. As beautiful, restful places go, northern New Mexico is an area he might want to get to know better, and this is an appropriate opportunity to reach out. It's a nice thought—on which, with the support of his vast national audience, would make an even nicer reality."

However, a year earlier, many New Mexicans hadn't been so sanguine toward the brothers Imus. In November 1997, Fred started a maelstrom of controversy when he characterized northern New Mexicans as Mexicans who get pregnant young and would rather drink beer than read, during a call in to *Imus in the Morning*. He also announced he wouldn't hire any Mexicans to work in his mail order business. Fred was piqued because while trying to re-create Ansel Adams's famous photo *Moonrise over Hernandez* on the fiftieth anniversary of the photo being taken, he had been asked to leave the area by a Latino landowner, who complained that the villagers were tired of tourists stopping by.

The next day, Fred found his Santa Fe Auto-Body Express boutique being picketed by protesters holding signs calling for Fred to leave New Mexico and accusing *Imus in the Morning* of being ignorant and divisive. "We will not tolerate racism. Those attitudes don't belong in Santa Fe," said activist Gloria Mendoza, who helped organize the protest.

"I'm outraged someone would have the nerve," added Angela Marino. "People won't take it anymore. We'll drive him out of town."

For possibly the first time in his life, it was Fred under public fire for spewing racially insensitive remarks. Chastised, the younger Imus apologized in an interview the following week. "I'll admit I shot my mouth off and should've shut up. I offended a lot of people that didn't deserve to be offended and for that I apologize." For Don, it was just another day at the office. But by the time the ranch was under way, the incident, while not necessarily forgotten or forgiven, was put behind.

Although Don was able to raise most of the money for his ranch without twisting arms, there were occasions where he took individuals to task, most notably Ted Turner, about whom he has jokingly asked, "He doesn't have much of a sense of humor, does he? He's on medication, right? We don't want to go there."

While doing an *Imus in the Morning* remote in Atlanta, he taunted the media mogul for failing to make a promised donation to the ranch. At seven in the morning, during his simulcast on MSNBC, Imus had Bernard McGuirk pack fifty audience members into pickup trucks and drove them to CNN Center, where they picketed the building and Turner. The ploy worked. A $175,000 check was hand-delivered by a band of professional wrestlers, including Hulk Hogan, who personally handed the check to Imus.

For all the care and commitment Imus had shown helping the children of others, it would pale in comparison to the heart and soul he would put into his second chance at being a father and the parent he had never been. When they first got married, Imus had brushed aside questions about whether he and Deirdre would start a family by saying he was already marrying a baby. But in the autumn of 1997, Deirdre became pregnant, and suddenly Imus was facing the prospect of starting a new family at fifty-seven years of age. But Imus chose not to dwell on the age factor. "If you didn't know how old you were, how old would you be? So I figure I'd be about forty."

In preparation for the birth of their baby, Imus bought a

house in Westport, Connecticut, best known as the home of Martha Stewart, for $4.6 million, in late 1997. In keeping with the Imus way, he immediately pissed off neighbors when he threatened to tear down the two-story "historic" house then standing on the property in order to build a three-story, seven-bedroom, seven-bath house on the 3.8-acre waterfront estate. The plans included a nursery and nanny's room.

Then, in July 1998, Frederick Wyatt Imus was born, and Don's life took perhaps the most unexpected turn of all. Don was enthralled with all things Frederick Wyatt, even the birth.

"That was great. I know this is going to sound idiotic, but you actually have to love your wife, but you also have to really like them, because you're right in there, it's war. My wife is great because she's an athlete, so she looked at the pushing like an athletic event. She was great. I was helping her count."

Then Don described the moment when the baby was born. "The child, his head comes out, and I said, 'He's got red hair!' The doctor was saying, 'No I think that's blood.' Well, there's blood all over the place, but I could see it was red hair. Well, I had red hair fifty years ago."

The red hair had special significance for Don and Deirdre because, "from the time I married Deirdre, I had a baby picture of me and she keeps it on the dresser and all she talked about was wanting a kid who looked like that, for whatever reason. I was [a cute baby]. And then we had this little redheaded boy, I couldn't stop crying. I don't cry about anything. I couldn't stop crying the first week. I went to work [one morning], left the apartment about four-thirty and was crying on the way to work. I don't know why. This afternoon he slept on my chest for about three hours. There's no way to describe it.

"My baby picture and this child's baby picture are nearly identical. So we got what we wanted. We got a little redheaded, blue-eyed little angel." Then just to show that he hadn't mellowed too much, Imus added, "You don't want to have an ugly baby."

Looking back at his first brush with fatherhood, Don admits his experience with his son is a world apart. "Yeah, because it wasn't a great marriage and it wasn't my ex-wife's fault, it wasn't anybody's fault, it's just one of those deals. I wasn't there when they grew up and then we got divorced pretty early on."

Despite his acknowledged failings as a father to his daughters, Imus told Larry King that his grown children had been mostly supportive of their half brother. He had sent pictures of Frederick to Elizabeth and "I talked to Nadine, my oldest daughter, and she's excited about it. She's a sweetheart, she was genuinely, enthusiastically excited about it."

However, he added, "One of the other daughters I haven't heard from in a while because she's going through this stage where she's blaming me for their lives." Despite the occasional hostility, Don says it doesn't bother him. "No. I still love 'em. They get over it. They go through phases where I'm a no-good bastard, then I'm great, then I'm a no-good bastard. They have a point, but then you really do have to move on. I mean, you gotta get over it."

Perhaps for the first time in his life, Imus said he felt "like a father. There's no way to describe it." Before Frederick, Imus says that when Tim Russert or others would talk about their children, "it was so *annoying* to hear them go on about their kids. It's nice, I'm happy they like their little sons, I think it's great they went to the All-Star game—I don't want to hear about it. I want to talk about me or Kinky Friedman or something else."

However, now the tables have turned. "Most people feel about me talking about my kid as I feel about them talking about theirs. They don't want to hear about it. I mention a couple of things about him but I'm not going through diaper changes and stuff," he says à la Kathie Lee Gifford. "That's a wretched individual. A hideous, horrible person."

Although Don has no immediate plans to retire, he has thought about the kind of life he wants his son to have. "I'm going to take him out to the ranch and teach him to be a cowboy. I want him to grow up on a ranch like I did. At the risk of sounding like an idiot, I think it's going to be great for this kid to grow up helping other kids," Don says, referring to the Imus Ranch. "I think it's going to be great for him. I think it's going to be great growing up riding a horse, to grow up with his uncle Fred. It took me fifty years to figure it out, but it's going to be great for this kid to help other kids."

Don can also visualize a day when *Imus in the Morning* heads west permanently. "My wife's an actor, so when she goes back to work, it kind of depends on what she does. But I can do the radio show from any place. It's no big deal. We're going to do the radio show from the ranch during the summer. With the technology now, it's easy to do it from any place."

Nor does Don want his son to grow up surrounded by bodyguards, the way some celebrities fret over security. "I mean, it's not like I'm Mel Gibson. I'm on the radio. It's not a big deal."

Because of his obvious enjoyment of being a parent, Imus has been asked if he and Deirdre have plans for more children. At first he wasn't sure. "So, I don't know. We wanted this child so much, we focused so much on this child that I couldn't imagine getting this excited about another kid. But then I was talking to Mike Breen and he has three children and he said he thought the same thing, but they were just as excited." Now, he says after talking it over with Deirdre, he is more inclined to add to their family. "I would like another little boy," no doubt wanting Frederick to grow up having the bond that only two brothers can share.

Considering how close Imus came to losing everything during the depth of his addictions, he seems genuinely grateful for his present life. He's got a wife he loves, "and we have a lovely little child." He pauses, then asks reflectively, "I don't like being tedious, but isn't this a great kid?"

Chapter Twenty-one

FEW WHO REMEMBER DON RUNNING DOWN THE HALL OF WNBC IN his underwear in 1983 believed the I-Man's career would last out the decade, much less the millennium. However, Imus has not only survived and prospered—his penthouse apartment with a wraparound garden terrace that overlooks the twinkling lights of Tavern-on-the-Green in Central Park and a mansion in Southport, Connecticut, offer testament to his financial success—he's been positively legitimized by the very people he's made a career out of insulting and criticizing. In addition to being included on *Time* magazine's Most Influential list, *Newsweek* devoted a December 1998 cover story to the I-Man: *The Importance of Being Imus.*

But it would go against the Imus grain to ever truly go establishment, and if anything, he seems to be edgier than ever. When speculating on success, Imus tends to subtly but clearly make a distinction between himself and his show. He believes *Imus in the Morning* has succeeded because "it's a good place to sell a book. I think it's interesting and entertaining. There's a lot of talented people who work on the program. They are brilliant people who work on the program." While his supporting cast members are unquestionably integral to the show, Imus himself always was and remains the show itself. *Imus in the Morning* reflects his deepest interests and is a bully pulpit—although the message he preaches is usually up for interpretation.

Although things were undoubtedly going well for Imus personally, *Imus in the Morning* suffered the occasional bump that reminded everyone they weren't an untouchable juggernaut. In December 1998, the show's Denver affiliate, KRRF-AM, announced that after five years it was replacing *Imus in the Morning* with a local program headlined by Gus Mircos. The move came just as another Denver station, KPXK-FM, also owned by KRRF's Chancellor Broadcasting, was bringing Howard Stern to the Mile-High City.

"We've struggled with Imus's low ratings and low revenue [for five years]," said station manager Mason Lewis. "We decided the station would make more of an impact in morning drive with a local version of Imus's show."

Lewis claimed the arrival of Stern had nothing to do with the decision to cut Imus loose. "We've been thinking of making a change for quite a while. The Imus show is fairly expensive. When we told the syndicate we were planning to drop the show, they offered it at a lower price. But we think it's a good time to go local.

"We're aware Imus has a high profile among many professionals, particularly men. But that profile has never translated into audience ratings and revenue, and that's what counts in today's broadcasting world.

"I'm not claiming Gus is exactly like Imus. But I think listeners who have not spent much time listening to him will discover he has an Imus-type edge."

Part of the station's decision was based on Arbitron ratings, which are based on what a select number of respondents literally hand-write in diaries. Lewis commented that perhaps the Imus fans had been too busy to fill out Arbitron diaries. At least one Denver paper thought Lewis's remark indicative of the problem with how radio determines audience size. "It's ridiculous. In this computer age, a multibillion-dollar industry makes numerous decisions on what people write—or don't write—in old-fashioned diaries."

There had long been a similar complaint from producers and fans alike about the television Nielsen ratings, which determined show rank on the viewing habits of approximately 1,200 people. But radio programs did have an advantage over TV entertainment programs, which tend to have a built-in obsolescence because they tend to be stuck in one place and one time. Because *Imus in the Morning* runs on the fuel of current events, it will probably last as long as Don remains interested in keeping it going. In December 1998, he signed a new three-year deal with MSNBC, turning down advances from both CNN and the Fox News Channel to lure him away.

"I like the people at MSNBC and I have a great deal of loyalty to Bob Wright," he said, referring to the head of NBC. Despite his continued association with the cable network, radio will forever be Imus's primary domain.

"He's meant for the radio," says *Esquire*'s Martha Sherrill. "And I think he's going to be on the radio and be a sensation on the radio as long as he's behind a microphone."

Although brother Fred can see the day when Don pulls the plug on his microphone for good, 1998 was the kind of political year that keeps the I-Man professionally young and intellectually stimulated. Early on in the Monica Lewinsky scandal, Imus noted, "We've all been sitting around, those of us who thrive on current events, and reveling in the agony of others, waiting for that Jimmy Swaggert–like moment—remember when he was caught with the $20 hooker, he stands in front of the mike and the tears are streaming down his face and he said, 'I've sinned against God'? We've been waiting for Bill Clinton to do that. I want it to happen."

As for his opinion on the whole affair, Imus cracked, "Do not hug the fat girl on the rope line. You can't do that."

While Don might have rebuked *Newsweek* for suggesting he occasionally goes too far—"What do you mean too far? I'm the fucking I-Man"—the blurry line was ultimately a matter of individual taste. And because Imus made a living out of speaking his mind, he always ran the risk of inciting the not-so-stable to riot. After listening to a January 1998 show that spotlighted the Lewinsky situation, an apparently disgruntled fan named Michael P. Michalski of Cromwell, Connecticut, sent Imus a threatening e-mail:

> I hope that one day as you walk out of the studio, someone
> is on the street with a deer gun.

After a second e-mail implied Michalski was headed to New York, authorities were contacted and he was arrested. Under an agreement with prosecutors, the threatening and harassment charges against Michalski would be purged if he had no more run-ins with law enforcement. Apparently, Michalski wasn't aware that Imus carried a .357 Magnum, about which he admits, "it would be better if it were registered."

Although his commentary could goad people to potential violence, it was his more thoughtful musings that elevated Imus above the fray. And in more reflective moments, his take on Clinton said as much about Imus as it did the commander in chief.

"I think people like him. I like him. He's a gregarious guy, attractive. He hasn't been a horrible president. The economy is obviously good. Ted Koppel gave a great commencement address at Stanford University [on June 14, 1998] that ought to be required reading for everybody in this country. Essentially, he said we are treating the fact we have a great economy as an ethical issue. And if we didn't have a great economy, what would our opinion then be of Clinton?"

Imus also believes, contrary to the public's majority opinion, that the President's sex life *is* our business. "Well, yes, it is. Marriage vows are important. Yeah, it is, and he's the President of the United States. He can't be in the Oval Office getting bj's from the intern. You can't do that. It's not just sex."

And with the upcoming primaries and 2000 presidential election, Imus is as acerbic as ever. If he already has a favorite target, it's Al Gore, who, Imus predicts, is "not going to be president. I really think he's a disingenuous weasel. We want George Bush, Jr., or McCain, or Bob Kerry. McCain would be great because he's a little nuts. George Bush, Jr., I think he's mean enough to do anything. Carla Faye Tucker, George put the juice to her. He had the guts to do that."

And it's hard to imagine Imus not salivating over the prospect of Hillary Clinton making a run for the Senate in New York. "The last time we talked to her she was playing three-card monte with billing records in the book room and jerking your chain on Wall Street and hiding suicide notes and she wants to run for the Senate against the most vicious person on the planet, Rudolph Giuliani? What is she, nuts?"

But even with a bushel full of delicious current events percolating at work and a beloved wife and adored child at home, Don was still unpredictable and moody—a Byzantine puzzle. *Imus in the Morning* producer McGuirk, notes: "You know how it's sometimes uncomfortable to end a conversation with somebody? Well, Imus doesn't have a problem with that, because instead of saying good-bye, he simply tells everybody, 'Now get out.' "

And as so many journalists had learned during their attempts to profile Imus, it was hard knowing when he was serious and when he was pulling a gag. Such as in August 1998, when Imus "suspended" the show's Wise Guy movie reviewers, Bo Deitl and his sidekick, Joey DeKamma. Imus announced on his show the ban on Deitl, a former police detective turned private investigator and his sidekick, would last until "they learn to comport themselves." Later, Imus told the *New York Daily News:* "Everything they could possibly do wrong, they did. They violated ethics, morals, taste, you name it."

Deitl, of course, had a different opinion. "Joey and I, it's like we take over the show. We're the best part of the show!"

Imus called Deitl's "delusions of grandeur" comparable to "Geraldo Rivera asserting that he may take over Tom Brokaw's anchor job." He then suggested Deitl "should maybe go stick another perpetrator's head in the toilet, or hang an innocent person off a building."

But after all the bickering, by show's end Deitl and DeKamma had been "reinstated, despite my better judgment," by Imus.

But one contretemps that definitely wasn't staged occurred a few days later when Imus took on Howie Carr, the acerbic afternoon deejay on Boston's WRKO-AM, who has also been accused of promoting homophobia and racism on his show. The war of words began when Carr made a comment on air that Don wouldn't live long enough to see his son Frederick graduate from high school, referring to Don being an older dad. Imus came back swinging by casually commenting that he would live long enough to see Carr's wife performing oral sex on boxer Riddick Bowe, "again." Imus claimed he was merely repeating what he'd read somewhere on the Internet.

Carr was incensed. "It is an outrageous, slanderous statement that exceeds all bounds of propriety, and it's obviously false. I believe he made it with reckless disregard for the truth," claiming his wife was a private citizen, not a public figure and therefore legally protected from those kinds of insults.

Imus, who'd been down this road enough times before, said, "It was a joke. If he wants to go to court, let's go. Somebody else will have to characterize whether it's a slanderous comment or not." Then he added, "I was provoked. If he wants to say something about me, fine. If he wants to get personal, I'll get personal. Just leave my kid out of it."

Carr was unwilling to let the matter go and consulted with Alan Dershowitz, the noted and notorious defense attorney and Harvard Law School professor whose clients included Claus Von Bulow and O. J. Simpson. But as of this writing, no suit has been filed. When contacted, Carr was evasive about whether or not any legal action was still being considered.

"I really can't say much about it. I'm sworn to silence on the whole thing. It's my wife's suit. It's my wife's problem anyway. I'm a public figure, so there's nothing I can really do. Alan Dershowitz is the lawyer. He can speak if he wants to say anything. I think I'll just let it pass for the time being."

It's easy to see how Don can get under people's skin, tossing the sharpest of barbs as almost casual asides with no apparent regard for the impact and collateral damage his verbal bombs may cause. After the horrific TWA explosion over Long Island in 1997, Imus pointed blame at the airline. As it happens, his old high school and marine buddy, Bert Schenberger, is a pilot for TWA.

Phil Oelze relates that in Schenberger's opinion, the comments Imus made "were very unfair and Bert is a senior captain on TWA. Bert got so incensed that he called the station and left several messages for Don, asking him to call. I guess Don didn't call back. Finally Bert left the message that he needed to get real and be fair and not distort the facts that surrounded a tragic crash."

Oelze believes Imus needs to be responsible with the power he has and not use his broadcast aerie to taunt politicians, such as he does Clinton by decorating the wall of his studio with a RESIGN, YOU FAT BASTARD bumper sticker. "I would hope the growth that Don would attain would be that he can utilize the power that he has to be more forthright, more honest, more purposeful in the sense of setting some things right that are wrong in this country. Like the money in politics and its perverse use. It would take someone like Don to do that.

"He now has a chance to really do something. I hope he can meet that. It seems to me he's trying to shift gears in the way he's approaching what he does, if he wants to leave a real legacy, more than just *Resign, you fat bastard.*"

But aside from his charitable works, Imus has never indicated he wanted to lead any crusade. He wants to provide humor laced with thoughtful dialogue and commentary. From the moment he stepped foot onstage to perform in his high school talent contest, John Donald Imus wanted to be a performer, and regardless of whatever else he may be, that is his fundamental job function, even though the script may be written largely from his own ego and id.

"He's a genius in the sense he is able to entertain us, to interest us, even fascinate us with the trials and tribulations of one D. Imus," says James Carville. Mary Matalin agrees. "The audience feels like he's their friend, which is a very important element of radio."

There are others, however, who sense the I-Man might be slipping. "He's done very well, but I think he's going downhill now," says Les Thompson, who worked with Don at KXOA in Sacramento. "He still has some funny bits, but he stumbles and mumbles over his speech. You can't understand him."

It seems as if how one views the current state of Imus depends largely on whatever first impression he left. To Terry Nelson, Imus was and will always be someone who can be counted on. "I was at a dinner party with some people in Sacramento and they were saying, 'Hey I didn't know that you and Don Imus were such good friends. He was talking about you today on the radio. He said you were his best friend, you were one of the greatest disc jockeys in the country.' Don has never been one to forget any of his friends, never been too busy to take a phone call if there's some reason for me to give him a jingle or vice versa.

"I've got a lot of respect for Don. He's been through a lot of changes, and at the same time he's always been himself for the most part. He's done a lot of good things for this business, this industry, this medium, and he's opened a lot of doors for a lot of other people to be able to come on and do things that they would not have been able to do if he hadn't broken that ice and that barrier."

But to Ethel Tyson he's still the foul-mouthed, rude adolescent he was in the halls of Prescott High. She was particularly offended by Don's remarks about Phil Oelze after he appeared on camera during a segment of *A&E Biography* that profiled Imus.

"Phil was really the only dear friend he had, I think. And the morning after he said, 'My God, he's so fat, didn't he ever hear of salads?' For someone who was his dearest friend at one time, that's kind of . . .'" Her voice trailed off, unable to find the appropriate words of dismay.

In *GQ*, Peter Richmond once wrote:

> Imus consumes you in stages. At first, I was incensed. He made me want to jump on the hoods of people's cars, like Kevin McCarthy in *Invasion of the Body Snatchers*, and warn them about this self-serving scourge of the airwaves. After a year or so, I began to laugh at some of it. Now, I'm an addict.

How listeners ultimately judge Imus depends more on what they bring to the program than what Imus delivers. As was pointed out earlier, it is not a matter of love him or hate him, but a matter of get him or don't. He refuses to curry favor with either his guests or his audience, and he clings tenaciously to the independent thinking that got him through a troubled childhood, the uncertain years of scraping out a living and sleeping behind Laundromat dryers, and the early jobs when his radio career dangled tenuously over oblivion.

But what both admirers and critics can agree on is that for

better or worse, Imus is his own man, the ultimate endangered species in an ever-homogenized culture. And the fear of losing collective independence is arguably one of the reasons Americans continue to hold the cowboy myth so close to heart and a reason millions of listeners find Imus impossible to ignore.

Now, get out.

Index

Abell, Lyndon, 148, 172
A Drinking Life, 276
Air checks, 66
Alcoholics Anonymous (AA), 164, 281
All-talk radio, 86
AM radio, decline of, 106
American Graffiti, 109
Announcer, training at Don Martin radio school, 52
Antelope Valley College, 56, 68
Antelope Valley Press, 60, 70, 269
Antisemitism, charges of, 238
Arbitron ratings, 165, 192, 295
Augusta Chronicle, 271
Auto-Body Express, 211, 212, 272, 289

Bartlett, Rob, 180, 182, 184, 185, 186, 232, 237, 260
Bascom, Perry, 111, 130
Baywatch, 4
Beck School of Radio, 86
Begala, Paul, 200, 205
Belzer, Richard, 146
Berry, Chuck, 99
Bierne, Brian, 53, 58, 92, 96, 146
Billboard magazine
convention, 115
1969 deejay award, 95
1970 deejay award, 103

Billboard Top 40, 62
Bitter End, 120
Black Hawk Wars, 7
Black Panthers, 81
Blitzer, Wolf, 252
Blue-eyed soul music, 44
Bongarten, Randall, 164, 165, 169, 209
Book (ratings period), 102
Boss radio format, 92
Boston Globe, 279
Bottom Line, 121
Bowling for Dollars, 183
Boxing, 222
Breen, Mike, 180, 182
Bridgeport Post, 194, 195
Brink & Belzer, 146
Broadcast Music Incorporated (BMI), 62
Broadcast of Telephone Conversations, FCC ruling, 95
Brown, Jim Ed, 54
Brown, Steve, 51
Bruce, Lenny, 53, 91
Buffalo, Steve, 56, 61, 64
Bush, George Jr., 298

Camp Pendelton, 35
Camp Willows, 8
Carr, Howie, 299, 300
Carville, James, 200, 232, 262, 301

305

Castro, Bernadette, 192
Cattle barons, 1
Chancellor Broadcasting, 295
Characters, satire, 88
"Chicken rock," 76
C. J. Foundation for Sudden Infant
    Death Syndrome (SIDS), 282
Claven and Finch, 107
Clean as a Mother car wash
    routine, 131
Cleaver, Eldridge, 81, 83
Cleveland Plain Dealer, 103, 106
Clinton, Bill, 220, 248, 263, 297
    April 1993 interview, 206–207
    1992 primary, 200–204
Clinton, Hillary, 232, 249, 298
Coleman, Deirdre, 222–224, 227,
    241–242, 274, 291
Collier, Chuck, 98, 99, 104, 144
Colmes, Alan, 177
Colony Sports Network, 182
Connecticut Special Olympics, 284
Cornelius, Helen, 54
Corps Values: Everything You Need to
    Know I learned in the Marines, 271
Couric, Katie, 202, 203, 205, 219
Cowboy, myth of, 1
Crazy Bob, character, 89
"Crimson and Clover," 62

Dallas, 12
D'Amato, Alfonse, 220–221, 245
Daniel, Dandy Dan, 107
Davis, George (cousin), 8, 9, 10, 13,
    16, 22, 29, 45, 46, 47
DC-101, Washington, D.C., 161
Deejay. See Disc jockey
DeKamma, Joey, 298, 299
Denial, of alcoholism, 158
Dershowitz, Alan, 300
Dietl, Bo, 298, 299

Disc jockey
    function of, 54
    technical requirements, 51
Dole, Bob, 219
Don Imus Combo, 23
Don Imus-WFAN Pediatric Center,
    Hackensack University Medical
    Center, 283
Don Martin School of Radio and
    Television Arts, 50, 51, 53, 115
"Do-wop" hair, 20

Eldridge Cleaver look-alike contest,
    at KJOI, 81, 83
Emmis Broadcasting Corporation,
    174
Estes, Billy Sol, 20

Fear of success, 159
Federal Communications
    Commission (FCC), 93, 94, 213
Fibber McGee and Molly, 55
Flagstaff brawl, 30–32
FM radio, rise of, 106
Friedman, Richard ("Kinky"), 121,
    122, 172, 188, 189
Furtado, Art, 53, 65, 66

Gambling, John, 107, 170
Gellman, Marc, 187
Giant Frog (Brian Bierne), 92, 97,
    115
Gingrich, Newt, 230, 256
Gleason's Gym, Brooklyn, 223
Globe-Miami mining, 45
God's Other Son, 152, 153, 214, 215,
    267, 276
Golden Age of Radio, 55
Goldwater, Barry Jr., 60
Good Guys, WMCA, 107
Gore, Al, 298
GQ, 302

Graceland, 271, 272
Greenfield, Jeff, 3, 191, 198, 210, 229, 240, 245
Grodin, Charles, 233
Grove, Lloyd, 260
Guilty: The Collapse of Criminal Justice, 243
Gulf War, 198, 199
Gumbel, Bryant, 202, 205

Haley, Bill, 99
Hamill, Pete, 276
Harden, Jake, cattleman, 8
Harrison, Harry, 108
Hartman, Thomas, 187
Hauser, Eric, 199
Hazelden Clinic, 173, 174, 176
Hilborn, Robin, 63, 68
Hill, Rick, 234
Hoffman, Don, 82
Hogan, Hulk, 290
Hollander, Joel, 178, 193, 283
Hollaus, Meredith, 117, 130, 132–133, 138, 150
Hoover, J. Edgar, 81
Hot Air: All Talk, All the Time, 229
Hy from Hollywood, character, 101

"I'm a Hot Rodder," 46
Imus, Ashleigh Suzanne (daughter), 48, 68
Imus, Charles, Captain (great uncle), 7
Imus, Elizabeth Ann (daughter), 48, 68, 292
Imus fairy tale corner, 134
Imus family
poverty of in 1950's, 27–28
trek west, 5–7
Imus, Frances Elizabeth (mother), 5, 12, 27–29, 37, 48

Imus, Fred (brother), 10, 11, 17, 29, 46, 54, 115, 163, 180, 210–211, 289–290
Imus, Frederick Wyatt (son), 291
Imus, Hiram, Sr., (greatgrandfather), 5
Imus in the Morning
at KJOI, 77
syndication, 212
TV debut, 268
Imus in the Morning: One Sacred Chicken to Go, album, 120
Imus, John Donald, Jr. (Don)
at AA, 164, 172
absenteeism at WNBC, 129
and advertisers, 192–193
alcohol and cocaine use, 2, 128, 135–136, 159, 164, 171, 173
American Book Awards, 278
anger of, 136
behavior in school, 13
blue collar image, 62
charity work, 282
Clinton interviews, 202, 206
collapsed lung, 216–217
as court jester, 241
cowbow image, 91
as "cranky," 159
drum and bugle corps assignment, 38
as fatalist, 105
fictional character development, 89, 101
GED, 43
high school performances, 22–24
honesty of, 151
literary rivalry with Oprah Winfrey, 277–278
love of books, 11, 273–274
Marine Corps, 35, 42
marriage
Deirdre Colman, 226

Harriet Showalter, 71
mining work, 45
news deconstruction, 231
pubescent humor, 196
railroad accident, 49
railroad work, 47
ratings decline, 167
as influential, 279, 294
at KJOI, 76–83
at KUTY, 53, 56–70
as loose canon, 104
as mysogynist and racist, 3, 152, 236
as outsider, 15
as parent, 96–97, 137, 156, 291–293
as philosopher, 209
as shock jock, 3, 100
as "Rat Pack," 18, 22
religious beliefs, 188
rivalry with Howard Stern, 169, 207–208
rock-star mystique, 245
in Sacramento, CA, 97
self-promotion, 81
on star trip, 135
state congress campaign, 60–61
stunts at KXOA, 92–93
toned down, 145
at WGAR, Cleveland, 98–105
at WNBC, 108–139, 147
Wolfman Jack gag similarities, 109
writing, 80
Imus, John Donald, Sr. (father), 5, 10, 25–26, 40–41
Imus, May (grandmother), 12
Imus Plus, Metromedia, 142
Imus Ranch, Tomorrow's Children, 284–287
Imus Unabridged, 215
Infinity Broadcasting, 196
Ingram, Dan, 108, 126
I-Posse members, 180–187

Iron Butterfly, 62, 69
Irreverence, delivery style, 100, 110
I Was Amelia Earhart, 274, 275

Jennings, Peter, 253, 254
JJ Imus and Freddie Ford, 46
Jordan, Hamilton, 285
Judge Hangin', character, 89–90

Karmazin, Mel, 197, 214
Kaufman-Astoria Studios, 178
Kempton, Murray, 236, 240
Kenney, Larry, 180, 182, 183, 229
KFIV radio station, 83
KFRC, San Francisco, 87
Kingman, Arizona, 8
KJOI, Stockton, CA, 75
 Imus fired from, 82
Kondracke, Morton, 239–240
Kornheiser, Tony, 190
KPHN, Kansas City, 270
Krassner, Paul, 91, 143
KRRF-AM, Denver, 295
KSTN radio station, 76
Kurtz, Howard, 171, 209, 210, 229, 238, 239, 262, 277
KUTY, Palmdale, CA, 50, 53, 56
KXOA, Sacramento, 87, 88, 97

Lack, Andrew, 267
Lawson, Vern, 60, 70
Ledger-Gazette, 60
Libel suit, by Bob Zames, 103
Limbaugh, Rush, 186, 256, 262
Lofthus, Ort, 82
Lupica, Mike, 194, 245, 276
Lynn, Michael, 5, 132, 135, 142, 164, 179

Marine Recruit Platoon 187, 35
Mason, Stan, 36

Matalin, Mary, 218, 230, 253, 261, 301

McCord, Charles, 118, 119, 130, 136, 144, 148, 150, 155, 179, 196

McCurry, Mike, 258, 260

McDonald's hamburger stunt, at KXOA, 93–94

McDougal, Susan, 249

McGuirk, Bernard, 163, 180, 181, 218, 237, 238, 298

Mende, David and Kay, KUTY, 64, 65

Mendlesohn, Jane, 274, 275

Metheny, L. Kevin, 168

Michalski, Michael P., 297

Midnight Special, WNBC, 109

Miller, Zell, 271

Mircos, Gus, 295

Moby Worm, 120

Moran, Jim, 213, 214

Morning radio, format, 77

Morning shows, importance of, 111

Morrow, Cousin Brucie, 108, 126, 139

MSNBC, 267, 296

Muni, Scott, 185, 186

Murray the K, 108

Nathan, Alan, 224–225

National Indian Gaming Association, 234

Nationwide Communications, 138

Nelson, Terry, 67, 77, 81, 82, 88, 96, 122–124, 133, 135, 301

New Wave Communications, 273

New York City Marathon, 227

New York Times, 198, 209

Newberg, Esther, 240

Newsday, 236, 237

Nielsen ratings, 296

Nolan, Martin, 279

Oelze, Phil, 13, 16, 17, 20, 27, 28, 37, 39, 42, 300

Of Mice and Men, 12

Oldies format, 98

One True Thing, 274

Palmdale, California, 50, 53, 54, 55, 70

Parker, Freddie, 14

Payne, Les, 237, 239

Payola, 47

Penchina, Selkowitz, Inc., 165

Pequot Yacht Club, 194

Perris, California, 5, 10

Philbin, Regis, 218

Pittman, Bob, 112, 138, 139, 140, 147, 159

Political incorrectness, 121

Prescott, Arizona, 14, 15

Prescott, William Hickling, 14

Private Parts, 162, 215, 267

Pru, Marty, 70

Quien Sabe, family ranch, 8

Quindlen, Anna, 198, 208, 216, 245, 274

Quivers, Robin, 161

Race for the Cure, 227

Racism, charges of, 233, 239

Radio-telephone operator's first class license, 50–51

Rather, Dan, 219, 248, 252

Ratings period (book), 102

Rattlesnakes and Eggs, 70

Rawitch, Bernie, 64

Record countdowns, 86

Regis & Kathie Lee, 218

Reverend Billy Sol Hargis, character, 90, 116, 149, 153, 178

Rhythm and blues, 46

Rice, Henry, 7

Richmond, Peter, 302
RKO format, morning radio shows, 77, 106
Roberts, Cokie, 253, 261, 263
Rock Around the Clock, 99
Rothwax, Harold, 241, 242, 243, 244
Rubin, Jerry, 83

Sacramento Union, 92
Sahl, Mort, 53, 91
"Salad oil scandal," 20
Salamone, Antoinette, 48, 72, 75
Salamone, John, 48, 72
Salamone, Nadine, 48, 72, 75, 292
Santa Fe New Mexican, 289
Satire, Imus' use of, 88, 110, 120, 121
Schenberger, Bert, 32, 39, 42, 300
Scimeca, Charles, 114, 118, 135, 137, 156
Sclar, Rick, 108
Scott, Bill, 100, 106, 112, 133, 150
Scottsdale, Arizona, 14
Search for Idi Amin stunt, 149
Shannon, Scott, 167, 169
Shaw, Tim, 56, 59, 62, 65, 67, 70
Sherman, Robert, 146, 147, 161
Sherrill, Martha, 105, 130, 136, 159, 218, 296
Shock jocks, term coined, 145
Showalter, Harriet Ann, 48, 71, 72, 136–137, 147, 152
  custody battles with John Salamone, 73–75
  divorce from Imus, 160
Siegel, Norman, 243
Silavardo Broadcasting, 51
Simon and Schuster, 152, 154, 214, 215, 277
Sirkin, Phil, 214
Sloman, Larry "Ratso," 143
Soupy Sales, 171

Southern Pacific Railroad, 47, 50
Southport, Connecticut, 195
Spin Cycle, 277
Spook comments, at KJOI, 82, 83
Sports-talk format, 214
Statler Hilton Hotel, Cleveland, 98
Steele, Real Don, 53
Stern, Howard, 161, 162, 164, 165, 170, 196, 199, 207, 267, 273, 284, 295
  FCC indecency fines, 213
  firing by NBC, 169
  ratings rise, 166, 167
Stockton Hotel, 76
Stonyfield Farm Yogurt endorsement, 193

Taylor, Dan, 172
Thayer, Jack G., 86, 93, 97, 99, 101, 106, 138, 140
The Fred Book, 276
The Importance of Being Imus (Newsweek), 294
The Phrase That Pays, 125
The Realist, 91, 143
Thomas, Jay, 170
Thompson, Les, 87, 88, 301
Today morning show, 202, 203, 206, 207
Tommy James and the Shondells, 62
Tomorrow's Children's Fund, 282, 283
Top 40 radio, 100
Try-A-Bed, 192–193
Turner, Ted, 290
20–20 news format, 92
Two Guys, Four Corners, 276
Tyson, Ethel, 21, 22, 24, 25, 34, 302

"Underground" stations, 86
Unistar Radio Networks, 212

Vecsey, George, 209
"Veejay," VH-1, 167, 168
VH-1 cable, veejay, 167

WABC, New York, 108
Wallace, Mike, 171
Warner, Charlie, 138, 140
Washington Post, 209
Wayne, John, 1
WFAN, New York, 177, 190, 192
WGAR-AM, Cleveland, 97, 98
Whiskey Row, Prescott, Arizona, 15
White House correspondents'
    dinner 1996, 247, 249
Whitley, Pat, 111, 130
WHK-AM, Cleveland, 87, 143
Why the Chimes Rang, 22
WIBV-AM, St. Louis, 272
Williams, Roy, 51, 75, 81, 83
Williams, William B., 107
Willows Ranch, 10, 14
Wilson, Malcom John "Big", 116,
    117

Winfrey, Oprah, 277
WINS all-news, 191
WLOL, Minneapolis
WMCA, New York, 107
WNBC, New York, 105
    final broadcast, 177
WNEW, New York, 106–107
Wolfman Jack (Robert Smith), 19,
    108, 109, 111
WOR, New York, 107
WQXI-AM, Atlanta, 271
WTEM, Washington, D.C., 190
WXLO-WOR FM, New York, 122
WXRK-FM, K-Rock, 170, 192
Wynn, Mike, 79
WYST-FM, Detroit, 269

XELO, Del Rio, Texas, 19
XERF-AM, Mexico, 109, 145

Zames, Bob, 102, 103